Taste of Home

Make it!

TAKE IT

TASTE OF HOME BOOKS • RDA ENTHUSIAST BRANDS, LLC • MILWAUKEE, WI

PAGE 55

PAGE 17

PAGE 72

PAGE 46

CONTENTS

CHAPTERS

REFERENCE

PAGE 117

PAGE 90

PAGE 221

PAGE 79

Visit us at **tasteofhome.com** for other
Taste of Home books and products.

Chief Content Officer, Home & Garden:
Jeanne Sidner
Content Director: Mark Hagen
Creative Director: Raeann Thompson
Senior Editors: Christine Rukavena, Julie Schnittka
Senior Art Director: Courtney Lovetere
Art Director: Maggie Conners
Layout Designer: Carrie Peterson
Deputy Editor, Copy Desk: Dulcie Shoener
Copy Editor: Kara Dennison
Cover Photography: Taste of Home Photo Studio

Cover:
Photographer: Dan Roberts
Set Stylist: Melissa Franco
Food Stylist: Shannon Norris

Pictured on front cover:
Shredded Beef Burrito Filling, p. 159;
Luscious Lime Angel Squares, p. 201;
Summertime Tea, p. 19

Pictured on title page:
Chocolate-Covered Strawberry Cobbler, p. 196

Pictured on back cover:
Hot Italian Party Sandwiches, p. 113
Moist Chocolate Cake, p. 191
Grilled Summer Sausage Salad, p. 82
Healthy Wholesome Snack Board,
p. 231

**International Standard Book
Numbers:**
D 978-1-62145-978-1
U 978-1-62145-979-8
International Standard Serial Number:
2166-0522
Component Numbers:
D 118100112H
U 118100114H

Printed in China
1 3 5 7 9 10 8 6 4 2

More ways to connect with us:

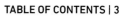

TIME TO SHINE
LET THESE RECIPES & TIPS UPGRADE YOUR NEXT POTLUCK!

The new *Make It, Take It!* is packed with hundreds of taste-tempting party foods and dozens of tips to make recipes in advance, transport dishes with ease and make your potluck contribution shine.

You'll enjoy each moment of party preparation with these reader-submitted recipes and expert pointers, all approved by the Test Kitchen pros at *Taste of Home*.

Inside, you'll discover 260 tasty new dishes! Also watch for these features:

BOARDS:
The ultimate potluck take-along is a charcuterie board, brimming with goodies and almost too pretty to eat. Our tutorial for building a basic charcuterie board (p. 218-219), plus the amazing ideas that follow, will inspire you to craft your own creation.

MAKE AHEAD recipes let you prep in advance, then keep a dish on ice for no-fuss serving later. Easy does it!

BRING IT
These tips sprinkled throughout the book provide insights for organizing the buffet, keeping foods hot or cold, and making sure your dish is a standout contribution.

PACK LIKE A PRO
These tips and tricks will have you hitting the road with confidence.

1 Build a DIY Multilevel Tote
If you have more dishes than hands, reach for a cooling rack with folding legs. Fold out the legs and use the rack to create sturdy, stable levels inside a carrying tote without crushing what's below. Get creative. You can also build layers by propping up a sheet pan with ring molds or cans.

2 Ensure a No-Slip Trip
Place grippy drawer liners or silicone baking mats in the car before loading your food. The lining will keep dishes from sliding and also contain any errant spills. An old yoga mat works well for this, too.

3 Keep a Lid on It
Use a bungee cord, painter's tape or thick ribbon to keep the lid for your slow cooker or Dutch oven in place. Secure the cord around the handles and over the top. Now you're ready to transport the dish without risk of a mess.

4 Bring a Salad
Yes, you can serve a crisp, freshly tossed salad when you're far from home. Just bring the fixings in a serving bowl, along with the utensils. Toss the salad at your destination. Voila! Remember to bring a grocery bag to corral the leftovers and dirty dishes.

5 Frosting Is Good Glue
If you're transporting a cake to a special event, make it easier to tote with this little tip: Secure the cake (or cardboard cake circle if you're using one) on to the presentation plate with a dab of frosting. This makes the cake less likely to slide around, even if you have to brake suddenly. And you're the only one who'll know the frosting is there!

6 Pack a Touch-Up Kit
Make a little touch-up kit of decorations and frosting (just in case) to take with your decorated cake. Pack the items with a clean dish towel and offset spatula. Transport the frosting in its pastry bag if you used one.

7 Tailgate Grill Skills
Place the grill on a solid surface away from any activities so no one bumps into it. Don't set the grill near shrubs, grass, overhangs or fences. Keep coolers away from the grill. Set the coolers out of direct sunlight and replenish the ice if possible.

8 Keep a Tailgate Kit
Store all your tailgate needs (such as linens, serve ware, games and sunblock) in a plastic bin inside a cooler. You'll be ready to go at a moment's notice.

PATRIOTIC
PEPPER PLATTER,
PAGE 33

Appetizers & Dips

Going to a holiday party or game-day get-together?
Find the perfect small bites and sips among these
tasty and toteable snacks, dips, spreads and more.

PIZZA MONKEY BREAD

I cannot throw a party without making this recipe. It's fast and easy, and my kids love it.
—*Courtney Wilson, Fresno, CA*

- -

Prep: 15 min. • **Bake:** 40 min. + cooling
Makes: 16 servings

- ⅓ cup olive oil
- 1 tsp. Italian seasoning
- 1 garlic clove, minced
- ¼ tsp. crushed red pepper flakes
- 2 cans (16.3 oz. each) large refrigerated flaky biscuits (8 count)
- 2 cups shredded part-skim mozzarella cheese
- ¼ cup grated Parmesan cheese
- 20 slices pepperoni, halved
- ½ cup marinara sauce
  Additional marinara sauce, warmed

1. Preheat oven to 350°. In a large microwave-safe bowl, combine first 4 ingredients; microwave, covered, on high for 30 seconds. Cool slightly.
2. Cut each biscuit into 4 pieces; add to oil mixture and toss to coat. Add cheeses and pepperoni; toss to combine. In a heavy 10-in. fluted tube pan coated with cooking spray, layer half of the biscuit mixture; drizzle with ¼ cup marinara sauce. Repeat layers.
3. Bake about 40 minutes or until golden brown. Cool in pan 10 minutes.
4. Run a knife around sides and center tube of pan. Invert onto a serving plate. Serve with additional marinara sauce if desired.
1 SERVING: 288 cal., 17g fat (5g sat. fat), 12mg chol., 723mg sod., 26g carb. (6g sugars, 1g fiber), 8g pro.

FLAVORFUL VARIATION

For a delicious twist, replace the marinara sauce with your favorite pesto. Bonus—it's colorful!

SOUTHERN DEVILED EGGS

Nothing is more simple or delicious than these deviled eggs. I make them for every BBQ, tailgate or picnic, and they're always a hit.
—*Ellen Riley, Murfreesboro, TN*

Takes: 20 min. • **Makes:** 1 dozen

- 6 hard-boiled large eggs
- 2 Tbsp. mayonnaise
- 2 Tbsp. sweet pickle relish, drained
- ½ tsp. prepared mustard
- ¼ tsp. salt
- ⅛ tsp. pepper
- Optional: Paprika and fresh dill

1. Slice eggs in half lengthwise. Remove yolks; set whites aside. In a small bowl, mash yolks. Stir in the mayonnaise, relish, mustard, salt and pepper.
2. Pipe or spoon mixture into egg whites. Refrigerate until serving. If desired, sprinkle with paprika and dill just before serving.
1 STUFFED EGG HALF: 57 cal., 4g fat (1g sat. fat), 94mg chol., 114mg sod., 1g carb. (1g sugars, 0 fiber), 3g pro.

PARTY PITAS

Whenever the ladies of our church host a shower, these pita sandwiches appear on the menu. Not only are they easy and delicious, they add color to the table.
—*Janette Root, Ellensburg, WA*

Takes: 15 min. • **Makes:** 16 pieces

- 1 pkg. (8 oz.) cream cheese, softened
- ½ cup mayonnaise
- ½ tsp. dill weed
- ¼ tsp. garlic salt
- 4 whole pita breads
- 1½ cups fresh baby spinach
- 1 lb. shaved fully cooked ham
- ½ lb. thinly sliced Monterey Jack cheese

1. Mix first 4 ingredients. Carefully cut each pita horizontally in half; spread 2 Tbsp. mixture onto each cut surface.
2. On 4 pita halves, layer spinach, ham and cheese. Top with remaining pita halves. Cut each sandwich into 4 wedges; secure with toothpicks.
1 PIECE: 225 cal., 15g fat (6g sat. fat), 45mg chol., 557mg sod., 10g carb. (1g sugars, 0 fiber), 12g pro.

CURRIED CHICKEN MEATBALL WRAPS

My strategy to get picky kids to eat healthy: letting everyone assemble their dinner at the table. We love these easy meatball wraps, topped with crunchy veggies and peanuts, sweet raisins, and a creamy dollop of yogurt.
—*Jennifer Beckman, Falls Church, VA*

Prep: 25 min. • **Bake:** 20 min.
Makes: 2 dozen

- 1 **large egg, lightly beaten**
- 1 **small onion, finely chopped**
- ½ **cup Rice Krispies**
- ¼ **cup golden raisins**
- ¼ **cup minced fresh cilantro**
- 2 **tsp. curry powder**
- ½ **tsp. salt**
- 1 **lb. lean ground chicken**

SAUCE
- 1 **cup plain yogurt**
- ¼ **cup minced fresh cilantro**

WRAPS
- 24 **small Bibb or Boston lettuce leaves**
- 1 **medium carrot, shredded**
- ½ **cup golden raisins**
- ½ **cup chopped salted peanuts**
   Additional minced fresh cilantro

1. Preheat oven to 350°. In a large bowl, combine the first 7 ingredients. Add chicken; mix lightly but thoroughly. With wet hands, shape mixture into 24 balls (about 1¼ in.).
2. Place the meatballs on a greased rack in a 15x10x1-in. baking pan. Bake 17-20 minutes or until cooked through.
3. In a small bowl, mix sauce ingredients. To serve, place 2 tsp. yogurt sauce and 1 meatball in each lettuce leaf; top with remaining ingredients.
1 APPETIZER: 72 cal., 3g fat (1g sat. fat), 22mg chol., 89mg sod., 6g carb. (4g sugars, 1g fiber), 6g pro. **DIABETIC EXCHANGES:** 1 lean meat, ½ starch.

CHEESE PUFFS

I based this recipe on one in my mother's old cookbooks and updated the flavor by adding cayenne and mustard. Tasty and quick for this busy season, these tender, golden puffs go together in minutes and simply disappear at parties!
—*Jamie Wetter, Boscobel, WI*

Prep: 15 min. • **Bake:** 15 min./batch
Makes: 4½ dozen

- 1 **cup water**
- 2 **Tbsp. butter**
- ½ **tsp. salt**
- ⅛ **tsp. cayenne pepper**
- 1 **cup all-purpose flour**
- 4 **large eggs, room temperature**
- 1¼ **cups shredded Gruyere or Swiss cheese**
- 1 **Tbsp. Dijon mustard**
- ¼ **cup grated Parmesan cheese**

1. In a large saucepan, bring the water, butter, salt and cayenne to a boil. Add flour all at once and stir until a smooth ball forms. Remove from the heat; let stand for 5 minutes. Add eggs, 1 at a time, beating well after each addition. Continue beating until mixture is smooth and shiny. Stir in Gruyere and mustard.
2. Drop by 1-in. balls 2 in. apart on greased baking sheets. Sprinkle with Parmesan cheese. Bake at 425° for 15-20 minutes or until golden brown. Serve warm or cold.
1 PUFF: 30 cal., 2g fat (1g sat. fat), 18mg chol., 62mg sod., 2g carb. (0 sugars, 0 fiber), 2g pro.

SAVORY TREATS
Known as *gourgeres* (goo-ZHAIR) in French, these are a savory version of cream puff. To make them even more amazing, split the puffs and fill with ham salad, egg salad or smoked fish pate right before serving.

HAM & CHEESE
CRESCENT BUNDLES

This hearty mini Danish is fluffy in the middle and crispy on the outside. Kids and adults alike love the fun design for snacking. For a breakfast or lunch entree, serve two per person.
—*Marisa Raponi, Vaughan, ON*

Prep: 20 min. • **Bake:** 15 min.
Makes: 1 dozen

- 1 pkg. (8 oz.) refrigerated crescent rolls
- ½ cup spinach dip
- 4 slices black forest ham (about 4 oz.)
- 1 cup shredded cheddar cheese

1. Preheat oven to 350°. Unroll crescent dough and separate into 4 rectangles; press perforations to seal.
2. Spread each rectangle with 2 Tbsp. dip to within ½ in. of edges. Top with ham and cheese. Roll up jelly-roll style, starting with a short side; pinch seam to seal. Cut each roll crosswise into thirds; place in greased muffin cups, cut sides down.
3. Bake bundle until golden brown, 12-15 minutes. Run a knife around edges to remove from pan.
1 APPETIZER: 149 cal., 10g fat (4g sat. fat), 17mg chol., 343mg sod., 9g carb. (2g sugars, 0 fiber), 5g pro.

MINI BURGERS
WITH THE WORKS

I started preparing these mini burgers several years ago as a creative way to use up bread crusts accumulating in my freezer. Their tiny size makes them simply irresistible.
—*Linda Lane, Bennington, VT*

Takes: 30 min. • **Makes:** 1 dozen

- ¼ lb. ground beef
- 3 slices American cheese
- 4 slices white bread (heels of loaves recommended)
- 2 Tbsp. prepared Thousand Island salad dressing
- 2 pearl onions, thinly sliced
- 4 baby dill pickles, thinly sliced
- 3 cherry tomatoes, thinly sliced

1. Shape beef into twelve 1-in. patties. Place on a microwave-safe plate lined with paper towels. Cover with another paper towel; microwave on high for 1 minute until meat is no longer pink. Cut each slice of cheese into fourths; set aside.
2. Using a 1-in. round cookie cutter, cut out 6 circles from each slice of bread. Spread half of the bread circles with dressing. Layer with burgers, cheese, onions, pickles and tomatoes. Top with remaining bread circles; secure with toothpicks.
1 BURGER: 68 cal., 3g fat (1g sat. fat), 11mg chol., 153mg sod., 5g carb. (1g sugars, 0 fiber), 4g pro.

EASY STRAWBERRY SALSA

My salsa is sweet and colorful, with just a little bit of a bite from jalapeno peppers. I use fresh strawberries and my own home-grown vegetables, but you can also use produce available year round. It's delicious with tortilla chips or even as a garnish to grill chicken or pork.
—*Dianna Wara, Washington, IL*

Prep: 20 min. + chilling
Makes: 16 servings

- 3 cups chopped seeded tomatoes (about 4 large)
- 1⅓ cups chopped fresh strawberries
- ½ cup finely chopped onion (about 1 small)
- ½ cup minced fresh cilantro
- 1 to 2 jalapeno peppers, seeded and finely chopped
- ⅓ cup chopped sweet yellow or orange pepper
- ¼ cup lime juice
- ¼ cup honey
- 4 garlic cloves, minced
- 1 tsp. chili powder
  Baked tortilla chip scoops

In a large bowl, combine the first 10 ingredients. Refrigerate, covered, at least 2 hours. Serve with chips.
NOTE: Wear disposable gloves when cutting hot peppers; the oils can burn skin. Avoid touching your face.
¼ CUP: 33 cal., 0 fat (0 sat. fat), 0 chol., 4mg sod., 8g carb. (6g sugars, 1g fiber), 1g pro. **DIABETIC EXCHANGES:** ½ starch.

GRILLED COCONUT CURRY WINGS

Everyone loves grilled wings and this is such a nice change from the usual version we see all summer long.
—*Carla Mendres, Winnipeg, MB*

Prep: 15 min. + marinating
Grill: 15 min. • **Makes:** 20 pieces

- 1 can (13.66 oz.) coconut milk
- 3 Tbsp. curry powder
- 4 garlic cloves, crushed
- 1 Tbsp. minced fresh gingerroot
- 2 lbs. chicken wingettes
- ½ tsp. salt
- ¼ tsp. pepper
- 2 Tbsp. honey, optional
  Thinly sliced green onions and lime wedges

1. In a large bowl or shallow dish, combine coconut milk, curry powder, garlic and ginger. Add chicken; turn to coat. Cover and refrigerate 8 hours or overnight.
2. Drain chicken, discarding marinade. Sprinkle chicken with salt and pepper. Grill, covered, over medium heat until juices run clear, 15-18 minutes, turning occasionally. If desired, drizzle with honey. Serve with green onions and lime wedges.
1 PIECE: 82 cal., 5g fat (2g sat. fat), 36mg chol., 236mg sod., 0 carb. (0 sugars, 0 fiber), 9g pro.

MARGARITA GELATIN SHOTS

Everyone's favorite cocktail becomes a celebratory shot! Serve them in shot glasses garnished to look like mini margaritas or, for a fun twist, pour the mixture into hollowed-out lime halves.
—Taste of Home *Test Kitchen*

Prep: 10 min. + chilling
Makes: 24 servings

- 3 envelopes unflavored gelatin
- 1 can (12 oz.) frozen limeade concentrate, thawed
- 1 cup tequila
- ¼ cup Triple Sec
  Optional: kosher salt and lime wedge

1. In a small saucepan, sprinkle gelatin over cold limeade; let stand 1 minute. Heat and stir over low heat until gelatin is completely dissolved. Remove from heat. Stir in tequila and triple sec.
2. Pour into 2-oz. shot glasses; chill until set. If desired, garnish rim with salt and lime. To serve in lime wedges instead of shot glasses, halve and juice 6 limes (save juice for another use). Scrape out pulp. Place halves in muffin tins for stability. Fill with mixture. Chill until set; cut each lime half into 2 wedges.
1 SERVING: 69 cal., 0 fat (0 sat. fat), 0 chol., 3mg sod., 10g carb. (9g sugars, 0 fiber), 1g pro.

SET 'EM UP FAST

There are a few tricks to make gelatin shots set faster. One way is to keep the tequila in the freezer before stirring it into the gelatin and limeade mixture. You can also freeze your shot glasses or lime halves before adding the gelatin. But don't pop them into the freezer once you've added the gelatin because the outer edges will start to freeze before the middles set.

SPRING PEA CROSTINI

Peas are an amazing power veggie full of flavor and nutrients. Use them with parsley for a colorful and crunchy topping on toast.
—*Ana Maria Avellar, Newport Beach, CA*

Takes: 30 min. • **Makes:** 40 appetizers

- 40 slices French bread baguette (¼ in. thick)
- 3 cups fresh or frozen peas
- 2 cups packed fresh parsley leaves
- ¾ cup plain Greek yogurt
- 5 Tbsp. olive oil, divided
- 1 garlic clove, minced
- ½ tsp. salt
- ½ tsp. pepper
- ½ cup crumbled goat or feta cheese
  Thinly sliced fresh basil or whole parsley sprigs

1. Preheat broiler. Place the baguette slices on ungreased baking sheets. Broil 3-4 in. from the heat until golden brown, 1-2 minutes.
2. In a large saucepan, bring 6 cups salted water to a boil. Add peas; cook, uncovered, 3-4 minutes or just until tender. Drain.
3. Place peas and parsley in a food processor; process until chopped. Add yogurt, 3 Tbsp. oil, garlic, salt and pepper; process just until blended.
4. To serve, spread pea mixture over baguette slices. Drizzle with remaining oil; top with cheese and basil.
1 APPETIZER: 43 cal., 3g fat (1g sat. fat), 3mg chol., 65mg sod., 4g carb. (1g sugars, 1g fiber), 1g pro.

OLIVE-STUFFED CELERY

My grandmother taught both me and my mom this appetizer recipe. We always serve it at Christmas and Thanksgiving. The stuffing is so yummy that even if you don't normally care for the ingredients on their own, you'll love the end result.
—*Stacy Powell, Santa Fe, TX*

Takes: 25 min. • **Makes:** 2 dozen

- 1 dill pickle spear plus 1 tsp. juice
- 3 sweet pickles plus 1 tsp. juice
- 6 pitted ripe olives plus 1 tsp. juice
- 6 pimiento-stuffed olives plus 1 tsp. juice
- 1 pkg. (8 oz.) cream cheese, softened
- ⅓ cup Miracle Whip
- ¼ tsp. salt
- ¼ cup finely chopped pecans, toasted
- 6 celery ribs, cut into 2-in. pieces

1. Finely chop the pickles and olives; set aside. In a small bowl, beat the cream cheese, Miracle Whip, juices and salt until blended. Stir in the pickles, olives and pecans.
2. Pipe or stuff filling into celery sticks. Store in the refrigerator.

1 PIECE: 61 cal., 5g fat (2g sat. fat), 12mg chol., 228mg sod., 2g carb. (1g sugars, 0 fiber), 1g pro.

LOADED COWBOY QUESO

This is the ultimate football dip. The easy appetizer loaded with cheese, beer, black beans, tomatoes and sausage is our favorite tailgating recipe. I often serve it with homemade tortilla chips sprinkled with taco seasoning.
—*Becky Hardin, St. Peters, MO*

Prep: 15 min. • **Cook:** 15 min.
Makes: 24 servings (6 cups)

- ½ lb. bulk spicy pork sausage
- 1 cup pale ale or other light beer
- 1 pkg. (16 oz.) Velveeta, cubed
- ½ cup shredded pepper jack cheese
- 1 tsp. salt
- 1 tsp. garlic powder
- 1 tsp. onion powder
- ½ tsp. cayenne pepper
- 1 can (10 oz.) diced tomatoes with mild green chiles, undrained
- 1 cup black beans, rinsed and drained
- ¼ cup minced fresh cilantro
  Optional: jalapenos and tortilla or corn chips

1. In a large skillet, cook sausage, crumbling meat, over medium heat until no longer pink, about 5 minutes. Add beer, cook until reduced slightly, 3-4 minutes, stirring occasionally. Add Velveeta, pepper jack cheese and seasonings; stir occasionally until melted. When melted, stir in tomatoes, beans, and cilantro.
2. If desired, garnish with jalapenos and additional cilantro and serve with tortilla or corn chips.

¼ CUP: 110 cal., 8g fat (4g sat. fat), 26mg chol., 461mg sod., 4g carb. (2g sugars, 1g fiber), 5g pro.

PICKLED PEPPERONCINI DEVILED EGGS

It's hard to resist these adorable deviled eggs that look like tiny Christmas trees on the buffet. The avocado filling has pepperoncini and cilantro for extra zip.
—*Carmell Childs, Orangeville, UT*

Takes: 30 min. • **Makes:** 1 dozen

- 6 hard-boiled large eggs
- 1 jar (16 oz.) garlic and dill pepperoncini
- 1 medium ripe avocado, peeled and pitted
- 1 Tbsp. minced fresh cilantro, divided
- ¼ tsp. salt
- ⅛ tsp. pepper
- 1 Tbsp. minced sweet red pepper
- ¼ tsp. chili powder

1. Cut eggs lengthwise in half. Remove yolks, reserving whites. Mash yolks. Stir in 1 tsp. minced garlic from the pepperoncini jar and 2 tsp. pepperoncini juice. Add 3 Tbsp. minced pepperoncini and the whole avocado; mash with a fork until smooth. Stir in 2 tsp. cilantro, salt and pepper.

2. Cut a small hole in the tip of a pastry bag; insert a medium star tip. Transfer avocado mixture to bag. Pipe into egg whites, swirling it upward to resemble Christmas trees. Sprinkle trees with minced red pepper, chili powder and remaining cilantro.

3. Cut open and seed 1 larger pepperoncini; slice into 12 small diamond shapes to top the Christmas trees. Refrigerate, covered, until serving. Save remaining pepperoncini for another use.

1 STUFFED EGG HALF: 59 cal., 4g fat (1g sat. fat), 93mg chol., 125mg sod., 1g carb. (0 sugars, 1g fiber), 3g pro.

BEST BOILED EGGS

Follow these steps for perfect hard-cooked eggs every time:

1. Place eggs in pot and just cover with cold water.

2. Bring to a full boil; as soon as the water boils, remove pan from heat.

3. Cover and set timer for 12 minutes.

4. Drain; run cold water over eggs to stop the cooking.

KALAMATA CHEESECAKE APPETIZER

The savory cheesecake filling tames the bold taste of kalamata olives, so even those who shy away from kalamatas will be glad they sampled this dish. For a milder flavor, use regular black olives.
—*Theresa Kreyche, Tustin, CA*

Prep: 30 min. • **Bake:** 25 min. + chilling
Makes: 24 servings

- 1¼ cups seasoned bread crumbs
- ½ cup finely chopped pecans
- ⅓ cup butter, melted

FILLING

- 11 oz. cream cheese, softened
- 1 cup sour cream
- 1 Tbsp. all-purpose flour
- ¼ tsp. salt
- ¼ tsp. pepper
- 1 large egg, room temperature
- 1 large egg yolk, room temperature
- ½ cup pitted kalamata olives, chopped
- 2 tsp. minced fresh rosemary
  Optional: Halved pitted kalamata olives and fresh rosemary sprigs

1. Combine bread crumbs and pecans; stir in butter. Press onto the bottom of a greased 9-in. springform pan. Place pan on a baking sheet. Bake at 350° for 12 minutes. Cool on a wire rack.
2. In a large bowl, beat the cream cheese, sour cream, flour, salt and pepper until smooth. Add egg and egg yolk; beat on low speed just until combined. Fold in chopped olives and minced rosemary. Pour over crust. Return pan to baking sheet.
3. Bake for 25-30 minutes or until center is almost set. Cool on a wire rack for 10 minutes. Loosen edge of cheesecake from pan with a knife. Cool 1 hour longer. Refrigerate overnight.
4. Remove rim from pan. If desired, top cheesecake with olives and rosemary.
1 PIECE: 142 cal., 12g fat (6g sat. fat), 45mg chol., 223mg sod., 6g carb. (1g sugars, 0 fiber), 3g pro.

SUMMERTIME TEA

You can't have a summer gathering around here without this sweet tea to cool you down. It's wonderful for sipping while basking by the pool.
—*Angela Lively, Conroe, TX*

Prep: 15 min. + chilling
Makes: 18 servings

- 14 cups water, divided
- 6 black tea bags
- 1½ cups sugar
- ¾ cup thawed orange juice concentrate
- ¾ cup thawed lemonade concentrate
- 1 cup tequila, optional
  Optional: Fresh mint leaves and lemon or lime slices

1. In a large saucepan, bring 4 cups water to a boil. Remove from heat; add tea bags. Cover and steep for 3-5 minutes. Discard tea bags.
2. Stir in the sugar, concentrates and remaining water. Add tequila if desired. Refrigerate until chilled. Garnish with mint and lemon or lime if desired.
¾ CUP: 102 cal., 0 fat (0 sat. fat), 0 chol., 1mg sod., 26g carb. (26g sugars, 0 fiber), 0 pro.

★ ★ ★ ★ ★ **READER REVIEW**

"We have been in a major heat wave. I made this today and took it to a pool party. Everyone loved it— extremely refreshing and delicious!"
BLBERGER TASTEOFHOME.COM

PEPPER SHOOTERS

Pop one of these savory peppers into your mouth for a tantalizing array of flavors. It's like an antipasto platter all in one bite.
—Taste of Home *Test Kitchen*

- -

Takes: 30 min. • **Makes:** 2 dozen

- 24 pickled sweet cherry peppers
- 4 oz. fresh mozzarella cheese, finely chopped
- 2¾ oz. thinly sliced hard salami, finely chopped
- 3 Tbsp. prepared pesto
- 2 Tbsp. olive oil

Cut tops off peppers and remove seeds; set aside. In a small bowl, combine the mozzarella, salami and pesto; spoon into peppers. Drizzle with oil. Chill until serving.

1 APPETIZER: 55 cal., 4g fat (1g sat. fat), 7mg chol., 313mg sod., 2g carb. (1g sugars, 1g fiber), 3g pro.

MAKE IT YOUR OWN

Swap out the mozzarella and salami in these pepper shooters for countless other options. Try shredded or diced provolone, olives, pepperoni, goat cheese, diced tomatoes and even croutons.

HOT SPINACH SPREAD WITH PITA CHIPS

Warm and cheesy, this spread is absolutely scrumptious served on toasted pita wedges. Its colorful appearance makes a stunning addition to any buffet.
—*Teresa Emanuel, Smithville, MO*

- -

Prep: 30 min. • **Bake:** 20 min.
Makes: 16 servings (4 cups spread)

- 2 cups shredded Monterey Jack cheese
- 1 pkg. (10 oz.) frozen chopped spinach, thawed and squeezed dry
- 1 pkg. (8 oz.) cream cheese, cubed
- 2 plum tomatoes, seeded and chopped
- ¾ cup chopped onion
- ⅓ cup half-and-half cream
- 1 Tbsp. finely chopped seeded jalapeno pepper
- 6 pita breads (6 in.)
- ½ cup butter, melted
- 2 tsp. lemon-pepper seasoning
- 2 tsp. ground cumin
- ¼ tsp. garlic salt

1. In a large bowl, combine the first 7 ingredients. Transfer to a greased 1½-qt. baking dish. Bake, uncovered, at 375° for 20-25 minutes or until bubbly.
2. Meanwhile, cut each pita bread into 8 wedges. Place in two 15x10x1-in. baking pans. Combine the butter, lemon pepper, cumin and garlic salt; brush over the pita wedges.
3. Bake for 7-9 minutes or until crisp. Serve with spinach spread.
NOTE: Wear disposable gloves when cutting hot peppers; the oils can burn skin. Avoid touching your face.
¼ CUP SPREAD WITH 3 PITA WEDGES: 231 cal., 16g fat (10g sat. fat), 46mg chol., 381mg sod., 15g carb. (1g sugars, 1g fiber), 8g pro.

MINI MAC & CHEESE BITES

Young relatives were coming for a Christmas party, so I wanted something fun for them to eat. Instead, the adults devoured my mini mac and cheese bites.
—*Kate Mainiero, Elizaville, NY*

- -

Prep: 35 min. • **Bake:** 10 min.
Makes: 3 dozen

- 2 cups uncooked elbow macaroni
- 1 cup seasoned bread crumbs, divided
- 2 Tbsp. butter
- 2 Tbsp. all-purpose flour
- ½ tsp. onion powder
- ½ tsp. garlic powder
- ½ tsp. seasoned salt
- 1¾ cups 2% milk
- 2 cups shredded sharp cheddar cheese, divided
- 1 cup shredded Swiss cheese
- ¾ cup biscuit/baking mix
- 2 large eggs, room temperature, lightly beaten

1. Preheat oven to 425°. Cook macaroni according to package directions; drain.
2. Meanwhile, sprinkle ¼ cup bread crumbs into 36 greased mini-muffin cups. In a large saucepan, melt butter over medium heat. Stir in flour and seasonings until smooth; gradually whisk in milk. Bring to a boil, stirring constantly; cook and stir until thickened, 1-2 minutes. Stir in 1 cup cheddar cheese and Swiss cheese until melted.
3. Remove from heat; stir in biscuit mix, eggs and ½ cup bread crumbs. Add macaroni; toss to coat. Spoon about 2 Tbsp. macaroni mixture into the prepared mini-muffin cups; sprinkle with remaining cheddar cheese and bread crumbs.
4. Bake until golden brown, 8-10 minutes. Cool in pans 5 minutes before serving.
1 APPETIZER: 91 cal., 5g fat (3g sat. fat), 22mg chol., 162mg sod., 8g carb. (1g sugars, 0 fiber), 4g pro.

SILLY SNAKE SUB

This slithering sub makes a fun and tasty centerpiece. Add your own zany, creative touches and feel free to mix and match the meat and cheeses to suit your family's tastes. You also can add breadsticks to make legs if you want the sub to look like a centipede.
—*Linda Overman, Wichita, KS*

Prep: 15 min. + rising
Bake: 15 min. + cooling
Makes: 12 servings

- 12 **frozen bread dough dinner rolls**
- ¼ **cup mayonnaise**
- 10 **slices cheddar cheese**
- ½ **lb. thinly sliced deli turkey**
- ½ **lb. thinly sliced deli ham**
- 2 **cups shredded lettuce**
- 1 **plum tomato, thinly sliced**
- ¼ **cup yellow mustard**
- 2 **pimiento-stuffed olives**
- 2-in. **piece thinly sliced deli ham, optional**

1. Arrange rolls ½ in. apart in an S-shape on a greased baking sheet. Cover and let rise in a warm place until doubled, about 3 hours.

2. Preheat oven to 350°. Bake rolls 15-20 minutes or until golden brown. Cool completely on pan on a wire rack.

3. Using a serrated knife, cut rolls crosswise in half, leaving halves intact. Spread bun bottoms with mayonnaise. Reserve 1 slice of cheese; layer bottoms with remaining cheese, turkey, ham, lettuce and tomato. Spread mustard over bun tops and replace tops. Using a frilly toothpick, attach an olive to front of snake for each eye. Cut reserved cheese into decorative shapes; place on back of snake. If desired, cut a snake tongue from ham; attach to snake. Discard toothpicks before serving.

1 SANDWICH: 278 cal., 15g fat (6g sat. fat), 44mg chol., 879mg sod., 20g carb. (2g sugars, 1g fiber), 17g pro.

TACO MEATBALL RING

While it looks complicated, this attractive meatball-filled ring is really very easy to assemble. My family loves tacos, and we find that the crescent roll dough is a nice change from the usual tortilla shells or chips.
—*Brenda Johnson, Davison, MI*

Prep: 30 min. • **Bake:** 15 min.
Makes: 16 servings

- 2 cups shredded cheddar cheese, divided
- 2 Tbsp. water
- 2 to 4 Tbsp. taco seasoning
- ½ lb. ground beef
- 2 tubes (8 oz. each) refrigerated crescent rolls
- ½ medium head iceberg lettuce, shredded
- 1 medium tomato, chopped
- 4 green onions, sliced
- ½ cup sliced ripe olives
- 2 jalapeno peppers, sliced
  Optional: Sour cream and salsa

1. In a large bowl, combine 1 cup cheese, water and taco seasoning. Crumble beef over mixture and mix lightly but thoroughly. Shape into 16 balls.
2. Place meatballs on a greased rack in a shallow baking pan. Bake, uncovered, at 400° until meat is no longer pink, about 12 minutes. Drain meatballs on paper towels. Reduce heat to 375°.
3. Arrange crescent rolls on a greased 15-in. pizza pan, forming a ring with pointed ends facing the outer edge of the pan and wide ends overlapping.
4. Place a meatball on each roll; fold point over meatball and tuck under wide end of roll (meatball will be visible). Repeat. Bake until rolls are golden brown, 15-20 minutes.

5. Transfer to a serving platter. Fill the center of the ring with lettuce, tomato, onions, olives, jalapenos, remaining cheese and, if desired, sour cream and salsa.
NOTE: Wear disposable gloves when cutting hot peppers; the oils can burn skin. Avoid touching your face.
1 PIECE: 203 cal., 12g fat (5g sat. fat), 24mg chol., 457mg sod., 14g carb. (3g sugars, 1g fiber), 8g pro.

★ ★ ★ ★ ★ **READER REVIEW**
"I usually make this on holidays. It's so yummy and everyone enjoys it. There are never any leftovers for me to take home."
MARGARETB TASTEOFHOME.COM

BLACK FOREST HAM PINWHEELS

Dried cherries are the sweet surprise alongside the savory ingredients in these delightfully different spirals. I roll up the tortillas and pop them in the fridge well before party time, and then I just slice and serve.
—*Kate Dampier, Quail Valley, CA*

Prep: 20 min. + chilling
Makes: about 3½ dozen

- 1 **pkg. (8 oz.) cream cheese, softened**
- 4 **tsp. minced fresh dill**
- 1 **Tbsp. lemon juice**
- 2 **tsp. Dijon mustard**
  Dash each salt and pepper
- ½ **cup dried cherries, chopped**
- ¼ **cup chopped green onions**
- 5 **flour tortillas (10 in.), room temperature**
- ½ **lb. sliced deli Black Forest ham**
- ½ **lb. sliced Swiss cheese**

1. In a small bowl, beat cream cheese, dill, lemon juice, mustard, salt and pepper until blended. Stir in cherries and onions. Spread over each tortilla; layer with ham and cheese.

2. Roll up tightly; securely wrap in waxed paper. Refrigerate at least 2 hours. Cut into ½-in. slices.
1 PIECE: 78 cal., 4g fat (2g sat. fat), 13mg chol., 151mg sod., 6g carb. (2g sugars, 0 fiber), 4g pro.
VEGGIE PINWHEELS: Omit dill, lemon juice, mustard, salt, pepper, cherries, onion, ham and cheese. Beat cream cheese with 1 cup sour cream, 1 can (4¼ oz.) drained chopped ripe olives, 1 can (4 oz.) well-drained chopped green chiles, 1 cup shredded cheddar cheese, ½ cup chopped green onions, dash garlic powder and dash salt until blended. Spread over tortillas and proceed as recipe directs.
REUBEN PINWHEELS: Omit dill, lemon juice, mustard, salt, pepper, cherries, onion, ham and cheese. Beat cream cheese with 3 Tbsp. spicy brown mustard and ¼ tsp. prepared horseradish. Spread 1 heaping Tbsp. of cream cheese mixture over each tortilla; layer each with 8 thin slices deli corned beef, 3 thin slices Swiss cheese and 1 heaping Tbsp. additional cream cheese mixture. Top each with ½ cup well-drained sauerkraut. Proceed as recipe directs.

JALAPENO POPPER SPREAD

I've been told by fellow partygoers that this recipe tastes exactly like a jalapeno popper. I like that it can be made without much fuss.
—*Ariane McAlpine, Penticton, BC*

Prep: 10 min. • **Bake:** 25 min.
Makes: 4 cups

- 2 **pkg. (8 oz. each) cream cheese, softened**
- 1 **cup mayonnaise**
- ½ **cup shredded Monterey Jack cheese**
- ¼ **cup canned chopped green chiles**
- ¼ **cup canned diced jalapeno peppers**
- 1 **cup shredded Parmesan cheese**
- ½ **cup panko bread crumbs**
  Sweet red and yellow pepper pieces and corn chips

In a large bowl, beat the first 5 ingredients until blended; spread into an ungreased 9-in. pie plate. Sprinkle with Parmesan cheese; top with bread crumbs. Bake at 400° until lightly browned, 25-30 minutes. Serve with peppers and chips.
¼ CUP: 239 cal., 23g fat (9g sat. fat), 43mg chol., 304mg sod., 3g carb. (1g sugars, 0 fiber), 5g pro.

VIDALIA ONION SWISS DIP

I've got one of those sweet, creamy dips you can't resist. Bake it in the oven, or use the slow cooker to make it ooey-gooey marvelous.
—*Judy Batson, Tampa, FL*

Prep: 10 min. • **Cook:** 25 min.
Makes: 20 servings

- 3 cups chopped Vidalia or other sweet onion (about 1 large)
- 2 cups shredded Swiss cheese
- 2 cups mayonnaise
- ¼ cup prepared horseradish
- 1 tsp. hot pepper sauce
  Fresh coarsely ground pepper, optional
  Assorted crackers or fresh vegetables

1. Preheat oven to 375°. In a large bowl, mix the first 5 ingredients. Transfer to a deep-dish pie plate.
2. Bake, uncovered, until edges are golden brown and onion is tender, 25-30 minutes. If desired, sprinkle with pepper. Serve warm with crackers.
¼ CUP: 212 cal., 21g fat (4g sat. fat), 18mg chol., 143mg sod., 3g carb. (1g sugars, 1g fiber), 3g pro.

PISTACHIO & DATE RICOTTA CROSTINI

My husband and I regularly have date night at home where we make a four-course meal. For appetizers, I like to keep things simple but dressed up. I've found that making a special appetizer helps transform the atmosphere into a fancy meal. We've grown to really cherish these long and luxurious evenings together in our living room.
—*Kristin Bowers, Gilbert, AZ*

Prep: 20 min. • **Bake:** 15 min.
Makes: 3 dozen

- 36 slices French bread baguette (¼ in. thick)
- 2 Tbsp. olive oil
- ⅛ tsp. plus ¼ tsp. salt, divided
- 1 cup whole-milk ricotta cheese
- 4 oz. cream cheese, softened
- 3 Tbsp. honey, divided
- 4 tsp. grated lemon zest, divided
- 10 pitted Medjool dates, chopped (about 1½ cups)
- ½ cup shelled pistachios, finely chopped

1. Preheat oven to 400°. Place bread slices on a large ungreased baking sheet. Brush tops with olive oil and sprinkle with ⅛ tsp. salt. Bake until golden brown, 12-15 minutes. Cool on baking sheet.
2. Meanwhile, place ricotta, cream cheese, 2 Tbsp. honey, 2 tsp. zest and remaining ¼ tsp. salt in a food processor; process until almost smooth. Spread mixture over bread slices. Top with dates and pistachios. Drizzle with remaining 1 Tbsp. honey and 2 tsp. zest. Serve immediately.
1 APPETIZER: 57 cal., 3g fat (1g sat. fat), 6mg chol., 74mg sod., 6g carb. (3g sugars, 0 fiber), 1g pro.

PINEAPPLE CHEESE BALL

Pineapple lends a fruity tang to this fun and tasty appetizer. Instead of forming one large cheese ball, you could make two smaller balls—one to serve before a meal and one to take to a party.
—*Anne Halfhill, Sunbury, OH*

- -

Prep: 20 min. + chilling
Makes: 1 cheese ball (3 cups)

- 2 pkg. (8 oz. each) cream cheese, softened
- 1 can (8 oz.) unsweetened crushed pineapple, drained
- ¼ cup finely chopped green pepper
- 2 Tbsp. finely chopped onion
- 2 tsp. seasoned salt
- 1½ cups chopped walnuts
  Assorted crackers and
  fresh vegetables

In a small bowl, beat cream cheese, pineapple, green pepper, onion and seasoned salt until blended. Cover and refrigerate for 30 minutes. Shape into a ball (mixture will be soft); coat in walnuts. Cover and refrigerate overnight. Serve with crackers and vegetables.
2 TBSP.: 87 cal., 8g fat (2g sat. fat), 10mg chol., 155mg sod., 3g carb. (1g sugars, 1g fiber), 3g pro.

★ ★ ★ ★ ★ **READER REVIEW**

"Love this recipe with pecans instead of walnuts and green onion instead of regular. It's important to thoroughly drain the pineapple. I get it drier using paper towels."

CARMEN412 TASTEOFHOME.COM

SMOKED SALMON BITES WITH SHALLOT SAUCE

Tangy Dijon-mayo sauce adds zip to layers of crisp arugula, smoked salmon and shaved Asiago cheese. I make these a couple of times a year.
—*Jamie Brown-Miller, Napa, CA*

- -

Takes: 30 min. • **Makes:** 25 appetizers

- 1 sheet frozen puff pastry, thawed

SAUCE
- 2 shallots
- 2 Tbsp. Dijon mustard
- 1 Tbsp. mayonnaise
- 1 Tbsp. red wine vinegar
- ¼ cup olive oil

FINISHING
- 1 cup fresh arugula or baby spinach, coarsely chopped
- 4½ oz. smoked salmon or lox, thinly sliced
- ½ cup shaved Asiago cheese

1. Preheat oven to 400°. Unfold puff pastry; cut into 25 squares. Transfer to greased baking sheets. Bake for 11-13 minutes or until golden brown.
2. Meanwhile, grate 1 shallot and finely chop the other. In a small bowl, combine shallots, mustard, mayonnaise and vinegar. While whisking, gradually add oil in a steady stream. Spoon a small amount of sauce onto each pastry; layer with arugula and salmon. Drizzle with remaining sauce and sprinkle with cheese.
1 APPETIZER: 89 cal., 6g fat (1g sat. fat), 3mg chol., 105mg sod., 6g carb. (0 sugars, 1g fiber), 2g pro.

TURKEY TEA SANDWICHES WITH BASIL MAYONNAISE

Basil mayonnaise is the secret to these tasty little sandwiches. Keep any extra mayo in the fridge to spread on other sandwiches, stir into egg salad or layer on pizza crust before topping it with other ingredients.
—*Lara Pennell, Mauldin, SC*

Takes: 15 min. • **Makes:** 20 tea sandwiches

- ½ cup mayonnaise
- ⅓ cup loosely packed basil leaves
- 10 slices white bread, crusts removed
- 10 oz. thinly sliced deli turkey
- 5 slices provolone cheese

Place mayonnaise and basil in a food processor; process until basil is finely chopped, scraping down sides as needed. Spread mayonnaise mixture over each bread slice. Layer 5 bread slices with turkey and cheese; top with remaining bread slices. Cut each into 4 long pieces.

1 TEA SANDWICH: 90 cal., 6g fat (2g sat. fat), 9mg chol., 230mg sod., 4g carb. (0 sugars, 0 fiber), 5g pro.

SPICY ROASTED CARROT HUMMUS

This is a wonderful appetizer for Easter, Mother's Day or any spring gathering. The roasted carrots give this hummus such a bright, fresh flavor. People who say they don't like hummus have loved this version!
—*Anne Ormond, Dover, NH*

Prep: 20 min. • **Roast:** 15 min. + cooling
Makes: 2 cups

- 1 cup chopped carrots
- 3 garlic cloves
- 3 Tbsp. olive oil, divided
- 1 can (15 oz.) garbanzo beans or chickpeas, rinsed and drained
- 2 Tbsp. lemon juice
- 2 Tbsp. tahini
- 1 Tbsp. water
- 1 tsp. hot pepper sauce, such as Tabasco
- ¼ tsp. sea salt
- ¼ tsp. ground turmeric
- ¼ tsp. ground cumin
- ⅛ tsp. cayenne pepper
- ¼ cup sunflower kernels
  Assorted fresh vegetables and pita wedges

1. Preheat oven to 400°. Place carrots and garlic in a rimmed baking sheet. Drizzle with 2 Tbsp. oil; toss to coat. Roast until the carrots are soft, 15-20 minutes. Cool on a wire rack.
2. Transfer carrot mixture to a food processor. Add garbanzo beans, lemon juice, tahini, water, hot sauce, salt and spices. While processing, add remaining 1 Tbsp. oil. Process until it's the desired consistency. Transfer to a serving dish. If desired, drizzle with additional oil and hot sauce. Top with sunflower seeds. Serve warm or chilled with vegetables and pita wedges.

¼ CUP: 155 cal., 11g fat (1g sat. fat), 0 chol., 175mg sod., 12g carb. (2g sugars, 3g fiber), 4g pro. **DIABETIC EXCHANGES:** 2 fat, 1 starch.

PESTO TWISTS

Use pesto made straight from your kitchen garden or purchase it prepared from the grocery store to fill these easy appetizers.

—*Jaye Beeler, Grand Rapids, MI*

Takes: 25 min. • **Makes:** 12 twists

- 1 pkg. (17.3 oz.) frozen puff pastry, thawed
- ½ cup prepared pesto
- ½ cup shredded Parmesan cheese
  Marinara sauce, warmed, optional

1. Preheat oven to 400°.
2. Unfold puff pastry sheets on a lightly floured surface. Roll each sheet into a 12-in. square. Spread pesto onto 1 pastry sheet to within ¼ in. of edges. Sprinkle with cheese. Top with remaining pastry, pressing lightly. Cut into twelve 1-in.-wide strips. Twist each strip 4 times. Place 2 in. apart on parchment-lined baking sheets, pressing down ends.
3. Bake until golden brown, 12-15 minutes. Serve warm with marinara sauce, if desired.

1 TWIST: 265 cal., 17g fat (4g sat. fat), 6mg chol., 270mg sod., 24g carb. (0 sugars, 3g fiber), 6g pro.

CHEDDAR TWISTS: Beat 1 egg and 1 Tbsp. water; brush over both sheets of pastry. Top 1 sheet with ¾ cup shredded cheddar cheese. Top with remaining pastry, egg wash side down. Cut and bake as directed.

SWEET ALMOND TWISTS: Beat 1 egg and 1 Tbsp. water; brush over both sheets of pastry. Top 1 sheet with ¼ cup almond cake and pastry filling 1 cup sliced almonds. Top with remaining pastry, egg wash side down. Cut and bake as directed.

★ ★ ★ ★ ★ **READER REVIEW**

"I took these to a luncheon along with a homemade salad. They were a nice addition to the salad and everyone seemed to like them. I will make them again."

POPOAGGIE TASTEOFHOME.COM

PATRIOTIC PEPPER PLATTER

Cream cheese stuffed peppers are easy to make, easy to travel with and wonderful to eat at room temperature. This platter can be made all summer long for each red, white and blue holiday! The dish also accommodates those who eat meat and those who don't. With or without the bacon, these peppers are delish!
—Tina Martino, Hewitt, NJ

Prep: 30 min. • **Bake:** 25 min.
Makes: 4 dozen

- 24 miniature sweet red peppers
- 1 pkg. (8 oz.) cream cheese, softened
- ½ cup grated Parmesan cheese
- 24 bacon strips, halved lengthwise
- 2 slices white cheddar cheese
- 1 jar (9½ oz.) pitted Greek olives, drained
  Crushed red pepper flakes, optional

1. Preheat oven 400°. Cut miniature peppers in half lengthwise and remove seeds; set aside. In a small bowl, beat cream cheese and Parmesan cheese until blended. Spoon into pepper halves. Cut bacon in half lengthwise. Wrap a half-strip of bacon around 24 pepper halves; place in a greased 15x10x1-in. baking pan. Place unwrapped pepper halves in another 15x10x1-in. baking pan.
2. Bake until bacon is cooked and filling is bubbly, 25-30 minutes. Meanwhile, using a star cookie cutter, cut stars out of cheese slices. Arrange peppers, olives and cheese stars on a serving platter to resemble an American flag. If desired, sprinkle bacon-wrapped peppers with red pepper flakes.
1 STUFFED PEPPER HALF: 60 cal., 5g fat (2g sat. fat), 10mg chol., 198mg sod., 1g carb. (0 sugars, 0 fiber), 2g pro.

BRIE-LEEK TARTLETS

I have a family of picky eaters, but everyone loves these little bites. I make dozens of them at a time because they're gone the second I turn my back.
—Colleen MacDonald, Port Moody, BC

Takes: 30 min. • **Makes:** 15 servings

- 1 medium leek (white portion only), finely chopped
- 3 Tbsp. butter
- 1 garlic clove, minced
- ½ cup heavy whipping cream
  Dash salt and white pepper
  Dash ground nutmeg
- 1 pkg. (1.9 oz.) frozen miniature phyllo tart shells
- 2 oz. Brie cheese, rind removed
  Minced fresh parsley, optional

1. In a small skillet, saute leek in butter until tender. Add garlic; cook 1 minute longer. Stir in cream, salt, pepper and nutmeg; cook and stir until thickened, 1-2 minutes.
2. Place tart shells on a baking sheet. Slice cheese into 15 pieces; place 1 piece in each tart shell. Top each with 1½ tsp. leek mixture.
3. Bake at 350° until heated through, 6-8 minutes. If desired, sprinkle with parsley. Refrigerate leftovers.
1 TARTLET: 86 cal., 7g fat (4g sat. fat), 21mg chol., 64mg sod., 4g carb. (0 sugars, 0 fiber), 2g pro.

BBQ CHICKEN GRITS BITES

I love grits and barbecued chicken, so I decided to combine them into a jaunty appetizer. You can also use shredded pork instead of chicken.
—*Jamie Jones, Madison, GA*

Prep: 30 min. • **Bake:** 15 min.
Makes: 2½ dozen

- 2 cups 2% milk
- ¾ cup quick-cooking grits
- ¼ tsp. salt
- ⅛ tsp. pepper
- 4 oz. crumbled goat cheese, divided
- ¼ cup apricot preserves
- ¼ cup barbecue sauce
- 1½ cups chopped rotisserie chicken
- 3 green onions, thinly sliced

1. Preheat oven to 350°. Grease 30 mini-muffin cups.
2. In a large saucepan, bring milk to a boil. Slowly stir in grits, salt and pepper. Reduce heat to medium-low; cook, covered, until thickened, about 5 minutes, stirring occasionally. Stir in half of the cheese. Spoon 1 Tbsp. mixture into each prepared muffin cup.
3. In a bowl, mix preserves and barbecue sauce; toss with chicken. Spoon about 1 tsp. chicken mixture into each cup; press lightly into grits.
4. Bake until heated through, 15-20 minutes. Top with remaining cheese; sprinkle with green onions. Cool 5 minutes before removing from pans. Serve warm.
1 APPETIZER: 56 cal., 2g fat (1g sat. fat), 12mg chol., 76mg sod., 7g carb. (3g sugars, 0 fiber), 4g pro.

ANTIPASTO PLATTER

We entertain often, and antipasto is one of our favorite crowd-pleasers. Guests love having their choice of so many delicious nibbles, including pepperoni and cubes of provolone.
—*Teri Lindquist, Gurnee, IL*

Prep: 10 min. + chilling
Makes: 16 servings (3 qt.)

- 1 jar (24 oz.) pepperoncini, drained
- 1 can (15 oz.) garbanzo beans or chickpeas, rinsed and drained
- 2 cups halved fresh mushrooms
- 2 cups halved cherry tomatoes
- ½ lb. provolone cheese, cubed
- 1 can (6 oz.) pitted ripe olives, drained
- 1 pkg. (3½ oz.) sliced pepperoni
- 1 bottle (8 oz.) Italian vinaigrette dressing
  Lettuce leaves

1. In a large bowl, combine pepperoncini, beans, mushrooms, tomatoes, cheese, olives and pepperoni. Pour vinaigrette over mixture; toss to coat.
2. Refrigerate at least 30 minutes or overnight. Arrange on a lettuce-lined platter. Serve with toothpicks.
1 CUP: 178 cal., 13g fat (4g sat. fat), 15mg chol., 852mg sod., 8g carb. (2g sugars, 2g fiber), 6g pro.

BRING IT
This dish is practical to bring on the road. Carry lettuce leaves and antipasto mix in separate resealable bags. On-site, line the platter with lettuce and pile high with the good stuff. You can hold back extra antipasto and replenish it as needed.

PUMPKIN FRENCH TOAST
WITH BACON MAPLE SYRUP,
PAGE 52

Breakfast for a Bunch

Morning meals are something to celebrate, thanks to delicious doughnuts, homey quiches, crowd-sized casseroles and more.

GLAZED CHERRY COFFEE CAKE

With its pretty layer of cherries and crunchy streusel topping, this coffee cake is fantastic for breakfast. Or you can even serve it for dessert.
—*Gail Buss, New Bern, NC*

Prep: 25 min. • **Bake:** 35 min. + cooling
Makes: 16 servings

- 1 pkg. yellow cake mix (regular size), divided
- 1 cup all-purpose flour
- 1 pkg. (¼ oz.) active dry yeast
- ⅔ cup warm water (120° to 130°)
- 2 large eggs, room temperature, lightly beaten
- 1 can (21 oz.) cherry pie filling
- ⅓ cup butter, melted

GLAZE
- 1 cup confectioners' sugar
- 1 Tbsp. corn syrup
- 1 to 2 Tbsp. water

1. Preheat oven to 350°. In a large bowl, combine 1½ cups cake mix, flour, yeast and water until smooth. Stir in eggs until blended. Transfer to a greased 13x9-in. baking dish. Gently spoon cherry pie filling over top.

2. In a small bowl, mix the butter and remaining cake mix; sprinkle over filling.

3. Bake 35-40 minutes or until lightly browned. Cool on a wire rack. In a small bowl, combine confectioners' sugar, corn syrup and enough water to achieve desired consistency. Drizzle over coffee cake.

1 PIECE: 264 cal., 6g fat (3g sat. fat), 33mg chol., 281mg sod., 51g carb. (30g sugars, 1g fiber), 3g pro.

APPLE COFFEE CAKE: Substitute apple pie filling for the cherry pie filling.

BLUEBERRY COFFEE CAKE: Substitute blueberry pie filling for the cherry pie filling.

RASPBERRY COFFEE CAKE: Substitute raspberry pie filling for the cherry pie filling.

GREAT GRANOLA

Nuts and dried fruit make a crunchy homemade topping for yogurt or for eating by the handful. It makes a delicious gift.
—*Johnna Johnson, Scottsdale, AZ*

Prep: 25 min. • **Bake:** 25 min. + cooling
Makes: 7 cups

- 2 cups old-fashioned oats
- ½ cup chopped almonds
- ½ cup salted pumpkin seeds or pepitas
- ½ cup chopped walnuts
- ¼ cup chopped pecans
- ¼ cup sesame seeds
- ¼ cup sunflower kernels
- ⅓ cup honey
- ¼ cup packed brown sugar
- ¼ cup maple syrup
- 2 Tbsp. toasted wheat germ
- 2 Tbsp. canola oil
- 1 tsp. ground cinnamon
- 1 tsp. vanilla extract
- 7 oz. mixed dried fruit (about 1⅓ cups)

1. In a large bowl, combine the first 7 ingredients; set aside.

2. In a small saucepan, combine the honey, brown sugar, syrup, wheat germ, oil and cinnamon. Cook and stir over medium heat until smooth, 4-5 minutes. Remove from the heat; stir in vanilla. Pour over the oat mixture and toss to coat.

3. Transfer to a greased 15x10x1-in. baking pan. Bake at 350° until golden brown, stirring occasionally, 22-27 minutes. Cool completely on a wire rack. Stir in dried fruit. Store in an airtight container.

½ CUP: 290 cal., 14g fat (2g sat. fat), 0 chol., 49mg sod., 38g carb. (25g sugars, 4g fiber), 6g pro.

HEARTY BREAKFAST EGG BAKE

I always fix this casserole ahead of time when overnight guests are visiting so I have more time to spend with them. Then I simply add some toast or biscuits and fresh fruit for a complete meal that everyone loves. This dish also reheats quite well.
—*Pamela Norris, Fenton, MO*

Prep: 10 min. + chilling
Bake: 45 min. + standing
Makes: 8 servings

- 1½ lbs. bulk pork sausage
- 3 cups frozen shredded hash brown potatoes, thawed
- 2 cups shredded cheddar cheese
- 8 large eggs, lightly beaten
- 1 can (10¾ oz.) condensed cream of mushroom soup, undiluted
- ¾ cup evaporated milk

1. Crumble sausage into a large skillet. Cook over medium heat until no longer pink; drain. Transfer to a greased 13x9-in. baking dish. Sprinkle with hash browns and cheese.
2. In a large bowl, whisk the remaining ingredients; pour over the top. Cover and refrigerate overnight.
3. Remove from refrigerator 30 minutes before baking. Bake, uncovered, at 350° for 45-50 minutes or until a knife inserted in center comes out clean. Let stand 10 minutes before cutting.
1 PIECE: 427 cal., 32g fat (15g sat. fat), 281mg chol., 887mg sod., 12g carb. (4g sugars, 1g fiber), 21g pro.

SWEET POTATO-CRANBERRY DOUGHNUTS

I grew up near Idaho where they're famous for spudnuts, a doughnut made from mashed potatoes. These use sweet potatoes and tart cranberries!
—*Joni Hilton, Rocklin, CA*

Prep: 25 min. + rising
Cook: 5 min./batch
Makes: 2 dozen

- ¼ cup sugar
- 1½ tsp. active dry yeast
- 1 tsp. ground cinnamon
- ½ tsp. salt
- 4 to 4½ cups all-purpose flour
- 1 cup 2% milk
- ¼ cup shortening
- 2 Tbsp. water
- 2 large eggs, room temperature
- ½ cup mashed sweet potatoes
- ½ cup finely chopped dried cranberries
  Oil for deep-fat frying
- 1 cup confectioners' sugar
- 2 to 3 Tbsp. apple cider or juice

1. In a large bowl, combine the sugar, yeast, cinnamon, salt and 1½ cups flour. In a small saucepan, heat the milk, shortening and water to 120°-130°; add to dry ingredients. Beat on medium speed for 2 minutes. Add the eggs, mashed potatoes and cranberries; beat 2 minutes longer. Stir in enough remaining flour to form a firm dough.
2. Do not knead. Place in a greased bowl, turning once to grease the top. Cover and let rise in a warm place until doubled, about 1 hour.
3. Punch dough down. Turn onto a lightly floured surface; roll out to ½-in. thickness. Cut with a floured 2½-in. doughnut cutter; reroll scraps. Place 1 in. apart
on greased baking sheets. Cover and let rise until doubled, about 30 minutes.
4. In an electric skillet or deep fryer, heat oil to 375°. Fry doughnuts, a few at a time, until golden brown on both sides. Drain on paper towels. Combine confectioners' sugar and apple cider; dip warm doughnuts in glaze.
1 GLAZED DOUGHNUT: 191 cal., 8g fat (1g sat. fat), 18mg chol., 63mg sod., 27g carb. (10g sugars, 1g fiber), 3g pro.

JALAPENO SAUSAGE QUICHE

This is a fantastic recipe for an office potluck. You can prepare the ingredients the night before, then mix together and pop it in the oven the next morning. You may want to double the recipe, because two is never enough.
—*Pamela Williams, Meridian, MS*

Prep: 30 min. + chilling
Bake: 30 min. + standing
Makes: 2 quiches (8 servings each)

    Dough for double-crust pie
1   lb. bulk pork sausage
5   large eggs
½   cup 2% milk
⅓   cup mayonnaise
1   tsp. salt
1   tsp. pepper
2   cups shredded sharp
    cheddar cheese
1   can (4 oz.) diced jalapeno peppers,
    drained
5   green onions, chopped

1. Preheat oven to 400°. On a lightly floured surface, roll half of dough to a ⅛-in.-thick circle; transfer to a 9-in. pie plate. Trim to ½ in. beyond rim of plate; flute edge. Repeat with remaining dough. Refrigerate 30 minutes. Line unpricked crusts with a double thickness of heavy-duty foil. Bake for 10 minutes. Remove the foil; bake 5 minutes longer. Cool on wire racks.

2. Meanwhile, in a large skillet, cook pork over medium heat until no longer pink, 7-9 minutes; drain. In a large bowl, whisk eggs, milk, mayonnaise, salt and pepper. Stir in cheese, jalapenos, green onions and cooked pork. Pour into crusts.

3. Bake until a knife inserted in center comes out clean, 30-35 minutes. Cover crust edge loosely with foil during the last 15 minutes if needed to prevent overbrowning. Remove foil. Let stand 10 minutes before cutting.

FREEZE OPTION: Cover and freeze unbaked quiches. To use, remove from freezer 30 minutes before baking (do not thaw). Preheat oven to 400°. Place quiches on baking sheets. Bake as directed, increasing the bake time to 40-45 minutes. Cover edges loosely with foil during the last 15 minutes if needed to prevent overbrowning.

1 PIECE: 357 cal., 27g fat (13g sat. fat), 118mg chol., 636mg sod., 17g carb. (1g sugars, 1g fiber), 11g pro.

DOUGH FOR DOUBLE-CRUST PIE (9 IN.): Combine 2½ cups all-purpose flour and ½ tsp. salt; cut in 1 cup cold butter until crumbly. Gradually add ⅓-⅔ cup ice water, tossing with a fork until dough holds together when pressed. Divide dough in half. Shape each into a disk; wrap tightly. Refrigerate 1 hour or overnight.

CHRISTMAS BREAKFAST CASSEROLE

Spicy sausage, herbs and vegetables pack this egg casserole. I like to make it for my family's Christmas breakfast, but it's a worthy meal addition any time of year.
—Debbie Carter, O'Fallon, IL

Prep: 20 min. • **Bake:** 25 min.
Makes: 12 servings

- 1 lb. bulk Italian sausage
- 1 cup chopped onion
- 1 jar (7 oz.) roasted red peppers, drained and chopped, divided
- 1 pkg. (10 oz.) frozen chopped spinach, thawed and well drained
- 1 cup all-purpose flour
- ¼ cup grated Parmesan cheese
- 1 tsp. dried basil
- ½ tsp. salt
- 8 large eggs
- 2 cups 2% milk
- 1 cup shredded provolone cheese

1. Preheat oven to 425°. In a skillet, cook sausage and onion over medium heat until sausage is no longer pink; drain. Transfer to a greased 3-qt. baking dish. Sprinkle with half of the red peppers and all the spinach.
2. In a bowl, combine flour, Parmesan cheese, basil and salt. Combine eggs and milk; add to dry ingredients and mix well. Pour over spinach.
3. Bake the casserole until a knife inserted in the center comes out clean, 20-25 minutes. Sprinkle with provolone cheese and remaining red peppers. Bake until cheese is melted, about 2 minutes longer. Let stand 5 minutes before cutting.
1 SERVING: 232 cal., 13g fat (6g sat. fat), 170mg chol., 531mg sod., 13g carb. (4g sugars, 1g fiber), 14g pro.

MAKE AHEAD
BAKED BANANA FRENCH TOAST

This easy overnight recipe makes a delightful breakfast or brunch entree. The decadent flavor is reminiscent of banana pudding, so I've also served it for dessert.
—Nancy Zimmerman, Cape May Court House, NJ

Prep: 20 min. + chilling
Bake: 55 min. + standing
Makes: 12 servings

- 2 cups sliced ripe bananas
- 2 Tbsp. lemon juice
- 9 cups cubed French bread
- 1 pkg. (8 oz.) cream cheese, cubed
- 9 large eggs
- 4 cups 2% milk
- ½ cup sugar
- ¼ cup butter, melted
- ¼ cup maple syrup
- ½ tsp. ground cinnamon

1. In a small bowl, toss bananas with lemon juice. Place half of bread in a greased 13x9-in. baking dish; layer with cream cheese, bananas and remaining bread.
2. In a large bowl, whisk eggs, milk, sugar, butter, syrup and cinnamon; pour over bread. Cover and refrigerate for 8 hours or overnight.
3. Remove from refrigerator 30 minutes before baking. Bake, uncovered, at 350° until a knife inserted in the center comes out clean, 55-65 minutes. Let stand for 10 minutes before serving.
1 PIECE: 348 cal., 16g fat (9g sat. fat), 196mg chol., 361mg sod., 40g carb. (20g sugars, 1g fiber), 13g pro.

★ ★ ★ ★ ★ **READER REVIEW**

"This was delicious; we all loved it! I'm planning to make it again for Easter. Since I didn't have a lemon handy, I substituted a little orange juice."

MMG-J TASTEOFHOME.COM

ALMOND-CHAI GRANOLA

Whether you snack on it by the handful or eat it with milk or yogurt, you'll be happy that you found this granola recipe.
—*Rachel Preus, Marshall, MI*

- -

Prep: 20 min. • **Bake:** 1¼ hours + cooling.
Makes: 8 cups (16 servings)

2	chai tea bags
¼	cup boiling water
3	cups quick-cooking oats
2	cups almonds, coarsely chopped
1	cup sweetened shredded coconut
½	cup honey
¼	cup olive oil
⅓	cup sugar
2	tsp. vanilla extract
¾	tsp. salt
¾	tsp. ground cinnamon
¾	tsp. ground nutmeg
¼	tsp. ground cardamom

1. Preheat oven to 250°. Steep tea bags in boiling water 5 minutes. Meanwhile, combine oats, almonds and coconut. Discard tea bags; stir remaining ingredients into tea. Pour tea mixture over oat mixture; mix well to coat.
2. Spread evenly in a greased 15x10-in. rimmed pan. Bake until golden brown, stirring every 20 minutes, about 1¼ hours. Cool completely without stirring; store in an airtight container.
½ CUP: 272 cal., 16g fat (3g sat. fat), 0 chol., 130mg sod., 29g carb. (16g sugars, 4g fiber), 6g pro. **DIABETIC EXCHANGES:** 3 fat, 2 starch.

MEASURING STICKY INGREDIENTS
For easy cleanup, spritz the measuring cup with a little cooking spray before measuring sticky ingredients such as honey and molasses.

MAKE AHEAD
MUFFIN-TIN SCRAMBLED EGGS

I made these one year at Christmas as a way to save time, and they were a big hit. I have to make a large batch because my husband and boys can polish them off in a short amount of time. These also freeze very well, if any are left!

—*Jill Darin, Geneseo, IL*

Prep: 15 min. • **Bake:** 20 min. + standing
Makes: 2 dozen

- 24 **large eggs**
- 1 **tsp. salt**
- ½ **tsp. pepper**
- ¼ **tsp. garlic powder**
- 1 **jar (4 oz.) sliced mushrooms, finely chopped**
- 1 **can (4 oz.) chopped green chiles**
- 3 **oz. sliced deli ham, finely chopped**
- ½ **medium onion, finely chopped**
- ½ **cup shredded cheddar cheese**
  Pico de gallo, optional

1. Preheat oven to 350°. In a large bowl, whisk eggs, salt, pepper and garlic powder until blended. Stir in the mushrooms, chiles, ham, onion and cheese. Spoon about ¼ cup mixture into each of 24 greased muffin cups.

2. Bake until eggs are set, 18-20 minutes, rotating pans halfway through baking. Let stand 10 minutes before removing from pans. If desired, serve with pico de gallo.

FREEZE OPTION: Freeze cooled, baked egg cups in airtight freezer containers. To use, microwave each serving on high for 1¼-1½ minutes or until heated through.

1 EGG CUP: 88 cal., 6g fat (2g sat. fat), 190mg chol., 257mg sod., 1g carb. (0 sugars, 0 fiber), 8g pro. **DIABETIC EXCHANGES:** 1 medium-fat meat.

CHAMPAGNE PUNCH

A blend of four fruit juices pairs well with bubbly champagne in this party-pleasing punch. A strawberry garnish adds a festive touch.
—*Amy Short, Milton, WV*

- -

Takes: 5 min. + chilling
Makes: 16 servings (3 qt.)

- 4   cups orange juice
- 1   cup ruby red grapefruit juice
- ½   cup lemon juice
- ½   cup lime juice
- 2   bottles (750 milliliters each)
      Champagne, chilled
      Lime slices

In a 3-qt. pitcher, combine the juices. Refrigerate until chilled. Just before serving, stir in Champagne. Serve in Champagne glasses. If desired, garnish with lime slices.

¾ CUP: 101 cal., 0 fat (0 sat. fat), 0 chol., 0 sod., 11g carb. (6g sugars, 0 fiber), 0 pro.

HOW TO CHILL WINE FAST

The quickest way to chill a bottle of wine is to immerse it in ice water with a small handful of salt. Turn the bottle periodically. It'll be ready in about 20 minutes!

LEAN TURKEY SAUSAGE PATTIES

Apple and sausage naturally go together. Add sage, and you've got a standout patty. They're freezer-friendly, so I make them ahead and grab when needed.
—*Scarlett Elrod, Newnan, GA*

- -

Prep: 35 min. + chilling
Cook: 10 min./batch • **Makes:** 16 servings

- 1   large apple
- 1   large egg, lightly beaten
- ½   cup chopped fresh parsley
- 3   to 4 Tbsp. minced fresh sage
- 2   garlic cloves, minced
- 1¼   tsp. salt
- ½   tsp. pepper
- ½   tsp. crushed red pepper flakes
- 1¼   lbs. lean ground turkey
- 6   tsp. olive oil, divided

1. Peel and coarsely shred apple; place apple in a colander over a plate. Let stand 15 minutes. Squeeze and blot dry with paper towels.
2. In a large bowl, combine the egg, parsley, sage, garlic, seasonings and apple. Add turkey; mix lightly but thoroughly. Shape into sixteen 2-in. patties. Place patties on waxed-paper-lined baking sheets. Refrigerate, covered, 8 hours or overnight.
3. In a large nonstick skillet, heat 2 tsp. oil over medium heat. In batches, cook patties 3-4 minutes on each side or until golden brown and a thermometer reads 165°, adding more oil as needed.
FREEZE OPTION: Place uncooked patties on waxed paper-lined baking sheets; wrap and freeze until firm. Remove from pans and transfer to a freezer container; return to freezer. To use, cook frozen patties as directed, increasing time to 4-5 minutes on each side.
1 PATTY: 79 cal., 5g fat (1g sat. fat), 36mg chol., 211mg sod., 2g carb. (1g sugars, 0 fiber), 8g pro. **DIABETIC EXCHANGES:** 1 lean meat, ½ fat.

SMOKED SALMON DEVILED EGGS

Flaky salmon and creamy sauce go so well over hard-boiled eggs. Drizzle the sauce or serve it on the side—it's fantastic either way.
—*Marinela Dragan, Portland, OR*

Prep: 30 min. • **Cook:** 20 min.
Makes: 32 appetizers

- 16 hard-boiled large eggs
- 4 oz. cream cheese, softened
- ⅓ cup mayonnaise
- 2 Tbsp. snipped fresh dill
- 1 Tbsp. capers, drained and finely chopped
- 1 Tbsp. lemon juice
- 1 tsp. horseradish sauce
- 1 tsp. prepared mustard
- ½ tsp. freshly ground pepper
- ¾ cup flaked smoked salmon fillet

SAUCE
- 1 cup mayonnaise
- ¼ cup plus 2 Tbsp. ketchup
- 1 Tbsp. horseradish sauce
- 1 Tbsp. prepared mustard
- ¼ cup smoked salmon fillets, optional

1. Cut eggs lengthwise in half. Remove yolks, reserving whites. In a small bowl, mash yolks. Mix in cream cheese, mayonnaise, dill, capers, lemon juice, horseradish sauce, mustard and pepper. Fold in salmon. Spoon into egg whites. Refrigerate, covered, until serving.
2. For sauce, in a small bowl, mix mayonnaise, ketchup, horseradish sauce and mustard. If desired, top eggs with salmon mixture; serve with sauce.

1 STUFFED EGG HALF: 129 cal., 12g fat (3g sat. fat), 115mg chol., 180mg sod., 1g carb. (1g sugars, 0 fiber), 4g pro.

MAKE AHEAD
HAWAIIAN HAM STRATA

I came up with this recipe because I love Hawaiian pizza and wanted a casserole I could make ahead and pop into the oven at the last minute. This is a perfect main dish to take to a potluck.
—*Lisa Renshaw, Kansas City, MO*

Prep: 20 min. + chilling
Cook: 30 min. + standing
Makes: 8 servings

- 8 English muffins, cut into eighths and toasted
- 3 cups cubed fully cooked ham
- 1 can (20 oz.) pineapple tidbits, drained
- 4 green onions, chopped
- 1 jar (4 oz.) diced pimientos, drained
- 1½ cups shredded cheddar cheese
- ¼ cup grated Parmesan cheese
- 1 jar (15 oz.) Alfredo sauce
- 1½ cups evaporated milk
- 4 large eggs, lightly beaten
- ½ tsp. salt
- ¼ tsp. cayenne pepper

1. Combine first 5 ingredients. Transfer to a 13x9-in. baking dish; top with cheeses.
2. Whisk together remaining ingredients. Pour sauce over layers, pushing down, if necessary, with the back of a spoon to ensure that the muffins absorb liquid. Refrigerate, covered, 1 hour or overnight.
3. Preheat oven to 350°. Remove strata from refrigerator while oven heats. Bake, uncovered, until strata is golden and bubbly, 30-40 minutes. Let stand 10 minutes before serving.

1 PIECE: 515 cal., 22g fat (12g sat. fat), 177mg chol., 1512mg sod., 48g carb. (16g sugars, 3g fiber), 31g pro.

MONTE CRISTO CASSEROLE WITH RASPBERRY SAUCE

My husband likes the ham and cheese sandwich known as the Monte Cristo, so I came up with a baked casserole based on the classic recipe. It makes a terrific brunch dish.

—*Mary Steiner, Parkville, MD*

- -

Prep: 20 min. + chilling
Bake: 30 min. + standing
Makes: 10 servings (1¾ cups sauce)

- 1   loaf (1 lb.) French bread, cut into 20 slices
- 2   Tbsp. Dijon mustard
- ½   lb. sliced deli ham
- ½   lb. sliced Swiss cheese
- ½   lb. sliced deli turkey
- 6   large eggs
- 1½ cups 2% milk
- 2   tsp. sugar
- 2   tsp. vanilla extract

TOPPING
- ½   cup packed brown sugar
- ¼   cup butter, softened
- ½   tsp. ground cinnamon

RASPBERRY SAUCE
- ⅓   cup sugar
- 1   Tbsp. cornstarch
- ¼   cup cold water
- ¼   cup lemon juice
- ¼   cup maple syrup
- 2   cups fresh or frozen raspberries

1. Line a greased 13x9-in. baking dish with half the bread. Spread mustard over bread. Layer with ham, cheese, turkey and remaining bread (dish will be full).
2. In a large bowl, whisk eggs, milk, sugar and vanilla; pour over top. Refrigerate, covered, overnight.
3. Preheat oven to 375°. Remove casserole from refrigerator while oven heats. In a small bowl, mix topping ingredients; sprinkle over casserole. Bake, uncovered, until golden brown, 30-40 minutes.

4. Meanwhile, in a small saucepan, combine sugar and cornstarch. Stir in water, lemon juice and maple syrup until smooth. Add raspberries. Bring to a boil; cook and stir until thickened, about 2 minutes. Cool slightly.
5. Let casserole stand 10 minutes before cutting. Serve with sauce.

1 PIECE WITH ABOUT 3 TBSP. SAUCE: 476 cal., 17g fat (8g sat. fat), 167mg chol., 906mg sod., 55g carb. (29g sugars, 3g fiber), 25g pro.

★ ★ ★ ★ ★ **READER REVIEW**
"We enjoyed this recipe and found we liked the compliment of the raspberry syrup drizzled on top. I will make this one again!"
JUSTMBETH TASTEOFHOME.COM

CHEESE & CRAB BRUNCH BAKE

Who doesn't love an easy, cheesy seafood casserole that can be pulled together in thirty minutes, refrigerated overnight and baked up the next morning?
—*Joyce Conway, Westerville, OH*

Prep: 30 min. + chilling
Bake: 50 min. • **Makes:** 12 servings

- 2 Tbsp. Dijon mustard
- 6 English muffins, split
- 8 oz. lump crabmeat, drained
- 2 Tbsp. lemon juice
- 2 tsp. grated lemon zest
- 2 cups shredded white cheddar cheese
- 12 large eggs
- 1 cup half-and-half cream
- 1 cup 2% milk
- ½ cup mayonnaise
- 1 tsp. salt
- ½ tsp. cayenne pepper
- ½ tsp. pepper
- 2 cups shredded Swiss cheese
- 1 cup grated Parmesan cheese
- 4 green onions, chopped
- ¼ cup finely chopped sweet red pepper
- ¼ cup finely chopped sweet yellow pepper

1. Spread mustard over bottom half of muffins. Place in a greased 13x9-in. baking dish. Top with crab and lemon juice and zest. Sprinkle with cheddar cheese. Top with muffin tops; set aside.

2. In a large bowl, whisk eggs, cream, milk, mayonnaise, salt, cayenne and pepper. Pour over muffins; sprinkle with Swiss cheese, Parmesan cheese, onions and peppers. Cover and refrigerate overnight.

3. Remove from refrigerator 30 minutes before baking. Preheat the oven to 375°. Cover and bake 30 minutes. Uncover; bake until set, 20-25 minutes longer. Let stand 5 minutes before serving. If desired, top with additional chopped green onions.

1 SERVING: 428 cal., 28g fat (13g sat. fat), 286mg chol., 844mg sod., 18g carb. (4g sugars, 1g fiber), 26g pro.

CROISSANT BAKED FRENCH TOAST

My best friend introduced me to this recipe. It is a perfect holiday or Sunday brunch dish. It's easy to make and is quite rich, so you feel fancy while eating it.
—Amanda Wilson, Milwaukee, WI

Prep: 10 min. • **Bake:** 25 min.
Makes: 8 servings

- 8 croissants
- 5 large eggs, beaten
- 1 cup half-and-half cream
- 1 tsp. vanilla extract
- 1 tsp. ground cinnamon
  Zest of 1 orange
- 2 Tbsp. maple syrup
  Optional toppings: Confectioners' sugar, assorted fresh fruit or maple syrup

1. Preheat oven to 375°. Coat a 13x9-in. baking dish with cooking spray; set aside.
2. Slice croissants in half lengthwise.
3. In a large bowl, whisk eggs, cream, vanilla, cinnamon, orange zest and maple syrup. Submerge croissant halves in liquid until completely soaked. Place croissants in baking dish, overlapping slightly if necessary. Bake until set, 25-30 minutes.
1 SERVING: 266 cal., 14g fat (8g sat. fat), 136mg chol., 261mg sod.,25g carb. (9g sugars, 1g fiber), 8g pro.

HASH BROWN NESTS WITH PORTOBELLOS & EGGS

Hash browns make a fabulous crust for these individual egg quiches. They look fancy but are actually easy to make. They've been a hit at holiday brunches and other special occasions.
—Kate Meyer, Brentwood, TN

Prep: 30 min. • **Bake:** 15 min.
Makes: 1 dozen

- 2 Tbsp. butter
- ½ lb. sliced baby portobello mushrooms, chopped
- ¼ cup chopped shallots
- 1 garlic clove, minced
- ½ tsp. salt
- ¼ tsp. pepper
  Dash cayenne pepper
- 2 Tbsp. sour cream
- 1 Tbsp. minced fresh basil or 1 tsp. dried basil
- 4 cups frozen shredded hash brown potatoes (about 1 lb.), thawed
- 7 large eggs, lightly beaten
- ¼ cup shredded Swiss cheese
- 2 bacon strips, cooked and crumbled

1. Preheat oven to 400°. In a large skillet, heat butter over medium-high heat; saute mushrooms and shallots until tender. Add garlic and seasonings; cook and stir 1 minute. Remove from heat; stir in sour cream and basil.
2. Press about ¼ cup potatoes onto bottom and up sides of each of 12 greased muffin cups. Fill each with about 2 Tbsp. beaten egg. Top with mushroom mixture, cheese and bacon.
3. Bake until eggs are set, 15-18 minutes.
1 SERVING: 105 cal., 7g fat (3g sat. fat), 118mg chol., 191mg sod., 6g carb. (1g sugars, 1g fiber), 6g pro. **DIABETIC EXCHANGES:** 1 medium-fat meat, ½ starch, ½ fat.

PUMPKIN FRENCH TOAST WITH BACON MAPLE SYRUP

My two great-grandsons helped me create this recipe. Each of the boys took turns prepping and offering suggestions. It's a wonderful holiday brunch dish, and it can even be made a day ahead and baked when ready to serve.
—*Barbara Estabrook, Appleton, WI*

Prep: 35 min. + chilling
Bake: 40 min.
Makes: 8 servings (1 cup sauce)

- 4 bacon strips
- 1¼ cups 2% milk
- 3 large eggs
- ½ cup plus 3 Tbsp. packed light brown sugar, divided
- ½ cup canned pumpkin
- 2 Tbsp. maple syrup
- 2½ tsp. pumpkin pie spice, divided
- 12 oz. challah or brioche bread, cut into ½-in. cubes
- ¼ cup quick-cooking oats
- ¼ cup chopped pecans, toasted
- 3 Tbsp. all-purpose flour
- 3 Tbsp. cold butter

SAUCE

- 3 Tbsp. butter
- 3 Tbsp. light brown sugar
- 3 Tbsp. maple syrup
- 3 Tbsp. 2% milk
- 3 Tbsp. canned pumpkin

1. In a large skillet, cook bacon over medium heat until crisp. Remove to paper towels to drain; crumble bacon. Discard drippings, reserving 1 Tbsp. for sauce. In a large bowl, whisk milk, eggs, ½ cup brown sugar, pumpkin, maple syrup and 2 tsp. pie spice until blended. Place half the bread cubes in a greased 2-qt. baking dish. Top with half the crumbled bacon and half the egg mixture. Repeat layers. Refrigerate, covered, overnight.

2. Preheat oven to 350°. Remove casserole from refrigerator while oven heats. Combine oats, pecans, flour, and the remaining 3 Tbsp. brown sugar and ½ tsp. pie spice. Cut in cold butter until mixture resembles coarse crumbs. Sprinkle over casserole.

3. Bake, uncovered, until a knife inserted near the center comes out clean, 40-45 minutes. Let stand for 5-10 minutes before serving.

4. Meanwhile, for sauce, in a small saucepan, melt butter and reserved bacon grease over medium heat. Stir in brown sugar and maple syrup. Add milk and pumpkin; heat through. Serve with French toast.

1 SERVING: 486 cal., 23g fat (12g sat. fat), 137mg chol., 386mg sod., 62g carb. (39g sugars, 2g fiber), 10g pro.

RICH YELLOW BREADS

Challah and brioche are bakery breads made with lots of butter and eggs. This gives them a characteristic rich yellow color. Chopped croissants are a good substitute if you can't find either of these.

HOMEMADE CRANBERRY JUICE

This refreshing and sweet cranberry juice has a mild tartness level. Its jewel red color looks very attractive served in glassware.
—*Carol Domes, Whitehorse, YT*

Prep: 35 min. + chilling
Makes: 8 servings (2 qt.)

  2 qt. water
  8 cups fresh or frozen cranberries
1½ cups sugar
  ½ cup lemon juice
  ½ cup orange juice

1. In a Dutch oven or large saucepan, bring water and cranberries to a boil. Reduce heat; cover and simmer until berries begin to pop, 20 minutes.
2. Strain through a fine strainer, pressing mixture with a spoon; discard berries. Return cranberry juice to the pan. Stir in the sugar, lemon juice and orange juice. Bring to a boil; cook and stir until sugar is dissolved.
3. Remove from the heat. Cool. Transfer juice to a pitcher; cover and refrigerate until chilled.

1 CUP: 227 cal., 0 fat (0 sat. fat), 0 chol., 31mg sod., 58g carb. (48g sugars, 0 fiber), 0 pro.

MAKE AHEAD
EGGS BENEDICT CASSEROLE

Here's a casserole as tasty as eggs Benedict, but without the hassle. Simply assemble the ingredients ahead, and bake it the next morning for an elegant breakfast or brunch.
—*Sandie Heindel, Liberty, MO*

Prep: 25 min. + chilling • **Bake:** 45 min.
Makes: 12 servings (1⅔ cups sauce)

 12 oz. Canadian bacon, chopped
  6 English muffins, split and
     cut into 1-in. pieces
  8 large eggs
  2 cups 2% milk
  1 tsp. onion powder
  ¼ tsp. paprika
HOLLANDAISE SAUCE
  4 large egg yolks
  ½ cup heavy whipping cream
  2 Tbsp. lemon juice
  1 tsp. Dijon mustard
  ½ cup butter, melted
     Minced chives, optional

1. Place half the Canadian bacon in a greased 3-qt. or 13x9-in. baking dish; top with English muffins and remaining bacon. In a large bowl, whisk eggs, milk and onion powder; pour over top. Refrigerate, covered, overnight.
2. Preheat oven to 375°. Remove casserole from refrigerator while oven heats. Sprinkle top with paprika. Bake, covered, 35 minutes. Uncover; bake for 10-15 minutes longer or until a knife inserted in the center comes out clean.
3. In top of a double boiler or a metal bowl over simmering water, whisk egg yolks, cream, lemon juice and mustard until blended; cook until mixture is just thick enough to coat a metal spoon and temperature reaches 160°, whisking constantly. Reduce heat to very low. Very slowly drizzle in warm melted butter, whisking constantly. Serve sauce immediately with casserole. If desired, sprinkle with chives.

1 PIECE WITH ABOUT 2 TBSP. SAUCE: 286 cal., 19g fat (10g sat. fat), 256mg chol., 535mg sod., 16g carb. (4g sugars, 1g fiber), 14g pro.

CHEESY HASH BROWN BAKE

Prepare this cheesy dish ahead of time for less stress on brunch day. You'll love it!
—*Karen Burns, Chandler, TX*

- -

Prep: 10 min. • **Bake:** 40 min.
Makes: 10 servings

- 1 pkg. (30 oz.) frozen shredded hash brown potatoes, thawed
- 2 cans (10¾ oz. each) condensed cream of potato soup, undiluted
- 2 cups sour cream
- 2 cups shredded cheddar cheese, divided
- 1 cup grated Parmesan cheese

1. Preheat oven to 350°. In a large bowl, combine potatoes, soup, sour cream, 1¾ cups cheddar cheese and the Parmesan cheese. Place in a greased 3-qt. baking dish. Sprinkle with the remaining cheddar cheese.
2. Bake, uncovered, until bubbly and cheese is melted, 40-45 minutes. Let stand 5 minutes before serving.

½ CUP: 305 cal., 18g fat (12g sat. fat), 65mg chol., 554mg sod., 21g carb. (3g sugars, 1g fiber), 12g pro.
PEPPER JACK HASH BROWN BAKE: Substitute pepper jack cheese for the cheddar and omit the Parmesan.
NACHO HASH BROWN BAKE: Substitute 1 can (10¾ oz.) condensed cream of celery soup and 1 can (10¾ oz.) condensed nacho cheese soup for the potato soup. Substitute Mexican cheese blend for the cheddar and omit the Parmesan.

BRING IT
These versatile potatoes can be served as a side for brunch or with your favorite main dishes for dinner. For take-and-bake ease, pack the potatoes in a disposable foil pan. You can even cook them in the foil pan on the upper shelf of a covered grill, away from direct heat.

CRUSTLESS SWISS QUICHE

I received this recipe from my mother-in-law, an all-around wonderfuk cook. Everyone raves about her rich quiche when she serves it at card parties and other occasions.
—*Marlene Kole, Highland Heights, OH*

- -

Prep: 15 min. + cooling • **Bake:** 40 min.
Makes: 2 quiches (10 servings each)

- ½ cup butter
- ½ cup all-purpose flour
- 1½ cups milk
- 2½ cups 4% cottage cheese
- 1 tsp. baking powder
- 1 tsp. salt
- 1 tsp. Dijon mustard
- 9 large eggs
- 1 pkg. (8 oz.) plus 3 oz. cream cheese, softened
- 3 cups shredded Swiss cheese
- ⅓ cup grated Parmesan cheese

1. Melt butter in a medium saucepan. Stir in flour; cook and stir until bubbly. Gradually add milk; cook over medium heat, stirring occasionally, until sauce thickens. Remove from the heat; set aside to cool, about 15-20 minutes. Meanwhile, combine the cottage cheese, baking powder, salt and mustard; set aside.
2. In a large bowl, beat eggs. Slowly add cream cheese, cottage cheese mixture and cream sauce. Fold in Swiss and Parmesan cheeses. Pour into 2 greased 10-in. pie plates. Bake at 350° for 40 minutes or until a knife inserted in the center comes out clean. Serve immediately.
1 PIECE: 248 cal., 19g fat (11g sat. fat), 150mg chol., 441mg sod., 6g carb. (3g sugars, 0 fiber), 13g pro.

ULTIMATE FRUITY GRANOLA

Honey, maple syrup and vanilla coat this wonderfully crunchy treat that is fantastic no matter how you serve it—on its own, with cold milk or in a yogurt parfait.
—*Sarah Vasques, Milford, NH*

Prep: 15 min. • **Bake:** 20 min. + cooling
Makes: 9 cups

- 5 cups old-fashioned oats
- 1 cup sliced almonds
- ½ cup sunflower kernels
- ½ cup ground flaxseed
- ½ cup packed brown sugar
- ¼ cup maple syrup
- ¼ cup honey
- 2 Tbsp. canola oil
- ½ tsp. salt
- ½ tsp. ground cinnamon
- 1 tsp. vanilla extract
- ½ cup dried cranberries
- ½ cup dried banana chips
- ½ cup dried apricots, halved

1. In a large bowl, combine the oats, almonds, sunflower kernels and flax. In a small saucepan, combine the brown sugar, maple syrup, honey, oil, salt and cinnamon. Cook and stir over medium heat for 2-3 minutes or until brown sugar is dissolved and mixture is heated through. Remove from heat; stir in vanilla. Pour over oat mixture and toss to coat.
2. Transfer to a 15x10x1-in. baking pan coated with cooking spray. Bake at 350° for 20-25 minutes or until golden brown, stirring every 8 minutes. Cool completely on a wire rack. Stir in dried fruits. Store in an airtight container.
½ CUP: 253 cal., 10g fat (2g sat. fat), 0 chol., 86mg sod., 38g carb. (18g sugars, 5g fiber), 6g pro.

FAVORITE BANANA CHIP MUFFINS

These muffins are one of the first things my husband, U.S. Army Maj. John Duda Jr., gets hungry for when he's home from deployment. I make sure to have the overripe bananas ready.
—*Kimberly Duda, Sanford, NC*

- -

Prep: 20 min. • **Bake:** 20 min.
Makes: 1 dozen

- 1½ cups all-purpose flour
- ⅔ cup sugar
- 1 tsp. baking soda
- ¼ tsp. ground cinnamon
- ⅛ tsp. salt
- 1 large egg
- 1⅓ cups mashed ripe bananas (about 3 medium)
- ⅓ cup butter, melted
- 1 tsp. vanilla extract
- ½ cup semisweet chocolate chips

1. Preheat oven to 375°. In a large bowl, whisk flour, sugar, baking soda, cinnamon and salt. In another bowl, whisk egg, bananas, melted butter and vanilla until blended. Add to flour mixture; stir just until moistened. Fold in chocolate chips.

2. Fill greased or paper-lined muffin cups three-fourths full. Bake for 17-20 minutes or until a toothpick inserted in center comes out clean. Cool 5 minutes before removing from pan to a wire rack. Serve warm.

1 MUFFIN: 207 cal., 8g fat (5g sat. fat), 31mg chol., 172mg sod., 33g carb. (18g sugars, 2g fiber), 3g pro. **DIABETIC EXCHANGES:** 2 starch, 1½ fat.

FRESHNESS POINTERS

To keep your muffins moist and fresh-tasting after baking, let them cool completely on a rack. Then, store them in an airtight container lined with paper towels. Before securing the lid, gently place another piece of paper towel on top of the muffins to absorb any excess moisture.

HAM & BISCUIT BREAKFAST BITES

I love using my grandfather's homemade horseradish in dishes. This particular dish is unique because it also calls for rosemary. I enjoy making these on the weekend and often share with my neighbors.
—*Danielle Lee, West Palm Beach, FL*

Prep: 20 min. • **Bake:** 20 min.
Makes: 1 dozen

- 3½ cups biscuit/baking mix
- 1 cup 2% milk
- ⅔ cup shredded cheddar cheese
- ½ cup chopped green pepper
- ⅔ cup cubed fully cooked ham or 3½ oz. Canadian bacon, cubed
- 4 large eggs or 1 cup egg substitute
- 2 to 3 Tbsp. prepared horseradish
- ½ tsp. salt
- ½ tsp. pepper
- 1½ tsp. minced fresh rosemary or ½ tsp. dried rosemary, crushed

1. Preheat oven to 375°. Stir together biscuit mix and milk to form a soft dough. On a lightly floured surface, pat dough to ¼-in. thickness; cut 12 biscuits using a floured 3½-in. round cutter. Press each onto bottom and up sides of a greased muffin cup.

2. Divide cheese, green pepper and ham among cups. Whisk together eggs, horseradish, salt and pepper; pour into cups. Sprinkle with rosemary.

3. Bake until eggs are set, 20-25 minutes. Let stand 5 minutes before removing from pan.

1 SERVING: 204 cal., 8g fat (3g sat. fat), 74mg chol., 640mg sod., 26g carb. (2g sugars, 1g fiber), 9g pro.

FESTIVE CRANBERRY FRUIT SALAD

This fruit salad is a tradition on my Christmas table. It goes together quickly, which is a plus on such a busy day.
—*Rousheen Arel Wolf, Delta Junction, AK*

Takes: 25 min. • **Makes:** 14 servings

- 1 pkg. (12 oz.) fresh or frozen cranberries
- ¾ cup water
- ½ cup sugar
- 5 medium apples, diced
- 2 medium firm bananas, sliced
- 1½ cups fresh or frozen blueberries, thawed
- 1 can (11 oz.) mandarin oranges, undrained
- 1 cup fresh or frozen raspberries, thawed
- ¾ cup fresh strawberries, halved

1. In a large saucepan, combine the cranberries, water and sugar. Cook and stir over medium heat until berries pop, about 15 minutes. Remove from the heat; cool slightly.

2. In a large bowl, combine the remaining ingredients. Add cranberry mixture; stir gently. Refrigerate until serving.

NOTE: If using frozen blueberries, use without thawing to avoid discoloring the batter. Heat 3 Tbsp. light corn syrup in microwave until warm; gently toss with 1 cup fresh or frozen cranberries, allowing excess syrup to drip off. Toss in ⅓ cup sugar to coat. Place on waxed paper; let stand until set, about 1 hour.

¾ CUP: 105 cal., 0 fat (0 sat. fat), 0 chol., 2mg sod., 27g carb. (21g sugars, 4g fiber), 1g pro.

MAKE AHEAD

BRIE & SAUSAGE BRUNCH BAKE

I've made this brunch bake for holidays as well as for a weekend at a friend's cabin, and I always get requests for the recipe. It's make-ahead convenient, reheats well and even tastes wonderful the next day.
—*Becky Hicks, Forest Lake, MN*

Prep: 30 min. + chilling
Bake: 50 min. + standing
Makes: 12 servings

- 1   lb. bulk Italian sausage
- 1   small onion, chopped
- 8   cups cubed day-old sourdough bread
- ½   cup chopped roasted sweet red peppers
- ½   lb. Brie cheese, rind removed, cubed
- ⅔   cup grated Parmesan cheese
- 2   Tbsp. minced fresh basil or 2 tsp. dried basil
- 8   large eggs
- 2   cups heavy whipping cream
- 1   Tbsp. Dijon mustard
- 1   tsp. pepper
- ½   tsp. salt
- ¾   cup shredded part-skim mozzarella cheese
- 3   green onions, sliced

1. In a large skillet, cook sausage and onion over medium heat until meat is no longer pink, 5-7 minutes; drain.
2. Place bread cubes in a greased 13x9-in. baking dish. Layer with the sausage mixture, red peppers, Brie and Parmesan cheeses and basil. In a large bowl, whisk eggs, cream, mustard, pepper and salt; pour over top. Cover and refrigerate overnight.
3. Remove from the refrigerator 30 minutes before baking. Preheat oven to 350°. Bake, uncovered, until a knife inserted in the center comes out clean, 45-50 minutes.

4. Sprinkle with mozzarella cheese. Bake until cheese is melted, 4-6 minutes. Let stand 10 minutes before cutting. Sprinkle with green onions.
1 PIECE: 451 cal., 34g fat (18g sat. fat), 217mg chol., 843mg sod., 16g carb. (3g sugars, 1g fiber), 19g pro.

POTLUCK EGGS BENEDICT

If you're looking for a hearty breakfast or brunch dish, look no further. Folks can't wait to dig in to the combination of eggs, ham, cheese and asparagus in this recipe.
—*Pauline Van Breemen, Franklin, IN*

Takes: 30 min. • **Makes:** 12 servings

- 1   lb. fresh asparagus, trimmed
- ¾   cup butter, cubed
- ¾   cup all-purpose flour
- 4   cups whole milk
- 1   can (14½ oz.) chicken broth
- 1   lb. cubed fully cooked ham
- 1   cup shredded cheddar cheese
- 8   hard-boiled large eggs, quartered
- ½   tsp. salt
- ⅛   tsp. cayenne pepper
- 12 biscuits, warmed

1. Cut the asparagus into ½-in. pieces, using only tender parts of spears. Cook in a small amount of boiling water until tender, about 5 minutes; drain. Set aside to cool.
2. Melt butter in a saucepan; stir in flour until smooth. Add milk and broth; bring to a boil. Cook and stir for 2 minutes. Add ham and cheese; stir until cheese is melted. Add eggs, salt, cayenne and asparagus; heat through. Serve over biscuits.
¾ CUP WITH 1 BISCUIT: 491 cal., 31g fat (18g sat. fat), 192mg chol., 1371mg sod., 33g carb. (7g sugars, 1g fiber), 21g pro.

SAUSAGE EGG BAKE

This hearty egg dish is wonderful for any meal of the day. I fix it frequently for special occasions, too, because it's easy to prepare and really versatile. For a change, use spicier sausage or substitute a flavored cheese blend.
—*Molly Swallow, Pocatello, ID*

Prep: 10 min. • **Bake:** 40 min.
Makes: 12 servings

- 1 lb. bulk Italian sausage
- 2 cans (10¾ oz. each) condensed cream of potato soup, undiluted
- 9 large eggs, lightly beaten
- ¾ cup 2% milk
- ¼ tsp. pepper
- 1 cup shredded cheddar cheese

1. In a large skillet, cook sausage over medium heat until no longer pink; drain. Stir in soup. In a large bowl, whisk eggs, milk and pepper; stir in sausage mixture.
2. Transfer to a lightly greased 2-qt. baking dish. Sprinkle with cheese. Bake, uncovered, at 375° for 40-45 minutes or until a knife inserted in the center comes out clean.

1 PIECE: 181 cal., 13g fat (6g sat. fat), 189mg chol., 484mg sod., 5g carb. (2g sugars, 0 fiber), 11g pro.

APPLE BUTTER BISCUIT BREAKFAST BAKE

My grandmother created this recipe to use up the leftovers from Christmas Eve dinner. By combining the leftover ham and biscuits with her homemade apple butter, milk and eggs, she could serve us all a warm, delicious breakfast and still have time to spend with the grandchildren.
—*Mary M Leverette, Columbia, SC*

Prep: 30 min. + chilling
Bake: 50 min. + standing
Makes: 12 servings

- 10 leftover biscuits (3-in. diameter)
- ¾ cup apple butter
- 2 cups shredded sharp cheddar cheese
- 1½ cups cubed fully cooked ham
- ¼ cup minced fresh parsley
- 6 large eggs
- 2½ cups 2% milk
- 1 tsp. salt
- ½ tsp. pepper
- ¼ tsp. ground mustard

1. Cut biscuits crosswise in half. Spread apple butter over cut sides of biscuits. Replace tops. Cut each biscuit into quarters; arrange in a single layer in a greased 13x9-in. baking dish. Top with cheese, ham and parsley.
2. In a large bowl, whisk eggs, milk, salt, pepper and mustard. Pour over biscuits. Cover and refrigerate overnight.
3. Preheat oven to 325°. Remove strata from refrigerator while oven heats. Bake, uncovered, until puffed and edges are golden brown, 50-60 minutes. Let stand 10 minutes before cutting.

1 PIECE: 331 cal., 15g fat (7g sat. fat), 126mg chol., 976mg sod., 31g carb. (12g sugars, 1g fiber), 16g pro.

★ ★ ★ ★ ★ **READER REVIEW**

"Amazing! I didn't have leftover biscuits, so I just baked up a tube of flaky biscuits and used those. We loved the sweetness and spice of the apple butter with the ham and cheddar."

CURLYLIS85 TASTEOFHOME.COM

RASPBERRY CRUMBLE COFFEE CAKE

Don't be intimidated by the recipe directions for this coffee cake—it really isn't difficult to make. Try it sometime as a nice brunch item. Don't limit it to that, though ... it's also a delicious dessert.
—*Shirley Boyken, Mesa, AZ*

Prep: 20 min. • **Bake:** 40 min.
Makes: 20 servings

FILLING
- ⅔ cup sugar
- ¼ cup cornstarch
- ¾ cup water or cranberry-raspberry juice
- 2 cups fresh or frozen raspberries
- 1 Tbsp. lemon juice

COFFEE CAKE
- 3 cups all-purpose flour
- 1 cup sugar
- 3 tsp. baking powder
- 1 tsp. salt
- 1 tsp. ground cinnamon
- ¼ tsp. ground mace
- 1 cup cold butter, cubed
- 2 large eggs, lightly beaten
- 1 cup whole milk
- 1 tsp. vanilla extract

TOPPING
- ¼ cup cold butter, cubed
- ½ cup all-purpose flour
- ½ cup sugar
- ¼ cup sliced almonds

1. For filling, in a large saucepan, combine the sugar, cornstarch and water until smooth. Bring to a boil over medium heat. Cook and stir until thickened, 1-2 minutes. Add berries and lemon juice. Set aside to cool.

2. In a large bowl, combine the flour, sugar, baking powder, salt, cinnamon and mace. Cut in butter to form fine crumbs. Stir in the eggs, milk and vanilla until blended. Divide in half.

3. Spread half of the batter in 2 greased 8-in. round baking pans. Divide filling and spread evenly over each. Drop remaining batter by small spoonfuls and spread evenly over filling.

4. For topping, cut butter into flour and sugar; stir in nuts. Sprinkle over tops of coffee cakes. Bake at 350° until golden brown, 40-45 minutes.

NOTE: If desired, 1 coffee cake can be baked in 13x9-in. baking pan. Bake for 45-50 minutes or until golden brown.

1 PIECE: 299 cal., 13g fat (8g sat. fat), 54mg chol., 307mg sod., 42g carb. (23g sugars, 2g fiber), 4g pro.

PUMPKIN OAT MUFFINS

It isn't considered Thanksgiving or Christmas in my house until these lovely muffins are on the table! Enjoy the flavors of pumpkin-pie in easy-to-eat muffin form.
—*Carol Hale, Sarver, PA*

Prep: 20 min. • **Bake:** 15 min.
Makes: 1½ dozen

- 1 cup all-purpose flour
- ½ cup packed brown sugar
- 2 tsp. baking powder
- 1 tsp. pumpkin pie spice
- ½ tsp. salt
- ¼ tsp. baking soda
- 1 large egg, lightly beaten
- ¾ cup canned pumpkin
- ¼ cup 2% milk
- ¼ cup canola oil
- 1 cup old-fashioned oats
- ½ cup raisins

TOPPING

- ⅓ cup packed brown sugar
- 1 Tbsp. all-purpose flour
- ¾ tsp. pumpkin pie spice
- 1 Tbsp. cold butter

1. Preheat oven to 375°. In a large bowl, combine the first 6 ingredients. Combine the egg, pumpkin, milk and oil; add to the dry ingredients just until moistened. Stir in oats and raisins.

2. Fill 18 greased or paper-lined muffin cups two-thirds full. In a small bowl, combine the brown sugar, flour and pie spice; cut in butter until crumbly. Sprinkle 1 rounded tsp. over each muffin. Bake until a toothpick comes out clean, 15-20 minutes.

3. Cool for 5 minutes before removing from pan to a wire rack. Serve warm.

1 MUFFIN: 138 cal., 5g fat (1g sat. fat), 12mg chol., 151mg sod., 23g carb. (13g sugars, 1g fiber), 2g pro. **DIABETIC EXCHANGES:** 1½ starch, 1 fat.

CHEESE & SAUSAGE BREAKFAST PIZZA

My unusual breakfast pizza with salsa and sausage is a crowd-pleaser at church events. Try it with a dash of sweet and spicy Tiger Sauce.
—*Kelly Buckley, Norton, KS*

Prep: 25 min. • **Bake:** 25 min.
Makes: 12 servings

- 1 lb. bulk pork sausage
- 1 medium onion, finely chopped
- ¼ cup salsa
- ½ tsp. onion powder
- ½ tsp. ground coriander
- ½ tsp. ground cumin
- 2 tubes (8 oz. each) refrigerated crescent rolls
- 2 cups shredded cheddar cheese
- 8 large eggs
- ¼ cup grated Parmesan cheese
- ¼ cup 2% milk
- ¼ tsp. salt
- ¼ tsp. pepper
  Tiger Sauce, optional

1. Preheat oven to 350°. In a large skillet, cook sausage and onion over medium heat, breaking up sausage into crumbles, until the sausage is no longer pink, 5-7 minutes; drain. Stir in salsa and seasonings. Remove from heat.

2. Unroll both tubes of crescent dough and press onto bottom and up sides of an ungreased 15x10x1-in. baking pan. Press perforations to seal. Top with sausage mixture and cheddar cheese. In a bowl, whisk eggs, Parmesan cheese, milk, salt and pepper until blended; pour over sausage and cheese.

3. Bake on a lower oven rack until crust is lightly browned and egg mixture is set, 23-28 minutes. If desired, serve with Tiger Sauce.

NOTE: This recipe was tested with TryMe brand Tiger Sauce, a sweet and mildly spicy sauce. Look for it in the condiments section of your grocery store.

1 PIECE: 380 cal., 26g fat (10g sat. fat), 165mg chol., 798mg sod., 18g carb. (4g sugars, 0 fiber), 16g pro.

TURKEY POTPIES,
PAGE 97

Main Dishes

You signed up to bring an entree to the shindig. A winning dish is ensured when you turn here for casseroles, sandwiches, cookout classics and more. Time to shine!

CHICKEN TETRAZZINI

A good friend shared a version of this recipe with me 35 years ago. I pay it forward by bringing the second casserole to friends when they are unable to cook.
—*Helen McPhee, Savoy, IL*

- -

Prep: 30 min. • **Bake:** 20 min.
Makes: 2 casseroles (4 servings each)

- 1 pkg. (12 oz.) spaghetti
- ⅓ cup butter, cubed
- ⅓ cup all-purpose flour
- ¾ tsp. salt
- ¼ tsp. white pepper
- 1 can (14½ oz.) chicken broth
- 1½ cups half-and-half cream
- 1 cup heavy whipping cream
- 4 cups cubed cooked chicken
- 3 cans (4 oz. each) mushroom stems and pieces, drained
- 1 jar (4 oz.) sliced pimientos, drained
- ½ cup grated Parmesan cheese

1. Cook spaghetti according to package directions. Meanwhile, in a Dutch oven, melt butter. Stir in the flour, salt and pepper until smooth. Gradually add the broth, half-and-half and whipping cream. Bring to a boil; cook and stir until thickened, about 2 minutes.

2. Remove from the heat. Stir in the chicken, mushrooms and pimientos. Drain spaghetti; add to the chicken mixture and toss to coat.

3. Transfer to 2 greased 11x7-in. baking dishes. Sprinkle with cheese. Bake, uncovered, at 350° until heated through, 20-25 minutes.

FREEZE OPTION: Cover and freeze casseroles for up to 2 months. Thaw in the refrigerator overnight. Cover and bake at 350° for 30 minutes. Uncover; bake until heated through, 15-20 minutes more. Stir before serving.

1 CUP: 576 cal., 30g fat (17g sat. fat), 144mg chol., 814mg sod., 41g carb. (4g sugars, 2g fiber), 31g pro.

SAUSAGE & ASPARAGUS PASTA WITH CAJUN CREAM SAUCE

I needed to use up some ingredients in my refrigerator, so I threw together this dish. It's delicious and everyone loves it. I only use Tony Chachere's Creole seasoning mix.
—*Angela Lively, Conroe, TX*

Takes: 25 min. • **Makes:** 8 servings

- 1 pkg. (16 oz.) spiral pasta
- 1 lb. fresh asparagus, trimmed and cut into 2-in. pieces
- 1 pkg. (14 oz.) smoked sausage, sliced
- 2 garlic cloves, minced
- 1 cup heavy whipping cream
- ½ cup shredded Parmesan cheese
- 1 Tbsp. Creole seasoning
- ¼ tsp. pepper

1. In a Dutch oven, cook pasta according to package directions, adding asparagus during the last 4 minutes of cooking. Meanwhile, in a large nonstick skillet, cook sausage over medium heat until browned. Add garlic; cook 1 minute longer. Stir in the cream, Parmesan cheese, Creole seasoning and pepper; cook and stir until slightly thickened, about 3 minutes.

2. Drain pasta mixture, reserving ½ cup cooking water; add to sausage mixture. Toss to coat, gradually adding enough reserved cooking water to reach the desired consistency.

1¼ CUPS: 496 cal., 26g fat (14g sat. fat), 71mg chol., 909mg sod., 46g carb. (4g sugars, 2g fiber), 18g pro.

GRILLED THIGHS & DRUMSTICKS

This chicken is juicy, has fantastic barbecue flavor and makes a big batch, so it's perfect for summer picnics and family reunions.
—*Brenda Beachy, Belvidere, TN*

Prep: 10 min. + marinating
Grill: 30 min. • **Makes:** 18 servings

- 2½ cups packed brown sugar
- 2 cups water
- 2 cups cider vinegar
- 2 cups ketchup
- 1 cup canola oil
- 4 Tbsp. salt
- 3 Tbsp. prepared mustard
- 4½ tsp. Worcestershire sauce
- 1 Tbsp. reduced-sodium soy sauce
- 1 tsp. pepper
- 1 tsp. Liquid Smoke, optional
- 10 lbs. bone-in chicken thighs and chicken drumsticks
- ½ tsp. seasoned salt

1. In a large bowl, combine the first 11 ingredients. Pour into 2 large shallow dishes; add equal amounts of chicken to dish; turn to coat. Cover and refrigerate chicken overnight.
2. Drain and discard marinade. Sprinkle chicken with seasoned salt. Grill the chicken, covered, over indirect medium heat until a thermometer reads 170°-175°, 15-20 minutes on each side.

5 OZ. COOKED CHICKEN: 384 cal., 19g fat (4g sat. fat), 128mg chol., 970mg sod., 16g carb. (15g sugars, 0 fiber), 36g pro.

GRILLING TIP

Using a charcoal grill as opposed to a gas grill just calls for keeping a closer eye on the meat. Because charcoal grills typically run a bit hotter, your chicken may cook more quickly than on a gas grill.

SLOPPY JOE DOGS

There are so many different ways to top a hot dog, but this tasty sloppy joe version beats them all!
—*Kimberly Wallace, Dennison, OH*

Prep: 20 min. • **Cook:** 15 min.
Makes: 16 servings

SLOPPY JOE TOPPING

- 2 lbs. ground beef
- 2 celery ribs, chopped
- 1 small green pepper, finely chopped
- 1 small onion, chopped
- 1 can (10¾ oz.) condensed tomato soup, undiluted
- ¼ cup packed brown sugar
- ¼ cup ketchup
- 1 Tbsp. cider vinegar
- 1 Tbsp. prepared mustard
- 1½ tsp. Worcestershire sauce
- 1 tsp. pepper
- ½ tsp. salt
- ¼ tsp. garlic powder

DOGS

- 16 hot dogs
- 16 hot dog buns, split
  Optional: Warmed cheese dip and grilled onions

1. In a Dutch oven, cook beef, celery, green pepper and onion over medium heat, crumbling beef, until meat is no longer pink, 5-7 minutes; drain. Stir in tomato soup, brown sugar, ketchup, vinegar, mustard, Worcestershire sauce, pepper, salt and garlic powder; heat through.
2. Grill hot dogs, covered, over medium heat until heated through, 6-10 minutes, turning occasionally. Serve on buns. Top each with ¼ cup beef mixture. If desired, top the dogs with warmed cheese dip and grilled onions.

1 SERVING: 422 cal., 23g fat (9g sat. fat), 68mg chol., 959mg sod., 31g carb. (10g sugars, 1g fiber), 22g pro.

SICILIAN PIZZA (SFINCIONE)

My favorite pizza from childhood is still my favorite today. The crunchy bread-crumb topping sets it apart from its American counterpart. I like to top this pie with torn fresh basil.
—*Susan Falk, Sterling Heights, MI*

Prep: 20 min. • **Bake:** 20 min.
Makes: 12 servings

- 2 loaves (1 lb. each) fresh or frozen pizza dough, thawed
- 3 Tbsp. olive oil, divided
- 1 can (28 oz.) whole tomatoes, drained and crushed
- 1 medium onion, finely chopped
- 1 can (2 oz.) anchovy fillets, drained and broken into ¼-in. pieces
- 1 cup shredded mozzarella cheese
- ½ cup soft bread crumbs
  Fresh torn basil leaves

1. Preheat oven to 425°. Grease a 15x10x1-in. baking pan. Press dough to fit bottom and ½ in. up sides of pan. Brush with 2 Tbsp. oil; top with tomatoes, onion and anchovies. Sprinkle with mozzarella. Combine bread crumbs and remaining 1 Tbsp. oil; sprinkle over pizza.
2. Bake on a lower oven rack until edges are golden brown and cheese is melted, 20-25 minutes. Sprinkle pizza with basil before serving.

1 PIECE: 277 cal., 9g fat (2g sat. fat), 11mg chol., 527mg sod., 38g carb. (4g sugars, 3g fiber), 11g pro.

COMPANY MAC & CHEESE

I'm not usually a fan of homemade macaroni and cheese, but when a friend served this, I had to have the recipe. This is by far the creamiest, tastiest and most special macaroni and cheese I have ever tried. Since it's simple to make and well received, it's a terrific potluck dish.
—*Catherine Ogden, Middlegrove, NY*

Takes: 30 min. • **Makes:** 8 servings

- 1¾ cups uncooked elbow macaroni
- 6 Tbsp. butter, divided
- 3 Tbsp. all-purpose flour
- 2 cups whole milk
- 1 pkg. (8 oz.) cream cheese, cubed
- 2 cups shredded cheddar cheese
- 2 tsp. spicy brown mustard
- ½ tsp. salt
- ¼ tsp. pepper
- ¾ cup dry bread crumbs
- 2 Tbsp. minced fresh parsley

1. Preheat oven to 400°. Cook macaroni according to the package directions. Meanwhile, melt 4 Tbsp. butter in a large saucepan. Stir in the flour until smooth. Gradually add milk. Bring to a boil; cook and stir for 2 minutes.
2. Reduce heat; add cheeses, mustard, salt and pepper. Stir until cheese is melted and sauce is smooth. Drain macaroni; add to cheese sauce and stir to coat.
3. Transfer to a greased shallow 3-qt. or 13x9-in. baking dish. Melt remaining butter; toss with bread crumbs and parsley. Sprinkle over macaroni. Bake, uncovered, until golden brown, 15-20 minutes.

1 CUP: 468 cal., 31g fat (18g sat. fat), 86mg chol., 604mg sod., 33g carb. (6g sugars, 1g fiber), 15g pro.

WINTER VEGETABLE SHEPHERD'S PIE

We seem to eat for comfort during the holidays—but comfort foods aren't necessarily healthy. To make a classic comfort food dish more healthy, I came up with this lovely take on shepherd's pie. It's perfect for putting out on your holiday buffet table.
—*Ann Sheehy, Lawrence, MA*

Prep: 55 min. • **Bake:** 30 min. + standing
Makes: 10 servings

- 3 cups cubed peeled butternut squash (1-in. pieces)
- 1 large potato, peeled and cut into 1-in. cubes (about 2 cups)
- 2 medium carrots, thinly sliced
- 2 cups vegetable broth
- ½ tsp. plus ¾ tsp. salt, divided
- ¾ tsp. pepper, divided
- 2 lbs. ground turkey
- 1 large onion, chopped
- 1 Tbsp. olive oil
- ¾ lb. sliced fresh mushrooms
- 3 garlic cloves, minced
- ½ cup white wine
- 1 tsp. dried thyme
- ¼ cup all-purpose flour
- 2 cups frozen peas (about 8 oz.)

1. Preheat oven to 350°. Place first 4 ingredients in a large saucepan; bring to a boil. Reduce heat; simmer, covered, until vegetables are tender, 10-15 minutes. Drain vegetables, reserving broth. Mash vegetables until smooth, stirring in ½ tsp. salt and ¼ tsp. pepper.

2. In 2 batches, cook turkey and onion in a Dutch oven over medium-high heat, breaking turkey into crumbles, until turkey is no longer pink, 5-7 minutes. Remove from pan.

3. In same pan, heat oil over medium-high heat; saute mushrooms until tender, 7-9 minutes. Add garlic; cook and stir 1 minute. Add wine, thyme and the remaining salt and pepper; bring to a boil, stirring to remove browned bits from pan. Cook until liquid is evaporated. Stir in flour until blended; gradually stir in reserved broth. Bring to a boil; cook and stir until thickened. Stir in peas and turkey mixture; heat through.

4. Transfer to a greased 2½-qt. baking dish. Spread with mashed vegetables. Bake, uncovered, until filling is bubbly, 30-35 minutes. Let stand 10 minutes before serving.

1 SERVING: 314 cal., 11g fat (2g sat. fat), 75mg chol., 654mg sod., 29g carb. (6g sugars, 5g fiber), 28g pro. **DIABETIC EXCHANGES:** 3 lean meat, 2 starch.

★ ★ ★ ★ ★ **READER REVIEW**

"Excellent recipe! Perfect blend of flavors that makes a light, yet rich-tasting, dish."

DANIELHARMON TASTEOFHOME.COM

SPANISH-STYLE PAELLA

If you enjoy cooking ethnic foods, this hearty rice dish is a fantastic one. It's brimming with generous chunks of sausage, shrimp and veggies.
—Taste of Home *Test Kitchen*

Prep: 10 min. • **Cook:** 35 min.
Makes: 8 servings

- ½ lb. Spanish chorizo links, sliced
- ½ lb. boneless skinless chicken breasts, cubed
- 1 Tbsp. olive oil
- 1 garlic clove, minced
- 1 cup uncooked short grain rice
- 1 cup chopped onion
- 1½ cups chicken broth
- 1 can (14½ oz.) stewed tomatoes, undrained
- ½ tsp. paprika
- ¼ tsp. ground cayenne pepper
- ¼ tsp. salt
- 10 strands saffron, crushed or ⅛ tsp. ground saffron
- ½ lb. uncooked medium shrimp, peeled and deveined
- ½ cup sweet red pepper strips
- ½ cup green pepper strips
- ½ cup frozen peas
  Optional: Minced fresh parsley and lemon wedges

1. In a large saucepan or skillet over medium-high heat, cook sausage and chicken in oil for 5 minutes or until sausage is lightly browned and chicken is no longer pink, stirring frequently. Add garlic; cook 1 minute longer. Drain if necessary.
2. Stir in rice and onion. Cook until onion is tender and rice is lightly browned, stirring frequently. Add the broth, tomatoes, paprika, cayenne, salt and saffron. Bring to a boil. Reduce heat to low; cover and cook for 10 minutes.

3. Stir in the shrimp, peppers and peas. Cover and cook 10 minutes longer or until rice is tender, shrimp turn pink and liquid is absorbed. Top with fresh parsley and lemon wedges, if desired.
1 CUP: 237 cal., 7g fat (2g sat. fat), 62mg chol., 543mg sod., 27g carb. (5g sugars, 2g fiber), 16g pro.

ROMANO BASIL TURKEY BREAST

Guests will be impressed when you slice this golden, grilled turkey breast, dressed up with a flavorful layer of basil and cheese under the skin.
—Darlene Markham, Rochester, NY

Prep: 15 min. • **Grill:** 1¾ hours + standing
Makes: 12 servings

- 1 cup shredded Romano cheese
- ½ cup fresh basil leaves, chopped
- 4 lemon slices
- 4 garlic cloves, minced
- 1 bone-in turkey breast (5 to 6 lbs.)
- 2 Tbsp. olive oil
- ½ tsp. salt
- ¼ tsp. pepper

1. Combine the cheese, basil, lemon slices and garlic. With fingers, carefully loosen skin from the turkey breast; place mixture under the skin. Secure skin to underside of breast with toothpicks. Rub skin with oil and sprinkle with salt and pepper.
2. Prepare grill for indirect heat, using a drip pan. Place the turkey breast over drip pan. Grill, covered, over indirect medium heat until a thermometer reads 170°, 1¾-2¼ hours. Remove toothpicks. Cover turkey and let stand for 10 minutes before slicing.
6 OZ. COOKED TURKEY: 321 cal., 15g fat (5g sat. fat), 112mg chol., 327mg sod., 1g carb. (0 sugars, 0 fiber), 44g pro.

ZUCCHINI ENCHILADAS

When my garden is bursting with zucchini, I turn to this recipe to make the most of it. My family loves the freshness of this dish.
—*Angela Leinenbach, Mechanicsville, VA*

Prep: 1½ hours • **Bake:** 30 min.
Makes: 12 servings

- 1 medium sweet yellow pepper, chopped
- 1 medium green pepper, chopped
- 1 large sweet onion, chopped
- 2 Tbsp. olive oil
- 2 garlic cloves, minced
- 2 cans (15 oz. each) tomato sauce
- 2 cans (14½ oz. each) no-salt-added diced tomatoes, undrained
- 2 Tbsp. chili powder
- 2 tsp. sugar
- 2 tsp. dried marjoram
- 1 tsp. dried basil
- 1 tsp. ground cumin
- ¼ tsp. salt
- ¼ tsp. cayenne pepper
- 1 bay leaf
- 3 lbs. zucchini, shredded (about 8 cups)
- 24 corn tortillas (6 in.), warmed
- 4 cups shredded reduced-fat cheddar cheese
- 2 cans (2¼ oz. each) sliced ripe olives, drained
- ½ cup minced fresh cilantro
  Reduced-fat sour cream, optional

1. In a large saucepan, saute peppers and onion in oil until tender. Add garlic; cook 1 minute longer. Stir in tomato sauce, tomatoes, chili powder, sugar, marjoram, basil, cumin, salt, cayenne and bay leaf. Bring to a boil. Reduce heat; simmer, uncovered, 30-35 minutes or until slightly thickened. Discard the bay leaf.

2. Preheat oven to 350°. Place ⅓ cup zucchini down the center of each tortilla; top with 2 Tbsp. cheese and 2 tsp. olives. Roll up and place seam side down in two 13x9-in. baking dishes coated with cooking spray. Pour sauce over the top; sprinkle with remaining cheese.

3. Bake, uncovered, 30-35 minutes or until heated through. Sprinkle with cilantro. Serve with sour cream if desired.

2 ENCHILADAS: 326 cal., 13g fat (6g sat. fat), 27mg chol., 846mg sod., 42g carb. (10g sugars, 7g fiber), 16g pro. **DIABETIC EXCHANGES:** 2 starch, 2 medium-fat meat, 2 vegetable, ½ fat.

ARTICHOKE & SPINACH CHICKEN CASSEROLE

Try this homey and comforting casserole for an alternate main dish at Thanksgiving. The spinach adds nice color and the red pepper flakes add a pleasant, mild heat.
—*Janice Christofferson, Eagle River, WI*

Prep: 30 min. • **Bake:** 45 min.
Makes: 8 servings

- 3 cups uncooked bow tie pasta
- 2 Tbsp. butter
- ½ lb. sliced fresh mushrooms
- 1 medium onion, chopped
- 2 large eggs
- 1½ cups 2% milk
- 1 tsp. Italian seasoning
- ½ tsp. salt
- ¼ tsp. pepper
- ¼ to ½ tsp. crushed red pepper flakes
- 3 cups cubed cooked chicken
- 1 can (14 oz.) water-packed quartered artichoke hearts, rinsed and drained
- 1 pkg. (10 oz.) frozen chopped spinach, thawed and squeezed dry
- 2 cups shredded Monterey Jack cheese
- 2 Tbsp. grated Parmesan cheese

TOPPING
- ⅓ cup seasoned bread crumbs
- 2 Tbsp. grated Parmesan cheese
- 1 Tbsp. butter, melted
- ½ tsp. paprika

1. Preheat oven to 350°. Cook the pasta according to package directions; drain.
2. In a large skillet, heat the butter over medium-high heat; saute the mushrooms and onion until tender. Remove from heat.
3. In a large bowl, whisk together eggs, milk and seasonings. Stir in chicken, artichoke hearts, spinach, cheeses and mushroom mixture. Stir in pasta.
4. Transfer to a greased 13x9-in. baking dish. Bake, covered, 40 minutes.
5. Mix the topping ingredients; sprinkle over casserole. Bake, uncovered, until bubbly and topping is golden brown, 5-10 minutes.

1½ CUPS: 455 cal., 21g fat (11g sat. fat), 136mg chol., 713mg sod., 34g carb. (5g sugars, 3g fiber), 34g pro.

★ ★ ★ ★ ★ **READER REVIEW**

"This was wonderful. I didn't have artichokes so used fresh Brussels sprouts instead. I sauteed them a bit with the onions before adding to the casserole. I will definitely make this again."

SHARONISAACSON TASTEOFHOME.COM

TACO-FILLED PASTA SHELLS

I've been stuffing pasta shells with different fillings for years, but my family enjoys this version with taco-seasoned meat the most. Freezing is so convenient, because you can take out only the number you need. Just add zippy taco sauce and bake.
—*Marge Hodel, Roanoke, IL*

- -

Prep: 20 min. + chilling • **Bake:** 45 min.
Makes: 2 casseroles (6 servings each)

2 lbs. ground beef
2 envelopes taco seasoning
1½ cups water
1 pkg. (8 oz.) cream cheese, cubed
24 uncooked jumbo pasta shells
¼ cup butter, melted
ADDITIONAL INGREDIENTS
(FOR EACH CASSEROLE)
1 cup salsa
1 cup taco sauce
1 cup shredded cheddar cheese
1 cup shredded Monterey Jack cheese
1½ cups crushed tortilla chips
1 cup sour cream
3 green onions, chopped

1. In a Dutch oven, cook beef over medium heat until no longer pink; drain. Stir in taco seasoning and water. Bring to a boil. Reduce heat; simmer, uncovered, for 5 minutes. Stir in cream cheese until melted. Transfer to a bowl; cool. Chill for 1 hour.
2. Cook pasta according to package directions; drain. Gently toss with butter. Fill each shell with about 3 Tbsp. of the meat mixture.
3. For each casserole, spoon 1 cup salsa into a greased 9-in. square baking dish. Top with shells and 1 cup taco sauce. Cover and bake at 350° for 30 minutes. Uncover; sprinkle with 1 cup of each cheese and with 1½ cups chips. Bake 15 minutes longer or until heated through.

4. Serve the casseroles with sour cream and onions.
FREEZE OPTION: Place filled pasta shells in a freezer container. Cover and freeze for up to 3 months. To use frozen shells, thaw in the refrigerator for 24 hours (shells will be partially frozen). Spoon 1 cup salsa into a greased 9-in. square baking dish; top with shells and 1 cup taco sauce. Cover and bake at 350° for 40 minutes. Uncover; sprinkle with cheeses and chips. Bake 15 minutes longer or until heated through. Serve casseroles with sour cream and onions.
2 SHELLS: 492 cal., 31g fat (16g sat. fat), 98mg chol., 982mg sod., 29g carb. (4g sugars, 1g fiber), 23g pro.

★ ★ ★ ★ ★ **READER REVIEW**

"This was delicious! I made it as written but added chopped onion and a can of black beans to the meat."

MIKE_HOYT TASTEOFHOME.COM

WATERMELON SHRIMP SALAD

Sweet, spicy and easy to make, this salad travels well in a cooler to picnics and summer gatherings. I love the combination of flavors, the colorful presentation, and of course, I love to see the happy faces of my guests once they've tried it.
—*Judy Batson, Tampa, FL*

Prep: 30 min. + chilling
Makes: 10 servings

- 1 seedless watermelon, cut into 1-in. cubes (about 10 cups)
- 1 medium honeydew melon, cut into 1-in. cubes (about 4 cups)
- 2 lbs. peeled and deveined cooked shrimp (31-40 per lb.)
- 2 cups green grapes, halved
- 1 large cucumber, seeded and chopped
- 1 small navel orange, peeled and sectioned
- 1 small red onion, chopped
- 1 jalapeno pepper, seeded and finely chopped
- ⅓ cup lemon juice
- 1 Tbsp. brown sugar
- ¼ tsp. crushed red pepper flakes

In a large bowl, combine the first 8 ingredients. Whisk together the remaining ingredients. Drizzle over shrimp mixture and toss to coat. Refrigerate at least 20 minutes before serving. Toss before serving.
NOTE: Wear disposable gloves when cutting hot peppers; the oils can burn skin. Avoid touching your face.
2 CUPS: 309 cal., 2g fat (0 sat. fat), 138mg chol., 158mg sod., 56g carb. (50g sugars, 3g fiber), 21g pro.

GRILLED CHICKEN RANCH BURGERS

This is one of the most fantastic, flavorful burgers I've ever made. Ranch is a favorite in dips and dressings, and believe me, it doesn't disappoint in these burgers, either!
—*Kari Shifflett, Lake Mills, IA*

Prep: 15 min. + chilling
Grill: 10 min. • **Makes:** 16 servings

- ¾ cup ranch salad dressing
- ¾ cup panko bread crumbs
- ¾ cup grated Parmesan cheese
- 3 Tbsp. Worcestershire sauce
- 3 garlic cloves, minced
- 3 tsp. pepper
- 4 lbs. ground chicken
- 3 Tbsp. olive oil
- 16 hamburger buns, split
  Optional toppings: Tomato slices, lettuce leaves, sliced red onion, sliced cucumber, sliced avocado and ranch dip

1. In a large bowl, mix the first 6 ingredients. Add chicken; mix lightly but thoroughly. Shape mixture into sixteen ½-in.-thick patties. Brush both sides with oil; refrigerate, covered, 15 minutes to allow patties to firm up.
2. Grill burgers, covered, over medium heat or broil 3-4 in. from the heat for 5-6 minutes on each side or until a thermometer reads 165°. Serve on buns with toppings as desired.
1 BURGER: 371 cal., 19g fat (5g sat. fat), 79mg chol., 498mg sod., 26g carb. (4g sugars, 1g fiber), 24g pro.

BAYOU COUNTRY SEAFOOD CASSEROLE

Seafood is a popular food in our area. Since crabs and shrimp are so plentiful in our bayous and rivers, they're used in a variety of recipes.
—*Ethel Miller, Eunice, LA*

Prep: 35 min. • **Bake:** 30 min.
Makes: 8 servings

- 1 medium onion, chopped
- 1 medium green pepper, chopped
- 1 celery rib, chopped
- 6 Tbsp. butter
- 1 garlic clove, minced
- 1 can (10¾ oz.) condensed cream of mushroom soup, undiluted
- 1 lb. uncooked shrimp, peeled and deveined
- 1½ cups cooked rice
- 2 cans (6 oz. each) crabmeat, drained, flaked and cartilage removed
- 4 slices day-old bread, cubed
- ¾ cup half-and-half cream
- ¼ cup chopped green onion tops
- ½ tsp. salt
- ¼ tsp. pepper
  Dash cayenne pepper

TOPPING

- 2 Tbsp. butter, melted
- ⅓ cup dry bread crumbs
- 2 Tbsp. snipped fresh parsley

1. Preheat oven to 375°. Heat a large skillet over medium heat; add onion, green pepper and celery in butter. Cook and stir until tender, 2-3 minutes. Add garlic; cook 1 minute longer. Add soup and shrimp; cook until shrimp turn pink, 10 minutes, stirring occasionally. Stir in the rice, crab, bread cubes, cream, onion tops and seasonings.
2. Spoon into a greased 2-qt. baking dish. Combine topping ingredients; sprinkle over casserole. Bake uncovered until heated through, 25-30 minutes.
1 SERVING: 329 cal., 17g fat (10g sat. fat), 147mg chol., 822mg sod., 25g carb. (3g sugars, 2g fiber), 18g pro.

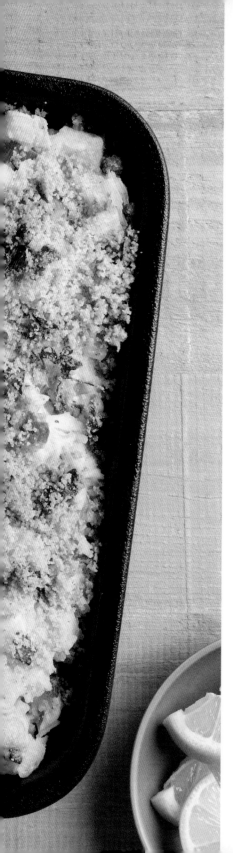

HAM & PINEAPPLE KABOBS

For a twist on the usual holiday fare, my family turns ham and pineapple into juicy kabobs. The marinade gets its unique zip from hoisin, teriyaki and soy sauces.
—*Chandra Lane Sirois, Kansas City, MO*

- -

Prep: 30 min. + marinating
Bake: 15 min. • **Makes:** 12 servings

- ¼ cup hoisin sauce
- ¼ cup unsweetened pineapple juice
- ¼ cup teriyaki sauce
- 1 Tbsp. honey
- 1½ tsp. rice vinegar
- 1½ tsp. reduced-sodium soy sauce
- KABOBS
- 2 lbs. fully cooked boneless ham, cut into 1-in. pieces
- 1 large fresh pineapple, peeled, cored and cut into 1-in. cubes (about 4 cups)

1. In a large shallow dish, combine the first 6 ingredients. Add ham; turn to coat. Refrigerate, covered, overnight.
2. Preheat oven to 350°. Drain ham, reserving marinade. For glaze, pour marinade into a small saucepan; bring to a boil. Reduce heat; simmer, uncovered, 5-7 minutes or until slightly thickened, stirring occasionally. Remove from heat.
3. Meanwhile, on 12 metal or soaked wooden skewers, alternately thread ham and pineapple; place in a foil-lined 15x10x1-in. baking pan. Brush with glaze. Bake, uncovered, 15-20 minutes or until lightly browned.
1 KABOB: 144 cal., 3g fat (1g sat. fat), 39mg chol., 1109mg sod., 15g carb. (12g sugars, 1g fiber), 15g pro.

BEEF STEW FOR A CROWD

Beef stew always seems to be popular at large gatherings. Everyone likes this hearty combination of beef, potatoes, carrots, celery and onion in a savory tomato-to-beef broth.
—*Jackie Holland, Gillette, WY*

- -

Prep: 30 min. • **Cook:** 2 hours
Makes: 22 servings (5½ qt.)

- 2½ lbs. beef stew meat, cut into ½-in. cubes
- 3 Tbsp. canola oil
- 12 cups water
- 2 cans (15 oz. each) tomato sauce
- ¼ cup beef bouillon granules
- 1 tsp. salt, optional
- ½ tsp. pepper
- 3½ lbs. potatoes, peeled and cubed
- 4 medium carrots, sliced
- 3 celery ribs, sliced
- 2 medium onions, coarsely chopped
- ¾ cup all-purpose flour
- 1½ cups cold water

1. In a soup kettle, brown beef in oil; drain. Stir in the water, tomato sauce, bouillon, salt if desired and pepper. Bring to a boil. Reduce heat; cover and simmer for 1½ hours or until the meat is tender.
2. Add the potatoes, carrots, celery and onions. Return to a boil. Reduce heat; cover and simmer for 25-30 minutes or until the vegetables are tender.
3. Combine flour and cold water until smooth; gradually stir into stew. Bring to a boil; cook and stir for 2 minutes or until thickened.
1 CUP: 183 cal., 6g fat (2g sat. fat), 32mg chol., 739mg sod., 22g carb. (0 sugars, 3g fiber), 13g pro. **DIABETIC EXCHANGES:** 1½ lean meat, 1 starch, 1 vegetable.

MEATBALL CALZONES

My family can't get enough of this savory entree. We have to have it at least once a month, or everyone goes through withdrawal. Leftovers freeze well for a quick meal later.
—Cori Cooper, Boise, ID

- -

Prep: 1½ hours + standing • **Bake:** 25 min.
Makes: 3 calzones (4 servings each)

- 3 large eggs, lightly beaten
- 1 cup seasoned bread crumbs
- 1 cup grated Parmesan cheese
- 3 tsp. Italian seasoning
- 2 lbs. ground beef
- 3 loaves (1 lb. each) frozen bread dough, thawed
- 3 cups shredded part-skim mozzarella cheese
- 1 large egg white, lightly beaten
  Additional Italian seasoning
- 1 jar (14 oz.) spaghetti sauce, warmed

1. In a large bowl, combine the eggs, bread crumbs, Parmesan cheese and Italian seasoning. Crumble beef over mixture and mix gently but thoroughly. Shape into 1-in. balls.
2. Place meatballs on a rack in a shallow baking pan. Bake, uncovered, at 400° for 10-15 minutes or until no longer pink. Drain on paper towels. Reduce heat to 350°.
3. On a floured surface, roll each portion of dough into an 18x12-in. rectangle. Spoon a third of the meatballs and mozzarella cheese down the center of each rectangle. Fold dough over filling; press edges firmly to seal.
4. Place on greased baking sheets. Brush tops with egg white; sprinkle with Italian seasoning. Let stand for 15-30 minutes. Bake for 25-30 minutes or until golden brown. Serve with spaghetti sauce.
1 PIECE: 1275 cal., 32g fat (8g sat. fat), 117mg chol., 2536mg sod., 176g carb. (17g sugars,15g fiber), 60g pro.

GRILLED SUMMER SAUSAGE SALAD

It's not often you see sausage in a salad, but I say why not? The grilled links and garden vegetables make for a garlicky, fresh-tasting, very filling salad. I'll even grill the romaine on occasion!
—Noelle Myers, Grand Forks, ND

- -

Takes: 30 min. • **Makes:** 8 servings

- 1 lb. garlic summer sausage, casing removed and quartered lengthwise
- 2 small zucchini, cut in half lengthwise
- 2 yellow summer squash, cut in half lengthwise
- 1 medium sweet red pepper, halved and seeded
- 1 medium sweet orange pepper, halved and seeded
- 2 Tbsp. olive oil
- ½ tsp. salt
- ¼ tsp. pepper
- 1 pkg. (5 oz.) spring mix salad greens
- ½ English cucumber, chopped
- 2 celery ribs with leaves, chopped
- ½ cup Italian salad dressing

1. Brush summer sausage, zucchini, yellow squash and peppers with olive oil; sprinkle with salt and pepper. Grill sausage and vegetables on an oiled rack, covered, over medium heat for 5-6 minutes on each side or until crisp-tender. Remove to cutting board; roughly chop vegetables and sausage.
2. Place salad greens in a large bowl; add cucumber, celery, grilled vegetables and sausage. Drizzle with dressing; toss to coat. Divide among 8 bowls. If desired, sprinkle with additional black pepper.
2 CUPS: 260 cal., 21g fat (6g sat. fat), 35mg chol., 1048mg sod., 10g carb. (4g sugars, 2g fiber), 10g pro.

CHICKEN BURRITOS

This mouthwatering southwestern recipe is wonderful to have on hand for quick meals or to take to potlucks.
—Sonya Nightingale, Burley, ID

- -

Prep: 30 min. • **Bake:** 35 min.
Makes: 2 casseroles (6 servings each)

6	Tbsp. butter
1	large onion, chopped
¼	cup chopped green pepper
½	cup all-purpose flour
3	cups chicken broth
1	can (10 oz.) diced tomatoes and green chiles, undrained
1	tsp. ground cumin
1	tsp. chili powder
½	tsp. garlic powder
½	tsp. salt
2	Tbsp. chopped jalapeno pepper, optional
1	can (15 oz.) chili with beans
1	pkg. (8 oz.) cream cheese, cubed
8	cups cubed cooked chicken
24	flour tortillas (6 in.), warmed
6	cups shredded Colby-Monterey Jack cheese
	Salsa, optional

1. Preheat oven to 350°. In a Dutch oven, heat butter over medium-high heat. Add onion and pepper; cook and stir until tender. Stir in the flour until blended; gradually stir in broth. Bring to a boil; cook and stir 2 minutes. Reduce heat; stir in tomatoes, seasonings and, if desired, jalapeno. Cook 5 minutes. Add chili and cream cheese; stir until cream cheese is melted. Stir in chicken.
2. Spoon about ½ cup filling across center of each tortilla; sprinkle each with ¼ cup Colby-Monterey Jack cheese. Fold bottom and sides over filling and roll up. Place in 2 greased 13x9-in. baking dishes.
3. Bake, covered, 35-40 minutes or until heated through. If desired, serve with salsa.

FREEZE OPTION: Cool unbaked burritos; cover and freeze. To use, partially thaw in refrigerator overnight. Remove from refrigerator 30 minutes before baking. Preheat oven to 350°. Cover burritos with foil; bake as directed, increasing baking time to 50-55 minutes or until heated through and a thermometer inserted in center reads 160°.
2 BURRITOS: 760 cal., 44g fat (23g sat. fat), 177mg chol., 1608mg sod., 40g carb. (2g sugars, 2g fiber), 51g pro.

BRING IT
The rich chicken filling is a creamy alternative to traditional beef on a taco bar. For this use, follow step 1 and heat through. Keep filling warm in a slow cooker set on low heat, and serve tortillas or taco shells, salsa and shredded cheese on the side.

CRANBERRY-WALNUT CHICKEN SALAD SANDWICHES

I made these simple, yet special, sandwiches for a birthday party. Tangy cranberries and crunchy celery pep up the chicken. Leftover turkey works well, too.
—*Shannon Tucker, Land O' Lakes, FL*

Takes: 15 min. • **Makes:** 8 servings

- ½ cup mayonnaise
- 2 Tbsp. honey Dijon mustard
- ¼ tsp. pepper
- 2 cups cubed rotisserie chicken
- 1 cup shredded Swiss cheese
- ½ cup chopped celery
- ½ cup dried cranberries
- ¼ cup chopped walnuts
- ½ tsp. dried parsley flakes
- 8 lettuce leaves
- 16 slices pumpernickel bread

1. In a large bowl, combine the mayonnaise, mustard and pepper. Stir in the chicken, cheese, celery, cranberries, walnuts and parsley.
2. Place lettuce on 8 slices of bread; top each with ½ cup chicken salad. Top with remaining bread.
1 SANDWICH: 411 cal., 22g fat (5g sat. fat), 49mg chol., 469mg sod., 35g carb. (7g sugars, 5g fiber), 20g pro.

JIM'S SECRET FAMILY RECIPE RIBS

For more than 30 years, my brother-in-law Jim kept his famous rib recipe a secret. When he finally shared it, we just had to pass it along because we loved it so much. This one's for you, Jim!
—*Vicki Young, Brighton, CO*

Prep: 20 min. + chilling
Cook: 3 hours 10 min.
Makes: 8 servings

- 2 racks pork baby back ribs (about 5 lbs.)
- ¼ cup soy sauce
- ¼ cup dried oregano
- 2 Tbsp. onion powder
- 2 tsp. garlic powder
- 1 liter lemon-lime soda
- ½ cup unsweetened pineapple or orange juice, optional

BARBECUE SAUCE

- ½ cup sugar or packed brown sugar
- ½ cup hot water
- 1 cup ketchup
- ¼ cup honey mustard
- ¼ cup barbecue sauce of choice
- 3 Tbsp. lemon juice
- 1½ tsp. white vinegar

1. Brush ribs with soy sauce. Combine oregano, onion powder and garlic powder; rub over both sides of ribs. Transfer to a large shallow roasting pan; refrigerate, covered, overnight.
2. Preheat oven to 225°. Add lemon-lime soda and, if desired, juice to roasting pan (do not pour over ribs). Bake, covered, until tender, about 3 hours.
3. Meanwhile, make barbecue sauce by dissolving sugar in hot water; combine with remaining ingredients, thinning with additional lemon-lime soda or juice if necessary. Reserve 1 cup for serving.
4. Remove ribs from oven; discard juices. Brush both sides with barbecue sauce. Grill ribs, covered, on a greased grill rack over low direct heat, turning and brushing occasionally with remaining sauce, until heated through, about 10 minutes. Cut into serving-size pieces; serve with reserved sauce.
1 SERVING: 483 cal., 27g fat (10g sat. fat), 102mg chol., 1107mg sod., 31g carb. (26g sugars, 1g fiber), 30g pro.

1. Preheat oven to 325°. In a Dutch oven, cook bacon over medium-low heat until crisp, stirring occasionally. Remove with a slotted spoon, reserving drippings; drain on paper towels.

2. In batches, brown beef in drippings over medium-high heat; remove from pan. Toss with flour, salt and pepper.

3. In same pan, heat 1 Tbsp. oil over medium heat; saute onions, carrots and mushrooms until onions are tender, 4-5 minutes. Add garlic and tomato paste; cook and stir 1 minute. Add wine and stock, stirring to loosen browned bits from pan. Add herbs, bacon and beef; bring to a boil.

4. Transfer to oven; bake, covered, until meat is tender, 2-2¼ hours. Remove bay leaves.

5. To serve, cook noodles according to package directions; drain. Serve stew with noodles; sprinkle with parsley.

FREEZE OPTION: Freeze cooled stew in freezer containers. To use, partially thaw in refrigerator overnight. Heat through in a saucepan, stirring occasionally; add a little stock or broth if necessary.

⅔ CUP STEW WITH ⅔ CUP NOODLES: 422 cal., 14g fat (4g sat. fat), 105mg chol., 357mg sod., 31g carb. (4g sugars, 2g fiber), 31g pro. **DIABETIC EXCHANGES:** 4 lean meat, 2 fat, 1½ starch, 1 vegetable.

MAKE AHEAD

SPECIAL OCCASION BEEF BOURGUIGNON

I've found many rich and satisfying variations for beef Bourguignon, including an intriguing peasant version that used beef cheeks for the meat and a rustic table wine.
—*Leo Cotnoir, Johnson City, NY*

Prep: 50 min. • **Bake:** 2 hours
Makes: 8 servings

- 4   bacon strips, chopped
- 1   beef sirloin tip roast (2 lbs.), cut into 1½-in. cubes and patted dry
- ¼   cup all-purpose flour
- ½   tsp. salt
- ½   tsp. pepper
- 1   Tbsp. canola oil
- 2   medium onions, chopped
- 2   medium carrots, coarsely chopped
- ½   lb. medium fresh mushrooms, quartered
- 4   garlic cloves, minced
- 1   Tbsp. tomato paste
- 2   cups dry red wine
- 1   cup beef stock
- 2   bay leaves
- ½   tsp. dried thyme
- 8   oz. uncooked egg noodles
     Minced fresh parsley

BEEF BOURGUIGNON SERVING TIPS

- This stew's origins are in Burgundy, France, an area celebrated for its wines.
- Prepare this recipe with an affordable wine made from pinot noir grapes, the same type used in red Burgundy wines.
- Serve the stew with mashed potatoes instead of egg noodles for traditional French flair.

GARLIC BREAD PASTA TORTE

My kids love to stuff spiral pasta inside bread for a clever dinner torte. We save the bread crusts to make garlicky croutons for salad.
—*Melissa Pelkey Hass, Waleska, GA*

- -

Prep: 40 min. • **Bake:** 25 min.
Makes: 12 servings

- 1 **pkg. (16 oz.) spiral pasta**
- 1 **pkg. (19½ oz.) Italian turkey sausage links, casings removed**
- 8 **oz. sliced fresh mushrooms**
- 1 **medium green pepper, chopped**
- 1 **medium onion, chopped**
- 1 **jar (24 oz.) marinara sauce**
- 1 **Tbsp. minced fresh basil or 1 tsp. dried basil**
- 3 **tsp. Italian seasoning**
- 2½ **cups shredded part-skim mozzarella cheese, divided**
- 6 **Tbsp. butter, cubed**
- 6 **garlic cloves, minced**
- 20 **slices white bread, crusts removed Additional marinara sauce, warmed, optional**

1. Preheat oven to 400°. In a 6-qt. stockpot, cook pasta according to package directions for al dente; drain and return to pot.

2. In a large skillet, cook sausage, mushrooms, green pepper and onion over medium-high heat 7-9 minutes or until sausage is no longer pink, breaking up sausage into crumbles; drain. Stir in sauce, basil and Italian seasoning. Add to pasta; stir in 2 cups cheese.

3. In a microwave, melt butter; stir in garlic. Lightly brush one side of bread with garlic butter. Line bottom and sides of a greased 10-in. springform pan with bread slices, trimming to fit and facing buttered sides against pan. Fill with pasta mixture; press firmly to pack down. Sprinkle with remaining cheese.

4. Bake, uncovered, 25-30 minutes or until golden brown and cheese is melted. Loosen sides from pan with a knife; remove rim. If desired, serve with additional marinara sauce.

1 PIECE: 409 cal., 16g fat (7g sat. fat), 49mg chol., 752mg sod., 48g carb. (7g sugars, 3g fiber), 19g pro.

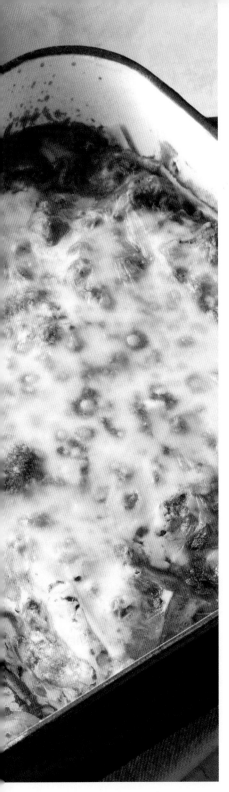

MAKE AHEAD

ARGENTINE LASAGNA

My family is from Argentina, which has a strong Italian heritage and large cattle ranches. This all-in-one lasagna is packed with meat, cheese and veggies.
—*Sylvia Maenenr, Omaha, NE*

Prep: 30 min. • **Bake:** 55 min. + standing
Makes: 12 servings

- 1 lb. ground beef
- 1 large sweet onion, chopped
- ½ lb. sliced fresh mushrooms
- 1 garlic clove, minced
- 1 can (15 oz.) tomato sauce
- 1 can (6 oz.) tomato paste
- ¼ tsp. pepper
- 4 cups shredded part-skim mozzarella cheese, divided
- 1 jar (15 oz.) Alfredo sauce
- 1 carton (15 oz.) ricotta cheese
- 2½ cups frozen peas, thawed
- 1 pkg. (10 oz.) frozen chopped spinach, thawed and squeezed dry
- 1 pkg. (9 oz.) no-cook lasagna noodles
  Grated Parmesan cheese, optional

1. Preheat oven to 350°. In a Dutch oven, cook the beef, onion, mushrooms and garlic over medium heat until meat is no longer pink, crumble beef; drain. Stir in the tomato sauce, tomato paste, pepper and 2 cups mozzarella cheese; set aside.
2. In a large bowl, combine the Alfredo sauce, ricotta cheese, peas and spinach.
3. Spread 1 cup meat sauce into a greased 13x9-in. baking dish. Layer with 4 noodles, 1¼ cups meat sauce and 1¼ cups spinach mixture. Repeat layers 3 times. Sprinkle with remaining 2 cups mozzarella cheese. (Pan will be full.)
4. Cover and bake for 45 minutes. Uncover; bake 10 minutes longer or until cheese is melted. Let stand for 10 minutes before cutting. Garnish with basil and, if desired, serve with Parmesan cheese.

FREEZE OPTION: Cover and freeze unbaked lasagna. To use, partially thaw in refrigerator overnight. Remove from refrigerator 30 minutes before baking. Bake lasagna as directed, increasing time as necessary to heat through and for a thermometer to read 165°.
1 PIECE: 406 cal., 18g fat (10g sat. fat), 69mg chol., 598mg sod., 33g carb. (8g sugars, 4g fiber), 28g pro.

FRENCH COUNTRY CASSEROLE

This delicious dish is ideal for busy nights when you don't have much time to devote to dinner. It's a quick-to-fix version of a traditional French cassoulet that was an instant hit with my husband, who enjoys smoked sausage. Just mix everything together and bake. The heavenly aroma will draw your family to the table.
—*Kim Lowe, Coralville, IA*

Prep: 10 min. • **Bake:** 1 hour
Makes: 9 servings

- 1 lb. smoked kielbasa or Polish sausage, cut into ¼ in. pieces
- 1 can (16 oz.) kidney beans, rinsed and drained
- 1 can (15½ oz.) great northern beans, rinsed and drained
- 1 can (15 oz.) black beans, rinsed and drained
- 1 can (15 oz.) tomato sauce
- 3 medium carrots, thinly sliced
- 2 small onions, sliced into rings
- ½ cup dry red wine or beef broth
- 2 Tbsp. brown sugar
- 2 garlic cloves, minced
- 1½ tsp. dried thyme

Combine all ingredients in a bowl; transfer to an ungreased 3-qt. baking dish. Cover and bake at 375° for 60-70 minutes or until the carrots are tender.
1 CUP: 268 cal., 5g fat (0 sat. fat), 33mg chol., 894mg sod., 39g carb. (0 sugars, 0 fiber), 19g pro.

PRESSURE-COOKER COLA BBQ CHICKEN

This recipe is rich with sweet and smoky deliciousness. The meat is juicy and tender, and I like to add a few tasty toppings, such as sliced dill pickles and a layer of pepper jack cheese, for a boost of flavor. This can also be cooked in the slow cooker on low for 8 hours.
—Ashley Lecker, Green Bay, WI

Prep: 10 min. • **Cook:** 10 min.
Makes: 14 servings

- 1   bottle (18 oz.) barbecue sauce
- 1   cup cola
- 2   Tbsp. cider vinegar
- 1   tsp. garlic powder
- 1   tsp. onion powder
- 1   tsp. salt
- ½   tsp. pepper
- 2½ lbs. boneless skinless chicken breasts
- 14 hamburger buns, split
- 14 slices pepper jack cheese
- 1   cup sliced sweet pickles

1. Place the first 7 ingredients in a 6-qt. electric pressure cooker; add chicken. Lock lid; close pressure-release valve. Adjust to pressure-cook on high for 7 minutes. Quick-release pressure. A thermometer inserted in chicken should read at least 165°.
2. Remove chicken; cool slightly. Reserve 2 cups cooking juices; discard remaining juices. Shred chicken with 2 forks. Combine with reserved juices. Serve on buns with cheese and pickles.
FREEZE OPTION: Freeze cooled meat mixture in freezer containers. To use, partially thaw in refrigerator overnight. Heat through in a saucepan, stirring occasionally; add water if necessary.
1 SANDWICH: 367 cal., 10g fat (5g sat. fat), 66mg chol., 971mg sod., 41g carb. (18g sugars, 1g fiber), 26g pro.

MAKEOVER TATER-TOPPED CASSEROLE

I love Tater Tots, and my casserole recipe is a delicious version. But I wanted it to be healthier. The experts at *Taste of Home* slashed the fat in this favorite dish, while keeping all the Tater Tots my family loves!
—Scott Woodward, Shullsburg, WI

Prep: 15 min. • **Bake:** 55 min.
Makes: 8 servings

- 1   lb. lean ground beef (90% lean)
- ½   lb. extra-lean ground turkey
- 1   pkg. (16 oz.) frozen mixed vegetables, thawed and drained
- ¾   cup french-fried onions
- 1   can (10¾ oz.) reduced-fat reduced-sodium condensed cream of celery soup, undiluted
- 1   can (10¾ oz.) reduced-fat reduced-sodium condensed cream of chicken soup, undiluted
- ½   cup fat-free milk
- 4   cups frozen Tater Tots, thawed

1. In a large skillet, cook and crumble beef and turkey over medium heat until no longer pink. In a 13x9-in. baking dish coated with cooking spray, layer the meat mixture, vegetables and french-fried onions.
2. In a small bowl, combine soups and milk; spread over onions. Top with Tater Tots. Bake, uncovered, at 350° until golden brown, 55-60 minutes.
1 CUP: 340 cal., 14g fat (4g sat. fat), 44mg chol., 657mg sod., 33g carb. (4g sugars, 4g fiber), 22g pro.

★ ★ ★ ★ ★ **READER REVIEW**

"I've made this about 20 times. The leftovers are just as good as the first day."

MELISSAZOMBOR TASTEOFHOME.COM

ROAST PORK WITH APPLES & ONIONS

The sweetness of the apples and onions nicely complements the roast pork. With its crisp skin and melt-in-your-mouth flavor, this is my family's favorite weekend dinner.
—*Lily Julow, Lawrenceville, GA*

Prep: 30 min. • **Bake:** 45 min. + standing
Makes: 8 servings

- 1 boneless pork loin roast (2 lbs.)
- ¼ tsp. salt
- ¼ tsp. pepper
- 1 Tbsp. olive oil
- 3 large Golden Delicious apples, cut into 1-in. wedges
- 2 large onions, cut into ¾-in. wedges
- 5 garlic cloves, peeled
- 1 Tbsp. minced fresh rosemary or 1 tsp. dried rosemary, crushed

1. Preheat oven to 350°. Sprinkle roast with salt and pepper. In a large nonstick skillet, heat oil over medium heat; brown roast on all sides. Transfer to a roasting pan coated with cooking spray. Place apples, onions and garlic around roast; sprinkle with rosemary.

2. Roast until a thermometer inserted in pork reads 145°, 45-55 minutes, turning apples, onion and garlic once. Remove from oven; tent with foil. Let stand 10 minutes before slicing roast. Serve with apple mixture.

1 SERVING: 210 cal., 7g fat (2g sat. fat), 57mg chol., 109mg sod., 14g carb. (9g sugars, 2g fiber), 23g pro. **DIABETIC EXCHANGES:** 3 lean meat, 1 starch, ½ fat.

★ ★ ★ ★ ★ **READER REVIEW**

"Fabulous. Pork was tender and juicy, apples and onions just right. Will make this again."

EUROTAHNY TASTEOFHOME.COM

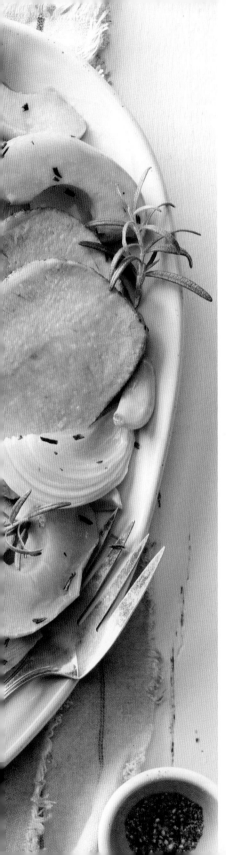

MAKE AHEAD

VEGGIE CALZONES

Bread dough makes it a breeze to assemble these savory meatless calzones. These freeze well, and once frozen, they can be heated in half an hour. If you have a favorite pizza dough, use it instead.

—Lee Ann Lowe, Gray, ME

Prep: 25 min. + rising
Bake: 35 min. • **Makes:** 8 servings

½ lb. fresh mushrooms, chopped
1 medium onion, chopped
1 medium green pepper, chopped
2 Tbsp. canola oil
3 plum tomatoes, seeded and chopped
1 can (6 oz.) tomato paste
1 cup shredded Monterey Jack cheese
1 cup shredded part-skim mozzarella cheese
½ cup grated Parmesan cheese
2 loaves (1 lb. each) frozen bread dough, thawed
1 large egg
1 Tbsp. water

1. In a large skillet, saute mushrooms, onion and green pepper in oil until tender. Add tomatoes; cook and stir 3 minutes. Stir in tomato paste; set aside. Combine cheeses and set aside.
2. On a lightly floured surface, divide dough into eight pieces. Roll each piece into a 7-in. circle. Spoon a scant ½ cup of vegetable mixture and ¼ cup of cheese mixture over 1 side of each circle. Brush edges of dough with water; fold dough over filling and press edges with a fork to seal. Place calzones 3 in. apart on greased baking sheets. Cover and let rise in a warm place for 20 minutes.
3. Preheat oven to 375°. Whisk egg and water; brush over calzones. Bake 33-37 minutes or until golden brown.
FREEZE OPTION: Bake calzones 15 minutes and cool. Place in resealable freezer bags; seal and freeze up to 3 months. To use, preheat oven to 350°. Place frozen calzones 2 in. apart on a greased baking sheet. Bake 30-35 minutes or until golden brown.
1 CALZONE: 503 cal., 15g fat (4g sat. fat), 45mg chol., 953mg sod., 67g carb. (9g sugars, 6g fiber), 23g pro.

LOADED SPAGHETTI BAKE

We used to go south in our RV for months at a time. One year when we arrived home after being gone for a while, my neighbor Jill came over with a pie plate filled with this wonderful spaghetti bake. Now I make it often for my family. I sometimes use leftover chicken instead of beef.
—*Marian Pappas, Lake Stevens, WA*

Prep: 25 min. • **Bake:** 30 min.
Makes: 8 servings

- 12 oz. uncooked spaghetti
- 1 lb. lean ground beef (90% lean)
- 1 cup chopped onion
- 1 cup chopped green pepper
- 1 jar (26 oz.) spaghetti sauce
- 1 can (4 oz.) mushroom stems and pieces, drained
- 1 can (2¼ oz.) sliced ripe olives, drained
- 2 cups shredded cheddar cheese, divided
- 1 can (10¾ oz.) condensed cream of chicken soup, undiluted
- 1 carton (10 oz.) refrigerated Alfredo sauce
- ¼ cup grated Parmesan cheese
- ½ cup cornflake crumbs

1. Preheat oven to 350°. Cook spaghetti according to package directions. Meanwhile, in a large skillet, cook the beef, onion and pepper over medium heat until meat is no longer pink; crumble meat; drain. Add the spaghetti sauce, mushrooms and olives. Drain spaghetti; add to skillet.
2. Transfer to a greased 13x9-in. baking dish. Sprinkle with 1 cup cheddar cheese. In a small bowl, combine soup, Alfredo sauce and Parmesan cheese; spread over cheddar cheese. In another bowl, combine cornflake crumbs and remaining 1 cup cheddar cheese; sprinkle over the top.

3. Bake, uncovered, until casserole is bubbly and cheese is melted, 30 minutes. Let stand 5 minutes before serving.
FREEZE OPTION: Cover and freeze casserole for up to 3 months. To use, remove from the freezer 30 minutes before baking (do not thaw). Cover and bake for 1 hour. Uncover casserole and bake until heated through and a thermometer reads 165°, 15-20 minutes longer.
1½ CUPS: 612 cal., 30g fat (14g sat. fat), 80mg chol., 1486mg sod., 55g carb. (10g sugars, 4g fiber), 29g pro.
MEATY LOADED SPAGHETTI BAKE: Reduce ground beef to ½ pound. Remove casings from ½ pound Italian sausage links. Crumble sausage into skillet and cook with ground beef.
HAM SPAGHETTI BAKE: Omit ground beef. Saute pepper and onions as directed. Stir in 3 cups cubed fully cooked ham.

☆ ☆ ☆ ☆ ☆ **READER REVIEW**

"Excellent casserole to feed a hungry group! Only changes I made were to serve the olives on the side (hubby hates them), and I used some crushed garlic croutons instead of cornflakes. I served it with a simple green salad and everyone was happy!"

ROBIN TASTEOFHOME.COM

PIZZA LOVER'S CASSEROLE

When you're looking for a surefire crowd-pleaser for a kids' party, it's hard to go wrong with pizza. This dish delivers the taste of pizza in a convenient and delicious casserole. Pair it with a salad and bread, and you have a wonderful meal for a table full of kids without the pizzeria tab!
—*Jackie Hannahs, Cedar Springs, MI*

Prep: 20 min. • **Bake:** 20 min.
Makes: 8 servings

- 7 cups uncooked wide egg noodles
- 1 lb. bulk Italian sausage
- 2 jars (14 oz. each) pizza sauce
- 6 oz. sliced pepperoni
- 2 cups shredded cheddar cheese

1. Cook noodles according to package directions. Meanwhile, crumble sausage into a large skillet. Cook over medium heat until meat is no longer pink; drain. Add pizza sauce.
2. Drain noodles and add to skillet; toss to coat. Transfer half of the noodle mixture to a greased 13x9-in. baking dish. Layer with half the pepperoni and half the cheese. Repeat layers. Bake, uncovered, at 350° for 20-25 minutes or until cheese is melted.
1½ CUPS: 537 cal., 32g fat (14g sat. fat), 112mg chol., 1423mg sod., 36g carb. (7g sugars, 3g fiber), 25g pro.

MAPLE-PEACH GLAZED HAM

This is one of my husband's favorite recipes. He makes it regularly for his group of friends on the weekends because it's so good and easy.
—*Bonnie Hawkins, Elkhorn, WI*

Prep: 5 min. • **Bake:** 2 hours
Makes: 16 servings (about 2 cups sauce)

- 1 fully cooked bone-in ham (7 to 9 lbs.)
- 2 cups peach preserves or orange marmalade
- ½ cup maple syrup
- ⅓ cup orange juice
- 2 Tbsp. ground ancho chile pepper, optional

1. Preheat oven to 325°. Place ham on a rack in a shallow roasting pan. Cover and bake 1¾-2¼ hours or until a thermometer reads 130°.
2. Meanwhile, in a small saucepan, mix preserves, syrup, orange juice and, if desired, chili pepper until blended. Remove ¾ cup mixture for glaze.
3. Remove ham from oven; brush with some of the glaze. Bake, uncovered, 15-20 minutes longer or until a thermometer reads 140°, brushing occasionally with remaining glaze.
4. In a saucepan over medium heat, bring preserves mixture to a boil, stirring occasionally. Cook and stir until slightly thickened, 1-2 minutes. Serve as a sauce with ham.
4 OZ. COOKED HAM WITH 2 TBSP. SAUCE: 294 cal., 5g fat (2g sat. fat), 87mg chol., 1040mg sod., 34g carb. (31g sugars, 0 fiber), 29g pro.

TURKEY POTPIES

With golden brown crust and scrumptious filling, these comforting potpies will warm you down to your toes. Because it makes two, you can eat one now and freeze the other for later. They bake and cut beautifully.
—*Laurie Jensen, Cadillac, MI*

Prep: 40 min. • **Bake:** 40 min. + standing
Makes: 2 pies (6 servings each)

- 2 medium potatoes, peeled and cut into 1-in. pieces
- 3 medium carrots, cut into 1-in. slices
- 1 medium onion, chopped
- 1 celery rib, diced
- 2 Tbsp. butter
- 1 Tbsp. olive oil
- 6 Tbsp. all-purpose flour
- 3 cups chicken broth
- 4 cups cubed cooked turkey
- ⅔ cup frozen peas
- ½ cup plus 1 Tbsp. heavy whipping cream, divided
- 1 Tbsp. minced fresh parsley
- 1 tsp. garlic salt
- ¼ tsp. pepper
- 2 sheets refrigerated pie crust
- 1 large egg

1. Preheat oven to 375°. In a Dutch oven, saute potatoes, carrots, onion and celery in butter and oil until tender. Stir in flour until blended; gradually add broth. Bring to a boil; cook and stir 2 minutes or until thickened. Stir in turkey, peas, ½ cup cream, parsley, garlic salt and pepper.
2. Spoon into 2 ungreased 9-in. pie plates. Unroll crusts; place over filling. Trim crusts and seal to edge of pie plates. Cut out a decorative center or cut slits in crusts. In a small bowl, whisk egg and remaining 1 Tbsp. cream; brush over crusts.
3. Bake pies until golden brown, 40-45 minutes. Let pies stand for 10 minutes before cutting.

FREEZE OPTION: Cover and freeze unbaked potpies up to 3 months. To use, remove from freezer 30 minutes before baking (do not thaw). Preheat oven to 425°. Place pie on a baking sheet; cover edge loosely with foil. Bake 30 minutes. Reduce oven setting to 350°; remove foil. Bake until golden brown and a thermometer inserted in center reads 165°, 55-60 minutes longer.
1 SERVING: 287 cal., 15g fat (7g sat. fat), 78mg chol., 542mg sod., 21g carb. (3g sugars, 2g fiber), 17g pro.

MIX UP THE VEGGIES
You can easily add different vegetables, such as sweet potatoes, turnips or cubed winter squash, in this recipe. If you're short on time or looking for an easy shortcut, you can also opt for your favorite frozen veggie mix. In that case, saute an onion or 2 in step 1 to build flavor, then add flour and broth to create a thick sauce. Stir in any frozen veggies at the same time you add the turkey and peas.

MILLION-DOLLAR CHICKEN CASSEROLE

Everyone at the table will love this family-friendly dish. Million-dollar chicken casserole is easy to get on the dinner table on busy weeknights. Stir in shredded cheddar, mozzarella or Monterey Jack cheese for extra flavor.
—Taste of Home *Test Kitchen*

Prep: 30 min. • **Bake:** 30 min.
Makes: 8 servings

    4   oz. cream cheese, softened
    ½   cup sour cream
    1   can (10½ oz.) condensed cream of
        chicken soup, undiluted
    ½   tsp. onion powder
    ½   tsp. garlic powder
    4   cups shredded cooked chicken
    1   cup 2% cottage cheese
   25   Ritz crackers, crushed
    3   Tbsp. butter, melted
    2   green onions, chopped

1. Preheat oven to 350°. In a large bowl, beat cream cheese and sour cream until smooth. Beat in soup, onion powder and garlic powder. Stir in chicken and cottage cheese. Transfer to a greased 9-in. square baking dish. Combine crackers and butter; sprinkle over casserole.
2. Bake, uncovered, until heated through, 25-30 minutes. Sprinkle with green onions.
1¼ CUPS: 363 cal., 24g fat (11g sat. fat), 105mg chol., 593mg sod., 12g carb. (3g sugars, 1g fiber), 26g pro.

ROTISSERIE CHICKEN JUMP-START

Store-bought rotisserie chicken is a convenient way to get a jump on chicken casserole recipes like this one. One rotisserie chicken will yield 4-5 cups of cubed or shredded meat.

GRILLED ITALIAN SAUSAGE SANDWICHES

Try these sausage sandwiches for a casual but hearty meal. Full of traditional Italian flavor, they're a snap to make.
—*Mike Yaeger, Brookings, SD*

Prep: 30 min. • **Grill:** 10 min.
Makes: 20 servings

    4   large green peppers, thinly sliced
    ½   cup chopped onion
    2   Tbsp. olive oil
    4   garlic cloves, minced
    1   can (15 oz.) tomato sauce
    1   can (12 oz.) tomato paste
    1   cup water
    1   Tbsp. sugar
    2   tsp. dried basil
    1   tsp. salt
    1   tsp. dried oregano
   20   uncooked Italian sausage links
   20   sandwich buns
        Shredded part-skim mozzarella
        cheese, optional

1. In a large saucepan, saute peppers and onion in oil until crisp-tender. Add garlic; cook 1 minute longer. Drain. Stir in the tomato sauce, tomato paste, water, sugar, basil, salt and oregano. Bring to a boil. Reduce heat; cover and simmer for 30 minutes or until heated through.
2. Meanwhile, grill sausages, covered, over medium heat for 10-16 minutes or until a thermometer reads 160°, turning occasionally. Serve on buns with sauce and cheese if desired.
1 SERVING: 525 cal., 28g fat (10g sat. fat), 60mg chol., 1327mg sod., 45g carb. (10g sugars, 2g fiber), 25g pro.

PORK & CHEESY MACARONI SLIDERS

I love sliders! This sweet and savory recipe was created out of leftover ingredients I had in my fridge. It is perfect for a weeknight meal or a special-occasion potluck.
—Rashanda Cobbins, Milwaukee, WI

Prep: 30 min. • **Bake:** 10 min.
Makes: 12 servings

- 1 cup uncooked cavatappi pasta
- 1 Tbsp. butter
- 1½ tsp. all-purpose flour
- ¼ tsp. pepper
- ½ cup 2% milk
- ¾ cup shredded sharp cheddar cheese
- 1 pkg. (18 oz.) Hawaiian sweet rolls
- 1 carton (16 oz.) refrigerated fully cooked barbecue shredded pork, warmed
- 2 Tbsp. melted butter
- 1 Tbsp. honey
- ½ tsp. ground mustard
- 1 jalapeno pepper, sliced, optional

1. Preheat oven to 375°. Cook pasta according to package directions.
2. Meanwhile, in a small saucepan, melt butter over medium heat. Stir in flour and pepper until smooth; gradually whisk in milk. Bring to a boil, stirring constantly; cook and stir until thickened, 3-5 minutes. Stir in cheese until melted. Drain pasta; stir into cheese sauce. Set aside.
3. Place roll bottoms in a greased 13x9-in. baking dish. Layer with pork, pasta mixture and roll tops. Combine melted butter, honey and mustard. Brush over roll tops.
4. Bake until tops are golden brown and filling is hot, 10-12 minutes. If desired, top with jalapeno pepper slices.
1 SLIDER: 305 cal., 10g fat (6g sat. fat), 48mg chol., 466mg sod., 39g carb. (17g sugars, 2g fiber), 14g pro.

TACO SALAD FOR A LARGE CROWD

I made this huge taco salad to bring to a party and people were scrambling to figure out who made it. Needless to say I only brought home an empty bowl and the guests went home with a full stomach! Everyone loves this taco salad recipe.
—Lisa Homer, Avon, NY

Prep: 25 min. • **Cook:** 10 min.
Makes: 26 servings (1⅓ cups each)

- 1½ lbs. ground beef
- 2 envelopes taco seasoning, divided
- 1 medium head iceberg lettuce
- 1 pkg. (10 oz.) nacho-flavored tortilla chips, coarsely crushed
- 2 pints grape tomatoes, halved
- 2 cans (16 oz. each) kidney beans, rinsed and drained
- 3 cans (2¼ oz. each) sliced ripe olives, drained
- 1½ cups shredded cheddar cheese
- 1 large sweet onion, chopped
- 2 cans (4 oz. each) chopped green chiles
- 1½ cups Thousand Island salad dressing
- 1⅓ cups salsa
- ⅓ cup sugar

1. In a Dutch oven over medium heat, cook beef with 1 envelope plus 2 Tbsp. taco seasoning until meat is no longer pink; drain.
2. In a very large serving bowl, combine the lettuce, chips, tomatoes, beans, olives, cheese, onion, chiles and the beef mixture.
3. In a small bowl, combine the salad dressing, salsa, sugar and remaining taco seasoning; pour over salad and toss to coat.
1⅓ CUPS: 262 cal., 15g fat (4g sat. fat), 24mg chol., 696mg sod., 23g carb. (7g sugars, 3g fiber), 10g pro.

FRUIT-PECAN PORK ROAST

This spectacular roast was a huge hit with members of the cooking club I belong to. The sweet, tangy fruit glaze looks lovely and is a wonderful complement to the juicy pork.
—Gay Flynn, Bellevue, NE

Prep: 20 min. • **Bake:** 70 min. + standing
Makes: 12 servings

- 1 boneless rolled pork loin roast (3½ lbs.)
- ½ cup chopped green onions
- 4 Tbsp. butter, divided
- ¼ cup orange juice
- 1 bay leaf
- 1 can (14 oz.) whole-berry cranberry sauce
- ½ cup chicken broth
- ½ cup chopped pecans
- 1 Tbsp. red wine vinegar
- ¼ tsp. salt
- ⅛ tsp. pepper
- ⅛ tsp. sugar
- ¼ cup apricot preserves

1. Place roast on a rack in a shallow roasting pan. Bake, uncovered, at 350° for 45 minutes.
2. Meanwhile, in a large skillet, saute onions in 1 Tbsp. of butter for 1 minute. Add orange juice and bay leaf; cook and stir over medium-high heat until thickened, about 4 minutes. Add the cranberry sauce, broth, pecans and vinegar; cook and stir until slightly thickened, about 5 minutes. Reduce heat; stir in the salt, pepper, sugar and remaining butter until butter is melted. Discard bay leaf.
3. Remove ¼ cup sauce and stir in preserves; spoon over roast. Set remaining sauce aside. Bake 20-25 minutes longer or until a thermometer reads 145°. Let meat stand for 10 minutes before slicing. Serve with reserved sauce.
1 SERVING: 306 cal., 13g fat (5g sat. fat), 76mg chol., 176mg sod., 20g carb. (14g sugars, 1g fiber), 26g pro.

GRILLED CHICKEN RAMEN SALAD

This is one of those recipes that I love because it's pretty much a complete meal in one bowl, and when it goes on the table, everyone says, Yeah!
—Karen Carlson, San Luis Obispo, CA

Takes: 30 min. • **Makes:** 8 servings

- 2 Tbsp. canola oil
- 2 pkg. (3 oz. each) ramen noodles, crumbled
- ⅔ cup canola oil
- 2 tsp. sesame oil
- ⅓ cup seasoned rice vinegar
- 1 Tbsp. sugar
- 2 Tbsp. reduced-sodium soy sauce
- 1½ lbs. boneless skinless chicken breast halves
- ½ tsp. pepper
- ¼ tsp. salt
- 1 pkg. (14 oz.) coleslaw mix
- ½ cup minced fresh cilantro
- 3 cups fresh snow peas, thinly sliced lengthwise
- 2 cups shredded carrots
- 4 cups torn mixed salad greens
- 3 thinly sliced green onions
- ⅓ cup crumbled cooked bacon, optional

1. In a large saucepan, heat oil over medium-low heat. Add ramen noodles; cook and stir until toasted, 5-8 minutes. Remove from pan; set aside.
2. In a small bowl, whisk oils, vinegar, sugar and soy sauce until blended; set aside.
3. Sprinkle chicken with pepper and salt. Place chicken on a lightly oiled grill rack. Grill, covered, over medium heat or broil 4-5 in. from heat until a thermometer reads 165°, 8-10 minutes on each side. Cool slightly and chop into ½-in. pieces.
4. In a large bowl, combine coleslaw mix and cilantro. Layer coleslaw mixture, peas, chicken, carrots, salad greens, noodles and green onions in an 8- to 10-qt. dish. Sprinkle with bacon; serve with vinaigrette.
1 SERVING: 458 cal., 29g fat (4g sat. fat), 47mg chol., 738mg sod., 28g carb. (10g sugars, 4g fiber), 22g pro.

10 flour tortillas (8 in.)
⅓ cup crumbled blue cheese
Optional: Chopped tomatoes, sliced
celery, shredded lettuce, sliced
green onions, minced fresh cilantro
and additional cheddar cheese

1. Preheat oven to 350°. In a large bowl, combine chicken, 1¾ cups shredded cheese, diced tomatoes and green chiles, enchilada sauce and wing sauce. In a small saucepan, heat soup, cream cheese, dressing and remaining ¼ cup shredded cheese over low heat until cheeses are melted, 5-10 minutes. Remove from heat.

2. Place ½ cup chicken mixture off center on each tortilla. Roll up and place in a greased 13x9-in. baking dish, seam side down. Top with sauce.

3. Bake, uncovered, until enchiladas are heated through and cheese is melted, 25-30 minutes. Sprinkle with blue cheese and additional toppings of your choice.

1 ENCHILADA: 472 cal., 26g fat (10g sat. fat), 76mg chol., 1387mg sod., 34g carb. (2g sugars, 3g fiber), 25g pro.

★ ★ ★ ★ ★ **READER REVIEW**

"I made these for the UFC fight, and my family loved them! I served them with a nice salad and celery sticks. Very rich but on point for Buffalo chicken fans."

CHERIBESSONEN TASTEOFHOME.COM

BUFFALO CHICKEN ENCHILADAS

This is not a drill! These buffalo chicken enchiladas, filled with tender rotisserie chicken and lots of cheese—and, of course, Buffalo sauce—will be the most craveable, easy and delicious meal you've ever tasted. The entire family will ask for them again and again.
—Becky Hardin, St. Peters, MO

- -

Prep: 15 min. • **Bake:** 25 min.
Makes: 10 servings

3 cups shredded rotisserie chicken
2 cups shredded cheddar cheese, divided
1 can (10 oz.) diced tomatoes and green chiles, drained
1 can (10 oz.) enchilada sauce
½ cup Buffalo wing sauce
1 can (10½ oz.) condensed cream of celery soup, undiluted
4 oz. reduced-fat cream cheese, cubed
½ cup blue cheese salad dressing

DECADENT SPINACH-STUFFED SHELLS

I created this comforting stuffed shells dish to serve on Christmas Eve, but it's so good we enjoy it all year long. It can easily be assembled and frozen to bake at a later date. If you have any leftover cheese mixture, it can be served as a dip, either cold or spooned into ramekins and baked until browned. If you don't like roasted red peppers, feel free to substitute chopped sun-dried tomatoes in the filling and any other pasta sauce.
—*Crystal Schlueter, Northglenn, CO*

Prep: 25 min. • **Cook:** 30 min.
Makes: 12 servings

1 pkg. (12 oz.) jumbo pasta shells
1 jar (24 oz.) roasted red pepper and garlic pasta sauce, divided
2 pkg. (8 oz. each) cream cheese, softened
1 cup roasted garlic Alfredo sauce
Dash salt
Dash pepper
Dash crushed red pepper flakes, optional
2 cups shredded Italian cheese blend
½ cup grated Parmesan cheese
1 pkg. (10 oz.) frozen chopped spinach, thawed and squeezed dry
½ cup finely chopped water-packed artichoke hearts
¼ cup finely chopped roasted sweet red pepper
Additional Parmesan cheese, optional

1. Preheat oven to 350°. Cook pasta shells according to package directions for al dente. Drain.
2. Spread 1 cup sauce into a greased 13x9-in. baking dish. In a large bowl, beat cream cheese, Alfredo sauce and seasonings until blended. Stir in cheeses and vegetables. Spoon into shells. Arrange in prepared baking dish.
3. Pour remaining sauce over top. Bake, covered, 20 minutes. If desired, sprinkle with additional Parmesan cheese. Bake, uncovered, 10-15 minutes longer or until cheese is melted.
3 STUFFED PASTA SHELLS: 389 cal., 22g fat (13g sat. fat), 70mg chol., 707mg sod., 33g carb. (7g sugars, 3g fiber), 14g pro.

DIJON-RUBBED PORK WITH RHUBARB SAUCE

This moist and tender pork loin roast is served with a rhubarb sauce that's just delicious! It's wonderful for company and makes an extra-special weeknight meal.
—Marilyn Rodriguez, Sparks, NV

Prep: 15 min. • **Bake:** 1 hour + standing
Makes: 12 servings (1½ cups sauce)

- 1 boneless pork loin roast (3 lbs.)
- ¼ cup Dijon mustard
- 6 garlic cloves, minced
- 1 Tbsp. minced fresh rosemary or 1 tsp. dried rosemary, crushed
- ¾ tsp. salt
- ½ tsp. pepper

SAUCE
- 3 cups sliced fresh or frozen rhubarb
- ⅓ cup orange juice
- ⅓ cup sugar
- 1 Tbsp. cider vinegar

1. Score the surface of the pork, making diamond shapes ¼ in. deep. In a small bowl, combine the mustard, garlic, rosemary, salt and pepper; rub over pork.
2. Coat a roasting pan and rack with cooking spray; place pork on rack in pan. Bake, uncovered, at 350° for 1 hour or until a thermometer reads 145°. Let stand for 10 minutes before slicing.
3. Meanwhile, in a small saucepan, bring the sauce ingredients to a boil. Reduce heat; cover and simmer for 8-12 minutes or until rhubarb is tender. Serve warm, with pork.
NOTE: If using frozen rhubarb, measure rhubarb while still frozen, then thaw completely. Drain in a colander, but do not press out liquid.

3 OZ. COOKED PORK WITH 2 TBSP. SAUCE: 181 cal., 6g fat (2g sat. fat), 56mg chol., 308mg sod., 9g carb. (7g sugars, 1g fiber), 23g pro. **DIABETIC EXCHANGES:** 3 lean meat, ½ starch.

SPINACH BEEF MACARONI BAKE

I serve this dish at family gatherings and church suppers and sometimes cut the recipe in half for smaller family dinners. My grandson-in-law and great-grandson often ask me to serve it when they stop by to visit.
—Lois Lauppe, Lahoma, OK

Prep: 55 min. • **Bake:** 25 min.
Makes: 2 casseroles (12 servings each)

- 5¼ cups uncooked elbow macaroni
- 2½ lbs. ground beef
- 2 large onions, chopped
- 3 large carrots, shredded
- 3 celery ribs, chopped
- 2 cans (28 oz. each) Italian diced tomatoes, undrained
- 4 tsp. salt
- 1 tsp. garlic powder
- 1 tsp. pepper
- ½ tsp. dried oregano
- 2 pkg. (10 oz. each) frozen chopped spinach, thawed and squeezed dry
- 1 cup grated Parmesan cheese

1. Cook macaroni according to package directions. Meanwhile, in a large Dutch oven, cook the beef, onions, carrots and celery over medium heat until meat is no longer pink; drain. Add the tomatoes, salt, garlic powder, pepper and oregano. Bring to a boil. Reduce heat; cover and simmer for 30 minutes or until vegetables are tender.
2. Drain macaroni; add macaroni and spinach to beef mixture. Pour into 2 greased 3-qt. baking dishes. Sprinkle with cheese. Bake, uncovered, at 350° for 25-30 minutes or until heated through.
1 SERVING: 173 cal., 6g fat (3g sat. fat), 26mg chol., 632mg sod., 18g carb. (4g sugars, 2g fiber), 13g pro.

CHURCH SUPPER HOT DISH

This recipe was in my mother's church cookbook, and now it's in my church cookbook! Apparently is was too good to miss a generation. I often make this dish to take along to potlucks.
—*Norma Turner, Haslett, MI*

Prep: 40 min. • **Bake:** 30 min.
Makes: 8 servings

- 1 lb. ground beef
- 2 cups sliced peeled potatoes
- 2 cups finely chopped celery
- ¾ cup finely chopped carrots
- ¼ cup finely chopped green pepper
- ¼ cup finely chopped onion
- 2 Tbsp. butter
- 1 cup water
- 2 cans (10¾ oz. each) condensed cream of mushroom soup, undiluted
- 1 can (5 oz.) chow mein noodles, divided
- 1 cup shredded cheddar cheese

1. Preheat oven to 350°. In a large skillet, cook beef over medium heat until no longer pink; drain and set aside.
2. In same skillet, saute potatoes, celery, carrots, green pepper and onion in butter 5 minutes. Add water; cover and simmer 10 minutes or until vegetables are tender. Stir in soup and cooked ground beef until blended.
3. Sprinkle half the chow mein noodles into a greased shallow 2-qt. baking dish. Spoon meat mixture over noodles. Cover and bake 20 minutes. Top with cheddar cheese and remaining noodles. Bake, uncovered, 10 minutes longer or until heated through.

1 SERVING: 339 cal., 20g fat (9g sat. fat), 53mg chol., 537mg sod., 25g carb. (2g sugars, 3g fiber), 16g pro.

EASY & ELEGANT TENDERLOIN ROAST

I love the simplicity of the rub in this recipe—olive oil, garlic, salt and pepper. Just add the tenderloin and pop it in the oven. In an hour or so you've got an impressive main dish to feed a crowd. This leaves you with more time to visit with family and less time fussing in the kitchen.
—*Mary Kandell, Huron, OH*

Prep: 10 min. • **Bake:** 45 min. + standing
Makes: 12 servings

- 1 beef tenderloin (5 lbs.)
- 2 Tbsp. olive oil
- 4 garlic cloves, minced
- 2 tsp. sea salt
- 1½ tsp. coarsely ground pepper

1. Preheat oven to 425°. Place roast on a rack in a shallow roasting pan. In a small bowl, mix the oil, garlic, salt and pepper; rub over roast.

2. Roast until meat reaches desired doneness (for medium-rare, a thermometer should read 135°; medium, 140°; medium-well, 145°), 45-65 minutes. Remove from oven; tent with foil. Let stand 15 minutes before slicing.

5 OZ. COOKED BEEF: 294 cal., 13g fat (5g sat. fat), 82mg chol., 394mg sod., 1g carb. (0 sugars, 0 fiber), 40g pro.
DIABETIC EXCHANGES: 5 lean meat, ½ fat.

MAKE AHEAD
HAM & CHEESE CASSEROLES

I got this recipe from my mother and love it because it's easy and I've usually got the ingredients on hand. Also, it freezes well and I can have it handy when extra guests show up. Everyone always likes it; there are never leftovers.
—Jan Schoshke, Brookville, KS

Prep: 20 min. • **Bake:** 25 min.
Makes: 2 casseroles (8 servings each)

- 24 oz. uncooked egg noodles
- 3 lbs. cubed fully cooked ham
- 4 cans (10¾ oz. each) condensed cream of chicken soup, undiluted
- 4 cups frozen cut green beans, thawed
- 1 cup 2% milk
- ¼ cup butter, melted
- 2 cups shredded Colby-Monterey Jack cheese

1. Preheat oven to 350°. Cook pasta according to package directions.
2. Meanwhile, in a large bowl, combine ham, soup, beans and milk. Drain pasta; pour over the ham mixture and toss to coat. Transfer to 2 greased 13x9-in. baking dishes.
3. Drizzle each with butter; sprinkle with cheese. Bake, uncovered, 25-30 minutes or until heated through.
FREEZE OPTION: Cool unbaked casseroles; cover and freeze up to 3 months. To use, partially thaw in refrigerator overnight. Remove from refrigerator 30 minutes before baking. Preheat oven to 350°. Bake, uncovered, 40-45 minutes or until heated through and a thermometer inserted in center reads 165°.
1⅓ CUPS: 470 cal., 21g fat (9g sat. fat), 109mg chol., 1786mg sod., 42g carb. (3g sugars, 3g fiber), 27g pro.

NEW ENGLAND BOILED DINNER

This has been a popular dinner with our family for a long time. When we moved to California in 1960, I'd make it often to remind us of New England. We're back home now and continue to enjoy this scrumptious dish.
—Natalie Cook, Scarborough, ME

Prep: 10 min. • **Cook:** 2 hours
Makes: 10 servings

- 1 smoked boneless pork shoulder butt roast (2 to 2½ lbs.)
- 1 lb. fresh carrots, sliced lengthwise and halved
- 8 medium red potatoes. peeled and halved
- 2 medium onions, cut into quarters
- 1 large head cabbage, cut into quarters
- 1 large turnip, peeled and cut into quarters
- 1 large rutabaga, peeled, halved and sliced

1. Place pork roast in a large Dutch oven; cover with water. Bring to a boil. Reduce heat; cover and simmer for 1 hour.
2. Add the remaining ingredients; return to a boil. Reduce the heat. Cover and simmer for 1 hour or until the vegetables are tender; drain.
1 SERVING: 350 cal., 17g fat (6g sat. fat), 52mg chol., 1120mg sod., 36g carb. (14g sugars, 9g fiber), 17g pro.

★ ★ ★ ★ ★ **READER REVIEW**

"I sometimes fix this recipe as a stew. The broth is so delicious, it's a shame to waste it. I have also made bean and ham soup with the leftover broth."

GAILMTIMMERMAN TASTEOFHOME.COM

SAUCY BARBECUE SHRIMP

This rustic Cajun dish is one of our family favorites. Don't remove the shells off the shrimp—the beauty of this dish is peeling the shrimp and dipping it in the sauce. We've doubled and even tripled the recipe to feed a crowd and it's always perfect!
—*Debbie Glasscock, Conway, AR*

Prep: 20 min. • **Bake:** 20 min.
Makes: 8 servings

- ½ cup butter, cubed
- 1 medium onion, chopped
- 1 bottle (18 oz.) barbecue sauce
- 1 bottle (12 oz.) pale ale beer or nonalcoholic beer
- 2 lbs. uncooked shell-on shrimp (31-40 per lb.), deveined
  French bread baguette, sliced

1. Preheat oven to 350°. In a large saucepan, melt butter over medium-high heat. Add onion; cook and stir until tender, 8-10 minutes. Stir in barbecue sauce and beer.
2. Place shrimp in a 13x9-in. baking dish. Pour barbecue mixture over top. Bake, uncovered, until shrimp turn pink, 20-25 minutes, stirring halfway through cooking. Serve with baguette slices.
1 CUP: 339 cal., 14g fat (8g sat. fat), 168mg chol., 883mg sod., 30g carb. (24g sugars, 1g fiber), 19g pro.

ROSEMARY TURKEY BREAST

I season turkey with a blend of rosemary, garlic and paprika. Because I rub that mixture directly on the meat under the skin, I can remove the skin before serving and not lose any of the flavor. The result is a lower-in-fat yet delicious entree that makes the perfect centerpiece for holiday meals.
—*Dorothy Pritchett, Wills Point, TX*

Prep: 10 min. • **Bake:** 1½ hours + standing
Makes: 15 servings

- 2 Tbsp. olive oil
- 8 to 10 garlic cloves, peeled
- 3 Tbsp. chopped fresh rosemary or 3 tsp. dried rosemary, crushed
- 1 tsp. salt
- 1 tsp. paprika
- ½ tsp. coarsely ground pepper
- 1 bone-in turkey breast (5 lbs.)

1. In a food processor, combine the oil, garlic, rosemary, salt, paprika and pepper; cover and process until garlic is coarsely chopped.
2. With your fingers, carefully loosen the skin from both sides of turkey breast. Spread half the garlic mixture over the meat under the skin. Smooth skin over meat and secure to underside of breast with toothpicks. Spread remaining garlic mixture over turkey skin.
3. Place turkey breast on a rack in a shallow roasting pan. Bake, uncovered, at 325° until a thermometer reads 165°, 1½-2 hours. (Cover loosely with foil if turkey browns too quickly.) Let stand for 15 minutes before slicing. Discard toothpicks.
4 OZ. COOKED TURKEY: 148 cal., 3g fat (0 sat. fat), 78mg chol., 207mg sod., 1g carb. (0 sugars, 0 fiber), 29g pro.
DIABETIC EXCHANGES: 4 lean meat.

MOUSSAKA

Moussaka is traditionally made with lamb, but I often use ground beef instead. The recipe looks a bit daunting, but if you prepare one step while working on another, it will save time.
—*Kim Powell, Knoxville, TN*

Prep: 45 min. • **Cook:** 30 min. + standing
Makes: 8 servings

- 3 **medium potatoes, peeled and cut lengthwise into ¼-in. slices**
- 1 **medium eggplant, cut lengthwise into ½-in. slices**
- 1½ **lbs. ground lamb or ground beef**
- 1 **small onion, chopped**
- 2 **garlic cloves, minced**
- 2 **plum tomatoes, chopped**
- 1¼ **cups hot water**
- 1 **can (6 oz.) tomato paste, divided**
- 1¼ **tsp. salt, divided**
- ½ **tsp. dried oregano**
- ½ **tsp. paprika**
- ½ **tsp. ground cinnamon**
- ½ **tsp. ground nutmeg, divided**

- 3 **Tbsp. butter**
- ¼ **cup all-purpose flour**
- 4 **cups 2% milk**
- 2 **cups shredded mozzarella cheese**

1. Preheat oven to 450°. Arrange the potato and eggplant slices in 2 greased 15x10x1-in. baking pans, overlapping as needed. Bake until cooked through, 20 minutes. Set aside; reduce oven setting to 400°.

2. In a large skillet, cook lamb, onion and garlic over medium heat, breaking into crumbles, until meat is no longer pink, 7-9 minutes; drain. Stir in tomatoes, water, tomato paste, ¼ tsp. salt, oregano, paprika, cinnamon and ¼ tsp. nutmeg. Bring to a boil. Reduce heat; simmer, uncovered, 5 minutes.

3. In a large saucepan, melt butter over medium heat. Stir in flour until smooth; gradually whisk in milk. Bring to a boil, stirring constantly; cook and stir until thickened, 2-3 minutes. Stir in remaining 1 tsp. salt and ¼ tsp. nutmeg.

4. Arrange parcooked potatoes in a greased 13x9-in. baking dish, overlapping as needed. Top with lamb mixture. Arrange eggplant over top, overlapping as needed.

5. Top with bechamel sauce. Sprinkle with mozzarella cheese. Bake, uncovered, until bubbly and golden brown, about 30 minutes. Let stand for 20 minutes before serving.

1 SERVING: 453 cal., 25g fat (13g sat. fat), 99mg chol., 700mg sod., 30g carb. (12g sugars, 4g fiber), 28g pro.

SPICE SURPRISE
Usually associated with sweet recipes, nutmeg is the secret ingredient in flavorful bechamel or white sauces. Be careful not to overdo it, as a small amount of the spice goes a long way.

HOT ITALIAN PARTY SANDWICHES

It doesn't get much easier or more delicious than these warm little Italian sandwiches. They are wonderful as an appetizer for gatherings or a hungry family, and are a fantastic party food that is quick to prepare.

—*Joan Hallford, North Richland Hills, TX*

Prep: 20 min. • **Bake:** 15 min.
Makes: 12 sandwiches

- 1 pkg. (12 oz.) Hawaiian sweet rolls
- ½ cup mayonnaise
- 2 Tbsp. prepared pesto
- 6 slices part-skim mozzarella or provolone cheese
- 6 thin slices deli ham
- 9 thin slices hard salami
- 6 thin slices deli pastrami
- 1¼ cups giardiniera
- ½ cup shredded Parmesan cheese
- 1 cup fresh basil leaves
- ½ cup sliced red onion
- ¼ cup prepared zesty Italian salad dressing
  Pepperoncini

1. Preheat oven to 350°. Cut rolls horizontally in half; place roll bottoms in a greased 11x7-in. baking dish. Mix mayonnaise and pesto until combined. Spread over cut sides of rolls. Layer bottoms with mozzarella cheese, ham, salami, pastrami, giardiniera, shredded Parmesan cheese, basil leaves and red onion. Place bun tops over filling and gently press to flatten.
2. Bake for 10 minutes. Remove from oven; brush with salad dressing. Bake until golden brown and cheese is melted, about 5 minutes longer. Cool slightly before cutting. Serve with pepperoncini and additional giardiniera if desired.
1 SANDWICH: 290 cal., 17g fat (6g sat. fat), 44mg chol., 1026mg sod., 20g carb. (7g sugars, 1g fiber), 15g pro.

BREADED CURRY CHICKEN DRUMMIES

These drumsticks are crispy with just the right amount of zing to get your mouth watering for more! They are super easy to make and are baked rather than fried so they save on fat but not on flavor. Boneless, skinless chicken breasts or assorted chicken pieces can be used instead of all drumsticks.

—*Lynn Kaufman, Mount Morris, IL*

Prep: 20 min. • **Bake:** 45 min.
Makes: 8 servings

- 1½ cups seasoned bread crumbs
- 1½ tsp. kosher salt
- 1½ tsp. onion powder
- 1½ tsp. garlic powder
- 1 tsp. curry powder
- 1 tsp. smoked paprika
- 1 tsp. dried parsley flakes
- ½ tsp. ground turmeric
- ¼ tsp. pepper
- ⅛ tsp. cayenne pepper
- ½ cup butter, cubed
- 3 Tbsp. lemon juice
- 16 chicken drumsticks (about 4 lbs.)

1. Preheat oven to 375°. In a shallow bowl, mix bread crumbs and seasonings. In a microwave, melt butter with lemon juice. Brush drumsticks with butter mixture, then coat with crumb mixture. Place chicken on greased racks in two 15x10x1-in. pans.
2. Bake until golden brown and a thermometer reads 170°-175°, 45-55 minutes, rotating the pans halfway through baking.
2 DRUMSTICKS: 380 cal., 24g fat (11g sat. fat), 125mg chol., 535mg sod., 9g carb. (1g sugars, 1g fiber), 31g pro.

RAITA DIPPING OPTION
The drumsticks are delicious on their own, but if you'd like to serve them with a dipping sauce, make a simple combination of plain yogurt, chopped seeded cucumber, cilantro and salt. This cool, creamy condiment is known as raita.

MAKEOVER
CHEDDAR BISCUITS,
PAGE 132

Sides & Salads

Round out the meal with heavenly biscuits, crisp coleslaws and salads, fiesta corn, creamy potatoes, and more. Discover wonderful sides for every season.

ORANGE-PISTACHIO QUINOA SALAD

Add this fresh and healthy salad to your holiday spread. Its citrusy, nutty taste is simply delicious.
—Jean Greenfield, San Anselmo, CA

Prep: 15 min. • **Cook:** 15 min. + cooling
Makes: 8 servings

1⅓ cups water
⅔ cup quinoa, rinsed
2 cups chopped romaine lettuce
1 can (15 oz.) garbanzo beans or chickpeas, rinsed and drained
1 can (15 oz.) mandarin oranges, drained
1 medium cucumber, halved and sliced
1 cup shelled pistachios, toasted
½ cup finely chopped red onion
1 medium navel orange
2 Tbsp. olive oil
½ tsp. salt
Pinch pepper

1. In a large saucepan, bring water to a boil. Add quinoa. Reduce heat; simmer, covered, 12-14 minutes or until liquid is absorbed. Remove from heat; fluff with a fork. Cool.
2. In a large bowl, combine romaine, beans, mandarin oranges, cucumber, pistachios, onion and cooled quinoa. In a small bowl, finely grate zest from orange. Cut orange crosswise in half; squeeze juice from orange and add to zest. Whisk in oil, salt and pepper. Drizzle over salad; toss to coat.

1 CUP: 257 cal., 12g fat (1g sat. fat), 0 chol., 287mg sod., 31g carb. (10g sugars, 6g fiber), 8g pro. **DIABETIC EXCHANGES:** 2 starch, 2 fat.

CARIBBEAN ISLAND COLESLAW

After trying a similar version of this coleslaw while visiting the island of St. Kitts, I returned home and wanted to make it myself. I've taken it to so many events, and it's always a hit.
—*Noreen McCormick Danek, Cromwell, CT*

Takes: 15 min. • **Makes:** 10 servings

- 2 pkg. (14 oz. each) coleslaw mix
- 1 cup unsweetened pineapple tidbits
- ½ cup sweetened shredded coconut
- ½ cup golden raisins
- ½ cup finely chopped sweet red pepper
- 1½ cups mayonnaise
- ½ cup unsweetened pineapple juice
- ¾ tsp. salt
- ¼ tsp. celery seed
- ¼ tsp. pepper

Place first 5 ingredients in a serving bowl. In a small bowl, combine the remaining ingredients. Pour over slaw mix; toss to coat. Chill until serving.

¾ CUP: 305 cal., 26g fat (5g sat. fat), 2mg chol., 378mg sod., 19g carb. (14g sugars, 3g fiber), 2g pro.

★ ★ ★ ★ ★ **READER REVIEW**

"Delicious. I made it exactly as written. May add a little more pineapple, coconut and raisins the next time I make it. This is replacing my go-to coleslaw recipe."

KATHYOCHENSKI TASTEOFHOME.COM

ROASTED BRUSSELS SPROUTS & CAULIFLOWER

My grandkids aren't huge fans of cauliflower, but toss a little bacon on it and they can't get enough! They like it even more with golden cauliflower instead of white.
—Patricia Hudson, Riverview, FL

Prep: 25 min. • **Cook:** 25 min.
Makes: 12 servings

- 8 bacon strips, chopped
- 6 garlic cloves, minced
- 1 Tbsp. olive oil
- 1 Tbsp. butter, melted
- ¼ tsp. kosher salt
- ¼ tsp. coarsely ground pepper
- 4 cups Brussels sprouts, halved
- 4 cups fresh cauliflowerets
- ¼ cup grated Parmesan cheese
  Additional grated Parmesan cheese, optional

1. In a large skillet, cook bacon over medium heat until crisp, stirring occasionally. Remove with a slotted spoon; drain on paper towels. Discard drippings, reserving 1 Tbsp.
2. In a large bowl, mix the garlic, oil, butter, salt, pepper and reserved drippings. Add Brussels sprouts and cauliflowerets; toss to coat. Transfer to 2 greased 15x10x1-in. baking pans.
3. Bake at 400° for 20-25 minutes. Sprinkle each pan with 2 Tbsp. cheese. Bake 5 minutes longer or until vegetables are tender. Sprinkle with bacon and, if desired, additional cheese.
½ CUP: 137 cal., 11g fat (4g sat. fat), 17mg chol., 221mg sod., 5g carb. (2g sugars, 2g fiber), 5g pro.

NOODLE KUGEL

I make this traditional dish along with other Jewish specialties for an annual Hanukkah/Christmas party with our friends.
—Lauren Kargen, Buffalo, NY

Prep: 20 min. • **Bake:** 50 min. + standing
Makes: 15 servings

- 1 pkg. (1 lb.) egg noodles
- ½ cup butter, melted
- 8 large eggs
- 2 cups sugar
- 2 cups sour cream
- 2 cups 4% cottage cheese

TOPPING
- ¾ cup cinnamon graham cracker crumbs (about 4 whole crackers)
- 3 Tbsp. butter, melted

1. Cook noodles according to package directions; drain. Toss with butter; set aside. In a large bowl, beat the eggs, sugar, sour cream and cottage cheese until well blended. Stir in noodles.
2. Transfer to a greased 13x9-in. baking dish. Combine the cracker crumbs and butter; sprinkle over top.
3. Bake, uncovered, at 350° until a thermometer reads 160°, 50-55 minutes. Let stand for 10 minutes before cutting. Serve warm or cold.
NOTE: This kugel recipe includes dairy, so be sure to keep that in mind if you or your guests follow strict kosher guidelines.
1 CUP: 432 cal., 19g fat (11g sat. fat), 191mg chol., 261mg sod., 54g carb. (30g sugars, 1g fiber), 12g pro.

SWEET, APPEALING TREAT
Sweet noodle kugel is a traditional Jewish side dish that can be served warm or cold at holiday gatherings, parties, potlucks and brunches.

DELIGHTFUL FRUIT SALAD

You can add as much or as little whipped topping as you like. I used this recipe as a salad, but my friends say it is good enough to be a dessert!
—Elaine Bailey, Bloomfield, IN

Prep: 35 min. + chilling
Makes: 24 servings (¾ cup each)

- 1 cup sugar
- 2 Tbsp. all-purpose flour
- ½ tsp. salt
- 1¾ cups unsweetened pineapple juice
- 2 large eggs, lightly beaten
- 1 Tbsp. lemon juice
- 1 pkg. (16 oz.) acini di pepe pasta
- 3 cans (11 oz. each) mandarin oranges, drained
- 2 cans (20 oz. each) pineapple chunks, drained
- 1 can (20 oz.) crushed pineapple, drained
- 1 cup miniature marshmallows
- 1 cup sweetened shredded coconut
- 1 carton (12 oz.) frozen whipped topping, thawed
  Maraschino cherries, optional

1. In a small saucepan, combine sugar, flour and salt. Gradually stir in pineapple juice. Bring to a boil, stirring constantly. Stir a small amount of hot mixture into eggs; return all to the pan, stirring constantly. Bring to a gentle boil; cook and stir 2 minutes longer. Remove from the heat. Gently stir in lemon juice.
2. Transfer to a large bowl. Cool to room temperature without stirring. Cover surface of dressing with waxed paper; refrigerate until cooled.
3. Cook pasta according to package directions; drain and rinse in cold water. Place in a very large bowl; stir in oranges, pineapple, marshmallows, coconut and dressing. Fold in whipped topping. Cover and refrigerate until chilled. If desired, garnish with cherries.

NOTE: Acini di pepe are tiny pellets of pasta. This recipe was tested with DaVinci brand pasta. You may substitute 1 pound of macaroni or other pasta if desired.
¾ CUP: 240 cal., 5g fat (4g sat. fat), 16mg chol., 72mg sod., 47g carb. (30g sugars, 2g fiber), 4g pro.

SALAD SERVING IDEAS
Spoon individual servings of this salad into bowls or parfait glasses, or prepare the fruit salad in a large trifle bowl and let guests scoop for themselves. For extra flair, garnish the top with stemmed maraschino cherries, sliced mandarin oranges or piped whipped cream.

YUMMY CORN CHIP SALAD

Corn chips give a special crunch and an unexpected flavor to this potluck favorite. Bacon adds a hint of smokiness, while the cranberries bring a touch of sweetness. It's the perfect picnic companion!
—*Nora Friesen, Aberdeen, MS*

Takes: 25 min. • **Makes:** 12 servings

- ¾ cup canola oil
- ¼ cup cider vinegar
- ¼ cup mayonnaise
- 2 Tbsp. yellow mustard
- ½ tsp. salt
- ¾ cup sugar
- ½ small onion
- ¾ tsp. poppy seeds

SALAD

- 2 bunches leaf lettuce, chopped (about 20 cups)
- 1 pkg. (9¼ oz.) corn chips
- 8 bacon strips, cooked and crumbled
- 1 cup shredded part-skim mozzarella cheese
- 1 cup dried cranberries

1. For dressing, place first 7 ingredients in a blender. Cover; process until smooth. Stir in poppy seeds.
2. Place salad ingredients in a large bowl; toss with dressing. Serve immediately.
1⅓ CUPS: 436 cal., 30g fat (4g sat. fat), 12mg chol., 456mg sod., 38g carb. (24g sugars, 2g fiber), 7g pro.

ASIAN SNOW PEA TOSS

My love for Asian flavors sparked the idea for this easy, healthy side dish. For this Asian salad, I use just-picked peas from our garden and serve it with grilled chicken.
—*Mary Ann Dell, Phoenixville, PA*

Takes: 20 min. • **Makes:** 12 servings

- ¼ cup orange marmalade
- ¼ cup seasoned rice vinegar
- 2 Tbsp. sesame oil
- 4 tsp. minced fresh gingerroot
- 1 pkg. (12 oz.) frozen shelled edamame
- 1 lb. fresh snow peas
- 1 can (15 oz.) black beans, rinsed and drained
- 1 small sweet red pepper, cut into thin strips
- 3 green onions, chopped
- 1 can (11 oz.) mandarin oranges, drained
- ¼ tsp. salt
- ¼ tsp. pepper

1. In a small bowl, whisk the marmalade, vinegar, sesame oil and ginger.
2. Cook edamame according to package directions, adding the snow peas during the last minute of cooking. Drain and rinse in cold water. Place in a large bowl. Stir in the black beans, red pepper and green onions. Add the marmalade mixture, mandarin oranges, salt and pepper; toss to coat.

NOTE: Edamame is a popular Asian food produced from the soybean that is harvested early, before the beans become hard. The young beans are parboiled and frozen to retain their freshness and can be found in the freezer of grocery and health food stores. Known as a good source of fiber, pro, calcium and vitamin C, edamame is a tasty addition to soups, salads, sandwiches and main dishes or eaten alone as a healthy snack.
¾ CUP: 148 cal., 4g fat (1g sat. fat), 0 chol., 304mg sod., 22g carb. (13g sugars, 4g fiber), 6g pro. **DIABETIC EXCHANGES:** 1 starch, 1 lean meat.

CREAMY PORTOBELLOS & CAULIFLOWER

When scalloped potatoes feel ho-hum, jazz things up with cauliflower and portobello mushrooms. We serve it with rolls and a light salad.
—*Donna Noel, Gray, ME*

Prep: 35 min. • **Bake:** 35 min.
Makes: 8 servings

- 1 large head cauliflower, broken into florets (about 7 cups)
- 1 lb. sliced baby portobello mushrooms
- ¾ cup water
- 6 Tbsp. butter, divided
- 4 shallots, finely chopped
- ¼ cup all-purpose flour
- ½ tsp. salt
- ¼ tsp. paprika
- 1¼ cups half-and-half cream
- ¾ cup shredded white cheddar cheese
- ¼ cup panko bread crumbs

1. Preheat oven to 350°. Place 1 in. of water and cauliflower in a 6-qt. stockpot; bring to a boil over high heat. Cook, covered, until tender, 7-10 minutes. Drain.

2. In a large saucepan, combine mushrooms and water; bring to a boil over medium-high heat. Reduce heat; simmer, covered, 10 minutes. Drain mushrooms, reserving ⅓ cup cooking liquid.

3. In same saucepan, heat 3 Tbsp. butter over medium heat until hot. Add shallots and drained mushrooms; cook and stir until shallots are tender and lightly browned. Stir in flour, salt and paprika until blended; gradually stir in cream and reserved mushroom liquid. Bring to a boil, stirring constantly; cook and stir until thickened, 2-3 minutes.

4. Place cauliflower in a greased 1½-qt. or 11x7-in. baking dish; cover with the mushroom sauce. Sprinkle with cheese, then bread crumbs. Dot with remaining butter. Bake, uncovered, until bubbly and golden brown, 35-40 minutes.

¾ CUP: 169 cal., 8g fat (5g sat. fat), 30mg chol., 275mg sod., 17g carb. (5g sugars, 3g fiber), 9g pro.

★ ★ ★ ★ ★ **READER REVIEW**

"Love this. I'm hooked. Perfect for Lent. I do add a little garlic salt. It tastes even better the second day."

GINA9870 TASTEOFHOME.COM

ROASTED BUTTERNUT SQUASH PANZANELLA

Squash was a hard sell with my family until I paired it with pumpkin seeds, cranberries and horseradish. Now they love it!
—*Devon Delaney, Westport, CT*

- -

Prep: 25 min. • **Bake:** 35 min.
Makes: 8 servings

- 4 cups cubed sourdough bread
- 5 Tbsp. olive oil, divided
- 1 medium butternut squash (about 3 lbs.), peeled and cut into 1-in. cubes
- ½ tsp. each salt, ground ginger, ground cumin and pepper
- 1 cup salted shelled pumpkin seeds or pepitas
- 1 cup dried cranberries
- 4 shallots, finely chopped (about ½ cup)

DRESSING
- ⅓ cup red wine vinegar
- ¼ cup maple syrup
- 2 Tbsp. prepared horseradish
- ½ tsp. salt
- ½ tsp. pepper
- ¼ tsp. dried rosemary, crushed
- ¼ cup olive oil

1. Preheat oven to 425°. Place bread cubes in a 15x10x1-in. baking pan; toss with 2 Tbsp. oil. Bake 10-15 minutes or until toasted, stirring twice.
2. Place squash in a greased 15x10x1-in. baking pan. Mix seasonings and remaining 3 Tbsp. oil; drizzle over squash and toss to coat. Roast for 35-45 minutes or until tender and lightly browned, stirring occasionally.
3. In a large bowl, combine bread cubes, squash, pumpkin seeds, cranberries and shallots. In a small saucepan, combine the first 6 dressing ingredients; heat through, stirring to blend. Remove from heat; gradually whisk in oil until blended.
4. Drizzle ½ cup dressing over salad and toss to combine. (Save remaining dressing for another use.)
1 CUP: 407 cal., 20g fat (3g sat. fat), 0 chol., 387mg sod., 54g carb. (19g sugars, 8g fiber), 9g pro.

LEMON-SCENTED BROCCOLINI

Even the most finicky eaters will eagerly eat this vegetable seasoned with lemon pepper, lemon zest and lemon juice. If you prefer, use broccoli instead.
—*Kim Champion, Phoenix, AZ*

- -

Takes: 30 min. • **Makes:** 12 servings

- 2½ lbs. Broccolini or broccoli spears
- 6 Tbsp. butter
- 1 Tbsp. plus 1½ tsp. lemon juice
- 1 Tbsp. lemon-pepper seasoning
- 1 tsp. grated lemon zest
- ¼ tsp. salt

1. In a large saucepan, bring 4 cups water to a boil. Add Broccolini; cook, uncovered, until just tender, 5-7 minutes. Drain and immediately place Broccolini in ice water. Drain and pat dry.
2. In a large skillet, melt butter. Stir in the lemon juice, lemon pepper, lemon zest and salt. Add broccolini; toss until heated through.
1 SERVING: 90 cal., 6g fat (4g sat. fat), 15mg chol., 232mg sod., 7g carb. (2g sugars, 1g fiber), 3g pro. **DIABETIC EXCHANGES:** 1 vegetable, 1 fat.
ZESTY BROCCOLINI: Cook Broccolini as directed. Saute 3 minced garlic cloves and 1 tsp. grated fresh ginger in ¼ cup olive oil for 1 minute. Add Broccolini and ¼ tsp. crushed pepper flakes; saute for 1-2 minutes or until heated through.

MAPLE-GINGER GLAZED CARROTS

I first made this dish for my family and friends one Thanksgiving. Not only are the carrots lovely on any table, but they taste terrific, too.
—*Jeannette Sabo, Lexington Park, MD*

Prep: 15 min. • **Cook:** 25 min.
Makes: 16 servings

- 4 lbs. medium carrots, cut into ¼-in. slices
- ¼ cup water
- 3 Tbsp. butter, divided
- 1 Tbsp. minced fresh gingerroot
- ⅓ cup maple syrup
- 1 Tbsp. cider vinegar
- ½ tsp. salt
- ¼ tsp. pepper
  Minced fresh parsley, optional

1. In a Dutch oven, combine carrots, water, 2 Tbsp. butter and ginger. Cover and cook for 10 minutes. Cook, uncovered, until the carrots are crisp-tender, 6-8 minutes longer.
2. Stir in the syrup, vinegar, salt and pepper. Cook, stirring frequently, until sauce is thickened, 5-6 minutes. Stir in remaining butter. If desired, garnish with parsley.

¾ CUP: 83 cal., 2g fat (1g sat. fat), 6mg chol., 168mg sod., 15g carb. (9g sugars, 3g fiber), 1g pro. **DIABETIC EXCHANGES:** 2 vegetable, ½ fat.

★ ★ ★ ★ ★ **READER REVIEW**

"I love these! My mom would also add a bit of grated orange peel and toasted almonds. Delicious and a staple during the holidays!"

MISSKELSI TASTEOFHOME.COM

MAKE AHEAD
RED POTATO & EGG SALAD

This flavorful red potato salad with egg is the perfect side for summer cookouts. The red potatoes really dress it up.
—*Margaret (Peggy) Blomquist, Newfield, NY*

Prep: 40 min. + chilling
Makes: 17 servings (¾ cup each)

- 5 lbs. medium red potatoes, halved
- 5 hard-boiled large eggs, chopped
- 1 celery rib, finely chopped
- ½ medium onion, finely chopped
- 1½ cups mayonnaise
- ¼ cup sweet pickle relish
- 3 Tbsp. sugar
- 2 Tbsp. dried parsley flakes
- 2 tsp. prepared mustard
- 1 tsp. salt
- 1 tsp. cider vinegar
- ⅛ tsp. pepper

1. Place potatoes in a large kettle; cover with water. Bring to a boil. Reduce heat; cover and cook until tender, 15-20 minutes. Drain and cool. Cut potatoes into ¾-in. cubes.
2. In a large bowl, combine potatoes, eggs, celery and onion. In a small bowl, combine the remaining ingredients. Pour over potato mixture and stir gently to coat. Cover and refrigerate for 6 hours or overnight.

¾ CUP: 276 cal., 17g fat (3g sat. fat), 69mg chol., 309mg sod., 25g carb. (5g sugars, 2g fiber), 5g pro.

BACON, CABBAGE & NOODLES

I received this recipe from a friend of Hungarian descent. Some folks turn up their noses when this is presented, but after one taste, they always come back for seconds—and thirds!
—*Jeanie Castor, Decatur, IL*

Takes: 30 min. • **Makes:** 12 servings

- 2 cups uncooked fine egg noodles
- ¾ lb. bacon strips, diced
- ½ medium head cabbage, thinly sliced
- ¼ tsp. salt
  Dash pepper

1. Cook egg noodles according to package directions. Meanwhile, in a large skillet, cook bacon over medium heat until crisp. Using a slotted spoon, remove to paper towels; drain, reserving 3 Tbsp. drippings.
2. Add cabbage to drippings; cover and cook on low for 20 minutes or until cabbage is tender, stirring occasionally. Drain noodles. Stir into skillet. Add bacon, salt and pepper; heat through.
¾ CUP: 89 cal., 7g fat (3g sat. fat), 13mg chol., 242mg sod., 2g carb. (1g sugars, 1g fiber), 4g pro.

BEST EVER BEANS & SAUSAGE

My wife cooked up this dish, which is very popular with our friends and family. When she asks what she should bring, the reply is always: Your beans and sausage—and a couple copies of the recipe!
—*Robert Saulnier, Clarksburg, MA*

Prep: 15 min. • **Bake:** 1 hour 20 min.
Makes: 16 servings

- 1½ lbs. bulk spicy pork sausage
- 1 medium green pepper, chopped
- 1 medium onion, chopped
- 1 can (31 oz.) pork and beans
- 1 can (16 oz.) kidney beans, rinsed and drained
- 1 can (15½ oz.) great northern beans, rinsed and drained
- 1 can (15½ oz.) black-eyed peas, rinsed and drained
- 1 can (15 oz.) pinto beans, rinsed and drained
- 1 can (15 oz.) chickpeas, rinsed and drained
- 1½ cups ketchup
- ¾ cup packed brown sugar
- 2 tsp. ground mustard

1. In a large skillet, cook and crumble sausage over medium heat until no longer pink; drain. Add green pepper and onion; saute until tender. Drain. Add remaining ingredients.
2. Pour into a greased 13x9-in. baking dish. Cover and bake at 325° for 1 hour. Uncover; bake 20-30 minutes longer or until bubbly.
¾ CUP: 316 cal., 9g fat (3g sat. fat), 15mg chol., 857mg sod., 48g carb. (19g sugars, 9g fiber), 13g pro.

QUINOA WITH ROASTED VEGETABLES

Grab all of your garden-fresh produce for this quinoa with roasted vegetables. The tangy dressing and fresh herbs really make the flavors shine.
—*Sonali Ruder, New York, NY*

Prep: 25 min. • **Bake:** 35 min.
Makes: 8 servings

- 1 small eggplant, chopped
- 1 medium zucchini, chopped
- 1 medium sweet yellow pepper, chopped
- 1 medium red onion, chopped
- 1 cup grape tomatoes, halved
- 2 garlic cloves, diced
- 4 Tbsp. olive oil, divided
- ½ tsp. salt
- ¼ tsp. pepper
- 3 cups reduced-sodium chicken broth
- 1½ cups quinoa, rinsed
- 3 Tbsp. balsamic vinegar
- ¾ tsp. Dijon mustard
- ¼ cup each minced fresh basil, parsley and chives

1. Place vegetables and garlic in an ungreased 15x10x1-in. baking pan. Toss with 2 Tbsp. oil; sprinkle with salt and pepper. Bake at 425° for 35-40 minutes or until tender, stirring once.
2. Meanwhile, in a large saucepan, bring broth to a boil. Add quinoa. Reduce heat; cover and simmer for 12-15 minutes or until liquid is absorbed. Remove from the heat; fluff with a fork.
3. Transfer vegetables and quinoa to a large bowl. Whisk vinegar, mustard and remaining 2 Tbsp. oil; drizzle over mixture. Sprinkle with herbs and toss to combine.
¾ CUP: 222 cal., 9g fat (1g sat. fat), 0 chol., 388mg sod., 31g carb. (4g sugars, 5g fiber), 7g pro. **DIABETIC EXCHANGES:** 1½ starch, 1½ fat, 1 vegetable.

DILLY POTATO & EGG SALAD

Everyone has a favorite potato salad, and this is mine. As a young bride 36 years ago, I was eager to learn how to cook and make things that my husband would love. I combined my mom's and his mom's recipes, and this is the delicious result.
—*Angela Leinenbach, Mechanicsville, VA*

Prep: 20 min. + chilling
Cook: 20 min. + cooling
Makes: 12 servings

- 4 lbs. medium red potatoes (about 14), peeled and halved
- 5 hard-boiled large eggs
- 1 cup chopped dill pickles
- 1 small onion, chopped
- 1½ cups mayonnaise
- 1 tsp. celery seed
- ½ tsp. salt
- ¼ tsp. pepper
  Paprika

1. Place potatoes in a large saucepan; add water to cover. Bring to a boil. Reduce heat; cook, uncovered, until tender, 15-20 minutes. Drain, then cool completely.
2. Cut potatoes into ¾-in. cubes; place in a large bowl. Chop 4 eggs; slice remaining egg. Add chopped eggs, pickles and onion to potatoes. Mix mayonnaise, celery seed, salt and pepper; stir gently into potato mixture.
3. Top with sliced egg and sprinkle with paprika. Refrigerate, covered, at least 2 hours before serving.
¾ CUP: 326 cal., 22g fat (4g sat. fat), 80mg chol., 413mg sod., 25g carb. (2g sugars, 3g fiber), 6g pro.

★ ★ ★ ★ ★ **READER REVIEW**

"I made this exactly as written. It was delicious and I loved the change from using my regular celery to using the chopped pickles instead."

KATLAYDEE3 TASTEOFHOME.COM

CHEDDAR & CHIVE MASHED POTATOES

My husband swears my cheddar mashed potatoes are the world's best. We always have some in the freezer. Sometimes I dollop individual servings in muffin cups and reheat them that way instead.
—*Cyndy Gerken, Naples, FL*

Prep: 45 min. • **Bake:** 1 hour
Makes: 16 servings

- 5 lbs. Yukon Gold potatoes, peeled and cut into 1-in. pieces (about 10 cups)
- 1 cup butter, cubed
- 1 cup sour cream
- 2 tsp. salt
- ¾ tsp. pepper
- ½ cup heavy whipping cream
- 1½ cups shredded cheddar cheese
- 1½ cups shredded Monterey Jack cheese
- ¼ cup grated Parmesan cheese
- 2 Tbsp. minced fresh chives

TOPPINGS
- 1 cup shredded cheddar cheese
- 1 can (6 oz.) french-fried onions

1. Preheat oven to 350°. Place the potatoes in a 6-qt. stockpot; add water to cover. Bring to a boil. Reduce heat to medium; cook, uncovered, until tender, 10-15 minutes. Drain; transfer to a large bowl.
2. Add butter, sour cream, salt and pepper; beat until blended. Beat in whipping cream. Stir in cheeses and chives.
3. Bake, covered, 45 minutes, stirring after 30 minutes. Sprinkle with toppings; bake, uncovered, until heated through, about 15 minutes.
¾ CUP: 474 cal., 32g fat (18g sat. fat), 70mg chol., 693mg sod., 37g carb. (3g sugars, 2g fiber), 11g pro.

FARMHOUSE APPLE SLAW

A friend from church gave me this apple coleslaw recipe that her grandmother handed down to her. The flavors complement each other well, while the fruit creates a refreshing change of pace from the usual coleslaw.
—*Jan Myers, Atlantic, IA*

Prep: 20 min. + chilling
Makes: 12 servings

- 4 cups shredded cabbage
- 1 large apple, chopped
- ¾ cup raisins
- ½ cup chopped celery
- ¼ cup chopped onion
- ¼ cup mayonnaise
- 2 Tbsp. lemon juice
- 1 Tbsp. sugar
- 1 Tbsp. olive oil
- ½ tsp. salt
- ⅛ tsp. pepper

In a serving bowl, combine cabbage, apple, raisins, celery and onion. In a small bowl, combine the remaining ingredients. Pour over cabbage mixture and toss to coat. Cover and refrigerate for at least 30 minutes.
⅔ CUP: 87 cal., 5g fat (1g sat. fat), 0 chol., 131mg sod., 12g carb. (8g sugars, 1g fiber), 1g pro. **DIABETIC EXCHANGES:** 1 vegetable, 1 fat, ½ starch.

BUTTERNUT & CHARD PASTA BAKE

This recipe is made for butternut squash lovers, with pureed squash in the sauce and squash pieces in the casserole alongside an ideal companion, Swiss chard. This is a veggie hybrid of ever-popular holiday sides.
—*Arlene Erlbach, Morton Grove, IL*

- -

Prep: 25 min. • **Bake:** 30 min.
Makes: 9 servings

- 3 cups uncooked bow tie pasta
- 2 cups fat-free ricotta cheese
- 4 large eggs
- 3 cups frozen cubed butternut squash, thawed and divided
- 1 tsp. dried thyme
- ½ tsp. salt, divided
- ¼ tsp. ground nutmeg
- 1 cup coarsely chopped shallots
- 1½ cups chopped Swiss chard, stems removed
- 2 Tbsp. olive oil
- 1½ cups panko bread crumbs
- ⅓ cup coarsely chopped fresh parsley
- ¼ tsp. garlic powder

1. Preheat oven to 375°. Cook pasta according to package directions for al dente; drain. Meanwhile, place the ricotta, eggs, 1½ cups squash, thyme, ¼ tsp. salt and nutmeg in a food processor; process until smooth. Pour into a large bowl. Stir in pasta, shallots, Swiss chard and remaining squash. Transfer to a greased 13x9-in. baking dish.
2. In a large skillet, heat oil over medium-high heat. Add bread crumbs; cook and stir until golden brown, 2-3 minutes. Stir in parsley, garlic powder and remaining ¼ tsp. salt. Sprinkle over pasta mixture.
3. Bake, uncovered, until set and topping is golden brown, 30-35 minutes.
1 CUP: 223 cal., 6g fat (1g sat. fat), 83mg chol., 209mg sod., 33g carb. (4g sugars, 2g fiber), 9g pro.

AUTHENTIC GERMAN POTATO SALAD

This recipe came from Speck's Restaurant, which was a famous eating establishment in St. Louis from the 1920s through the '50s. I ate lunch there almost every day and always ordered the potato salad. When the owner learned I was getting married, he gave me the recipe as a wedding gift!
—*Violette Klevorn, Washington, MO*

- -

Prep: 30 min. + cooling
Cook: 20 min. • **Makes:** 8 servings

- 3 lbs. medium red potatoes
- 5 bacon strips, diced
- 1 medium onion, chopped
- ¼ cup all-purpose flour
- 2 tsp. salt
- ¼ tsp. celery seed
- ¼ tsp. pepper
- 1¼ cups sugar
- 1 cup cider vinegar
- ¾ cup water
- 3 Tbsp. minced fresh parsley

1. Place potatoes in a Dutch oven; cover with water. Bring to a boil. Reduce heat; cover and simmer for 25-30 minutes or until tender. Drain and cool.
2. In a large skillet, cook bacon over medium heat until crisp; using a slotted spoon, remove to paper towels. Drain, reserving 4 Tbsp. drippings. In the drippings, saute onion until tender.
3. Stir in the flour, salt, celery seed and pepper until blended. Gradually add the sugar, vinegar and water. Bring to a boil over medium-high heat; cook and stir for 2 minutes or until thickened.
4. Cut the potatoes into ¼-in. slices. Add potatoes and bacon to the skillet; cook and stir gently over low heat until heated through. Sprinkle with parsley. Serve warm.
¾ CUP: 349 cal., 8g fat (3g sat. fat), 9mg chol., 706mg sod., 65g carb. (35g sugars, 3g fiber), 5g pro.

CRANBERRY GELATIN SALAD

My family has requested this delicious holiday salad every year since the first time I served it. The not-too-sweet flavor is a perfect pairing with just about any meat.
—*Jennifer Mastnick-Cook, Hartville, OH*

Prep: 30 min. + chilling
Makes: 12 servings

- 2 pkg. (3 oz. each) raspberry gelatin
- 2 cups boiling water, divided
- 1 can (14 oz.) whole-berry cranberry sauce
- 2 Tbsp. lemon juice
- 1 cup heavy whipping cream
- 1 pkg. (8 oz.) cream cheese, softened
- ½ cup chopped pecans

1. In a small bowl, dissolve gelatin in 1 cup boiling water. In another bowl, combine cranberry sauce and remaining water; add gelatin mixture and lemon juice. Pour into a 13x9-in. dish coated with cooking spray; refrigerate until firm, about 1 hour.
2. In a large bowl, beat cream until stiff peaks form. In another bowl, beat cream cheese until smooth. Stir in ½ cup whipped cream; fold in remaining whipped cream. Spread over gelatin mixture; sprinkle with pecans. Refrigerate for at least 2 hours.
1 PIECE: 241 cal., 14g fat (7g sat. fat), 34mg chol., 100mg sod., 28g carb. (22g sugars, 1g fiber), 3g pro.

MAKEOVER CHEDDAR BISCUITS

These biscuits have a cheesy richness that everyone will love. I like to serve them with steaming bowls of chili or a hearty beef soup.
—*Alicia Rooker, Milwaukee, WI*

Takes: 30 min. • **Makes:** 15 biscuits

- 1 cup all-purpose flour
- 1 cup cake flour
- 1½ tsp. baking powder
- ¾ tsp. salt
- ½ tsp. garlic powder, divided
- ¼ tsp. baking soda
- 4 Tbsp. cold butter, divided
- ⅓ cup finely shredded cheddar cheese
- 1 cup buttermilk
- ½ tsp. dried parsley flakes

1. In a large bowl, combine the flours, baking powder, salt, ¼ tsp. garlic powder and baking soda. Cut in 3 Tbsp. butter until mixture resembles coarse crumbs; add cheese. Stir in the buttermilk just until moistened.
2. Drop by 2 tablespoonfuls 2 in. apart onto baking sheets coated with cooking spray. Bake at 425° until golden brown, 10-12 minutes. Melt remaining 1 Tbsp. butter; stir in parsley and remaining ¼ tsp. garlic powder. Brush over the biscuits. Serve warm.
1 BISCUIT: 106 cal., 4g fat (3g sat. fat), 11mg chol., 233mg sod., 14g carb. (1g sugars, 0 fiber), 3g pro.

HARVEST SQUASH CASSEROLE

Flavored with autumn cranberries and pecans, this nutritious recipe works very well as a comforting side dish with roasted turkey or chicken.
—*Mary Ann Lee, Clifton Park, NY*

- -

Prep: 35 min. • **Bake:** 40 min.
Makes: 10 servings

- 1 large butternut squash (about 6 lbs.), peeled, seeded and cubed
- 1 large onion, finely chopped
- 1 Tbsp. butter
- 2 garlic cloves, minced
- 3 large eggs, lightly beaten
- 2 Tbsp. sugar
- 2 tsp. salt
- ½ tsp. pepper
- 1 cup chopped fresh or frozen cranberries
- ¾ cup chopped pecans

TOPPING
- 2 cups soft whole wheat bread crumbs
- 2 Tbsp. butter, melted

1. Place squash in a Dutch oven; cover with water. Bring to a boil. Reduce heat; cover and cook 15-20 minutes or just until tender. Drain. In a large bowl, mash squash and set aside.

2. Preheat oven to 350°. In a large nonstick skillet, saute onion in butter until tender. Add garlic; cook 1 minute longer. Add to squash. Stir in the eggs, sugar, salt and pepper. Gently fold in cranberries and pecans. Transfer to a 13x9-in. baking dish coated with cooking spray.

3. For topping, combine bread crumbs and melted butter; sprinkle over top. Bake 40-45 minutes or until a knife inserted in the center comes out clean.

FREEZE OPTION: Cool unbaked casserole. Sprinkle with topping; cover and freeze. To use, partially thaw in refrigerator overnight. Remove from refrigerator 30 minutes before baking. Preheat oven to 350°. Bake casserole as directed, increasing time as necessary for a knife inserted in the center to come out clean.

¾ CUP: 273 cal., 12g fat (3g sat. fat), 72mg chol., 593mg sod., 39g carb. (11g sugars, 10g fiber), 7g pro.

★ ★ ★ ★ ★ **READER REVIEW**

"This was a big hit at a party I had recently. I am making it again for Thanksgiving."
CMOLSON113 TASTEOFHOME.COM

SAGE SAUSAGE DRESSING

Port is a sweet red wine that's often served as a dessert beverage, but it adds a deep flavor to our family's hearty stuffing.
—*Denise Hruz, Germantown, WI*

Prep: 40 min. • **Bake:** 25 min.
Makes: 17 servings (¾ cup each)

- ¼ cup port wine or 2 Tbsp. grape juice plus 2 Tbsp. chicken broth
- ½ cup dried cherries
- 1 large tart apple, peeled, finely chopped
- 1 Tbsp. lemon juice
- 1 lb. bulk sage pork sausage
- 1 medium onion, chopped
- 2 celery ribs, sliced
- 2 Tbsp. olive oil
- 3 cups chicken broth
- ½ cup orange juice
- ¼ cup butter, cubed
- 1 pkg. (12 oz.) seasoned stuffing cubes
- 1 cup chopped walnuts, toasted
- ¼ cup thinly sliced fresh sage
  Additional thinly sliced fresh sage, optional

1. Preheat oven to 350°. In a small saucepan, bring wine to a boil. Stir in cherries; remove from the heat. In a small bowl, combine apple and lemon juice; toss to coat. Set aside cherry and apple mixtures.
2. In a Dutch oven, cook sausage over medium heat until no longer pink. Remove from pan with a slotted spoon; drain. In the same pan, saute onion and celery in oil until tender. Add the broth, orange juice and butter; heat until butter is melted.
3. Stir in the stuffing cubes, walnuts, sage, cherry mixture, apple mixture and sausage. Transfer to a greased 13x9-in. baking dish. Bake, uncovered, until lightly browned, 25-30 minutes. If desired, top with additional sliced fresh sage.
¾ CUP: 258 cal., 14g fat (4g sat. fat), 18mg chol., 641mg sod., 26g carb. (7g sugars, 2g fiber), 7g pro.

CAULIFLOWER BROCCOLI SALAD

This salad has been to as many family gatherings as I have! It holds well, and leftovers are still tasty a day later. When I'm not trying out new recipes, I enjoy crafts and being an at-home mom to our nine children, ages 5 months to 17 years.
—*Linda Kangas, Outlook, SK*

Prep: 15 min. + chilling
Makes: 20 servings

- 1 medium head cauliflower, broken into florets (about 7½ cups)
- 1 medium bunch broccoli, cut into florets (about 4 cups)
- 2 cups seedless red grapes
- 6 green onions with tops, sliced
- 2 cups shredded part-skim mozzarella cheese
- 2 cups mayonnaise
- ¼ cup grated Parmesan cheese
- 2 Tbsp. sugar
- 2 Tbsp. white vinegar
- ½ to 1 lb. sliced bacon, cooked and crumbled

1. In a large bowl, combine cauliflower, broccoli, grapes, onions and mozzarella cheese. Combine the mayonnaise, Parmesan cheese, sugar and vinegar; pour over vegetable mixture and toss to coat.
2. Cover and refrigerate for at least 2 hours. Just before serving, stir in bacon.
¾ CUP: 248 cal., 22g fat (4g sat. fat), 19mg chol., 269mg sod., 8g carb. (6g sugars, 2g fiber), 6g pro.

BRING IT
Mayonnaise-based salad should spend no more than 2 hours at room temperature (and even less if it's outside on a very hot day). For safety, nestle the serving bowl in a larger bowl of ice on the buffet and stir the salad often. If practical, use a small serving bowl and replenish the salad as needed from a refrigerator or cooler.

COMPANY RICE

This colorful side dish is a proven favorite with family and friends. One of my late son's friends always requested that rice when he came over for dinner. It's delicious served with grilled salmon, beef, turkey, lamb roast or ham.
—*Jayne Shiley, Campbellsport, WI*

Prep: 10 min. • **Cook:** 55 min.
Makes: 10 servings

- 1 celery rib, thinly sliced
- 1 large carrot, finely chopped
- 1 small onion, finely chopped
- 2 Tbsp. butter
- 5 cups chicken broth
- 1 cup uncooked wild rice
- 1 cup uncooked long grain rice
- ⅔ cup dried cherries or cranberries
- ½ cup chopped pecans, toasted

1. In a large saucepan, saute the celery, carrot and onion in butter until tender. Stir in broth and wild rice. Bring to a boil. Reduce heat; cover and simmer for 25 minutes.
2. Add long grain rice; cover and simmer 20 minutes longer. Stir in dried cherries; cook until the liquid is absorbed, about 5 minutes longer. Just before serving, stir in pecans.
⅔ CUP: 238 cal., 7g fat (2g sat. fat), 9mg chol., 516mg sod., 38g carb. (7g sugars, 2g fiber), 5g pro.
ALMOND WILD RICE: Omit the long grain rice, dried cherries and pecans. Add 1 cup uncooked brown rice with broth and wild rice. Bring to a boil. Reduce heat; cover and simmer for 45-50 minutes or until rice is tender and liquid is absorbed. Remove from the heat; stir in 1 cup toasted slivered almonds, ½ cup minced fresh parsley and ¼ tsp. each salt and pepper.

PINEAPPLE SWEET POTATO CASSEROLE WITH MARSHMALLOWS

Pineapple, sugar and marshmallows lend a super sweetness to sweet potatoes. I've been making the casserole for years, both for special occasions at home and for casual dinners.
—*Ruth Leach, Shreveport, LA*

Prep: 45 min. • **Bake:** 40 min.
Makes: 8 servings

- 6 medium sweet potatoes
- ½ cup butter, cubed
- ¾ cup sugar
- 1 can (20 oz.) crushed pineapple, drained
- 2 large eggs, beaten
- 1 tsp. vanilla extract
- ½ tsp. ground nutmeg
- ½ tsp. salt
- 15 large marshmallows

1. Place sweet potatoes in a large kettle and cover with water; bring to a boil. Boil gently until potatoes can easily be pierced with the tip of a sharp knife, 30-45 minutes. Drain; cool slightly.
2. Preheat oven to 350°. Peel potatoes and place in a large bowl with butter and sugar; mash. Add pineapple, eggs, vanilla, nutmeg and salt; stir to combine.
3. Spoon into a greased 2-qt. baking dish. Top with marshmallows. Bake, uncovered, until a knife inserted in the center comes out clean, 40-45 minutes.
1 CUP: 367 cal., 13g fat (8g sat. fat), 84mg chol., 295mg sod., 62g carb. (43g sugars, 3g fiber), 4g pro.

POMEGRANATE SPLASH SALAD

The sparkling pomegranate gems make this salad irresistibly beautiful. My family loves it at holiday gatherings when pomegranates are in season. Even the children can't get enough of this antioxidant-rich delight.
—*Emily Jamison, Champaign, IL*

Takes: 15 min. • **Makes:** 8 servings

- 4 **cups fresh baby spinach**
- 4 **cups spring mix salad greens**
- ¾ **cup crumbled feta cheese**
- ¾ **cup pomegranate seeds**
- ¾ **cup fresh or frozen raspberries**
- ⅓ **cup pine nuts, toasted**

CRANBERRY VINAIGRETTE
- ½ **cup thawed cranberry juice concentrate**
- 3 **Tbsp. olive oil**
- 2 **Tbsp. rice vinegar**
  Dash salt

In a large bowl, combine the first 6 ingredients. In a small bowl, whisk the vinaigrette ingredients. Serve with salad.

1 CUP WITH ABOUT 4½ TSP. VINAIGRETTE: 164 cal., 10g fat (2g sat. fat), 6mg chol., 140mg sod., 16g carb. (11g sugars, 2g fiber), 4g pro. **DIABETIC EXCHANGES:** 2 fat, 1 starch.

MACARONI COLESLAW

My friend Peggy brought this coleslaw to one of our picnics, and everyone liked it so much that we all had to have the recipe.
—*Sandra Matteson, Westhope, ND*

Prep: 25 min. + chilling
Makes: 16 servings

- 1 **pkg. (7 oz.) ring macaroni or ditalini**
- 1 **pkg. (14 oz.) coleslaw mix**
- 2 **medium onions, finely chopped**
- 2 **celery ribs, finely chopped**
- 1 **medium cucumber, finely chopped**
- 1 **medium green pepper, finely chopped**
- 1 **can (8 oz.) whole water chestnuts, drained and chopped**

DRESSING
- 1½ **cups Miracle Whip Light**
- ⅓ **cup sugar**
- ¼ **cup cider vinegar**
- ½ **tsp. salt**
- ¼ **tsp. pepper**

1. Cook macaroni according to package directions; drain and rinse in cold water. Transfer to a large bowl; add coleslaw mix, onions, celery, cucumber, green pepper and water chestnuts.
2. In a small bowl, whisk the dressing ingredients. Pour over salad; toss to coat. Cover and refrigerate for at least 1 hour.

¾ CUP: 150 cal., 5g fat (1g sat. fat), 6mg chol., 286mg sod., 24g carb. (12g sugars, 2g fiber), 3g pro. **DIABETIC EXCHANGES:** 1 starch, 1 vegetable, 1 fat.

ANGEL BISCUITS

Light, airy biscuits are irresistible when you serve them with butter and honey.
—*Faye Hintz, Springfield, MO*

Prep: 20 min. + rising
Bake: 10 min. • **Makes:** 2½ dozen

- 2 pkg. (¼ oz. each) active dry yeast
- ¼ cup warm water (110° to 115°)
- 2 cups warm buttermilk (110° to 115°)
- 5 to 5½ cups all-purpose flour
- ⅓ cup sugar
- 2 tsp. salt
- 2 tsp. baking powder
- 1 tsp. baking soda
- 1 cup shortening
  Melted butter

1. In a small bowl, dissolve yeast in warm water. Let stand 5 minutes. Stir in warm buttermilk; set aside.
2. In a large bowl, combine flour, sugar, salt, baking powder and baking soda. Cut in shortening with a pastry blender until mixture resembles coarse crumbs. Stir in yeast mixture.

3. Turn onto a lightly floured surface; knead lightly 3-4 times. Roll out to ½-in. thickness; cut with a 2½-in. biscuit cutter. Place 2 in. apart on lightly greased baking sheets. Cover with kitchen towels and let rise in a warm place until almost doubled, about 1 hour.
4. Bake at 450° for 8-10 minutes or until golden brown. Lightly brush tops with melted butter. Serve warm.

NOTE: To substitute for each cup of buttermilk, use 1 Tbsp. white vinegar or lemon juice plus enough milk to measure 1 cup. Stir, then let stand 5 min. Or, use 1 cup plain yogurt or 1¾ tsp. cream of tartar plus 1 cup milk.

1 BISCUIT: 150 cal., 7g fat (2g sat. fat), 1mg chol., 244mg sod., 19g carb. (3g sugars, 1g fiber), 3g pro.

HOW TO ENSURE TALL, FLUFFY BISCUITS

For perfectly raised biscuits, work quickly and avoid overhandling the dough. Press firmly and straight down with your biscuit cutter, rather than using a twisting motion. Twisting the cutter can pinch the biscuit edges together and inhibit rising.

BACON MAC & CHEESE CORNBREAD SKILLET

My cast-iron skillet is a workhorse in my kitchen. I just love it for cooking and baking. And this cast-iron mac and cheese recipe can be served as a main dish or as a smaller-portion side.
—*Lisa Keys, Kennett Square, PA*

Prep: 35 min. • **Bake:** 30 min. + standing
Makes: 8 servings

- 1¾ cups uncooked elbow macaroni
- 8 bacon strips, chopped
- 1 cup shredded smoked Gouda or cheddar cheese
- 1 cup shredded pepper jack cheese
- 4 oz. cream cheese, cubed
- 6 large eggs, divided use
- 3 cups 2% milk, divided
- 4 green onions, chopped
- 1 tsp. kosher salt, divided
- ½ tsp. pepper, divided
- 1 pkg. (8½ oz.) cornbread/muffin mix
- ½ tsp. smoked paprika
    Additional green onions

1. Preheat oven to 400°. Cook macaroni according to package directions. Meanwhile, in a 12-in. cast-iron or other ovenproof skillet, cook bacon over medium heat until crisp, stirring occasionally. Remove with a slotted spoon; drain on paper towels. Discard drippings, reserving 1 Tbsp. in pan.
2. Drain macaroni; add macaroni to drippings. Stir in shredded cheeses and cream cheese; cook and stir over medium heat until cheese is melted, 2-3 minutes. Whisk 2 eggs, 1 cup milk, green onions, ½ tsp. kosher salt and ¼ tsp. pepper; pour into skillet. Cook and stir until slightly thickened, 3-4 minutes. Remove from heat.
3. Reserve ¼ cup bacon for topping; sprinkle the remaining bacon over macaroni. Place cornbread mix, paprika and remaining 4 eggs, 2 cups milk, ½ tsp. kosher salt and ¼ tsp. pepper in a blender; cover and process until smooth. Pour over bacon.
4. Bake until puffed and golden brown, 30-35 minutes. Let stand 10 minutes before serving. Sprinkle with reserved ¼ cup bacon and additional green onions.
1 CUP: 497 cal., 27g fat (13g sat. fat), 203mg chol., 978mg sod., 40g carb. (12g sugars, 3g fiber), 23g pro.

ADD IN-SEASON VEGGIES
Give some seasonal flair to this recipe by adding cooked green peas for a touch of spring or tasty chunks of butternut squash for an autumn twist.

SHRIMP PASTA SALAD

I adore shrimp, so discovering it in this pasta salad recipe was a real treat for me. The lemon-dill sauce is light and bright.
—*Traci Wynne, Denver, PA*

Prep: 15 min. + chilling
Cook: 15 min. • **Makes:** 10 servings

- 8 oz. uncooked small pasta shells (about 2⅔ cups)
- 1 lb. peeled and deveined cooked shrimp, chopped
- 1 cup frozen peas, thawed
- 4 green onions, chopped
- ¼ cup minced fresh parsley
- 1 cup mayonnaise
- 1 cup plain yogurt
- ¼ cup lemon juice
- 2 Tbsp. snipped fresh dill
- ½ tsp. salt
- ¼ tsp. white pepper

1. Cook pasta according to package directions. Drain; rinse with cold water and drain again.
2. In a large bowl, combine pasta, shrimp, peas, green onions and parsley. Mix remaining ingredients; stir into pasta mixture. Refrigerate, covered, at least 2 hours.
¾ CUP: 306 cal., 18g fat (3g sat. fat), 74mg chol., 326mg sod., 21g carb. (3g sugars, 2g fiber), 14g pro.

EDDIE'S FAVORITE FIESTA CORN

When sweet corn is available, I love making this splurge of a side dish. Frozen corn works, but taste as you go and add sugar if needed.
—*Anthony Bolton, Bellevue, NE*

Prep: 15 min. • **Cook:** 25 min.
Makes: 8 servings

- ½ lb. bacon strips, chopped
- 5 cups fresh or frozen super sweet corn
- 1 medium sweet red pepper, finely chopped
- 1 medium sweet yellow pepper, finely chopped
- 1 pkg. (8 oz.) reduced-fat cream cheese
- ½ cup half-and-half cream
- 1 can (4 oz.) chopped green chiles, optional
- 2 tsp. sugar
- 1 tsp. pepper
- ¼ tsp. salt

1. In a 6-qt. stockpot, cook bacon over medium heat until crisp, stirring occasionally. Remove with a slotted spoon; drain on paper towels. Discard drippings, reserving 1 Tbsp. in pan.
2. Add corn, red pepper and yellow pepper to drippings; cook and stir over medium-high heat until tender, 5-6 minutes. Stir in the remaining ingredients until blended; bring to a boil. Reduce heat; simmer, covered, until thickened, 8-10 minutes.
⅔ CUP: 249 cal., 14g fat (7g sat. fat), 39mg chol., 399mg sod., 22g carb. (9g sugars, 2g fiber), 10g pro.

CALICO BEANS

Packed full of beef, beans and bacon, this calico beans recipe is one of my favorites. Serve it as a hearty side or main dish.
—*Betty Claycomb, Alverton, PA*

Prep: 25 min. • **Bake:** 45 min.
Makes: 10 servings

- 1 lb. lean ground beef (90% lean)
- 1 small onion, chopped
- 1 can (21 oz.) pork and beans
- 1 can (16 oz.) kidney beans, rinsed and drained
- 1 can (16 oz.) butter beans, rinsed and drained
- ½ cup packed brown sugar
- ½ cup ketchup
- 4 bacon strips, cooked and crumbled
- 1 Tbsp. cider vinegar
- 1 tsp. prepared mustard
- 1 tsp. salt

1. Preheat oven to 325°. In a large skillet, cook beef and onion over medium heat until meat is no longer pink, 5-7 minutes, breaking up beef into crumbles; drain. Stir in remaining ingredients. Transfer to a greased large cast-iron skillet or 2-qt. baking dish.
2. Bake, uncovered, until the beans are as thick as desired, 45-60 minutes.
1 SERVING: 260 cal., 5g fat (2g sat. fat), 32mg chol., 826mg sod., 39g carb. (19g sugars, 7g fiber), 18g pro.

HEARTY, ECONOMICAL BEANS
Beans pack a nutritional one-two punch of protein and fiber, which helps you feel fuller longer. They're an economical way to stretch the meat in a recipe.

COLCANNON POTATOES

Every Irish family has its own version of this classic dish. My recipe comes from my father's family in Ireland. It's part of my St. Patrick's Day menu, along with lamb chops, carrots and soda bread.
—*Marilou Robinson, Portland, OR*

Prep: 25 min. • **Cook:** 35 min.
Makes: 12 servings

- 1 medium head cabbage (about 2 lbs.), shredded
- 4 lbs. medium potatoes (about 8), peeled and quartered
- 2 cups whole milk
- 1 cup chopped green onions
- 1½ tsp. salt
- ½ tsp. pepper
- ¼ cup butter, melted
  Minced fresh parsley
  Crumbled cooked bacon

1. Place cabbage and 2 cups water in a large saucepan; bring to a boil. Reduce heat; simmer, covered, until cabbage is tender, about 10 minutes. Drain, reserving cooking liquid; keep the cabbage warm in separate dish.

2. In same pan, combine potatoes and reserved cooking liquid. Add additional water to cover potatoes; bring to a boil. Reduce heat; cook, uncovered, until potatoes are tender, 15-20 minutes. Meanwhile, place milk, green onions, salt and pepper in a small saucepan; bring just to a boil and remove from heat.

3. Drain potatoes; place in a large bowl and mash. Add milk mixture; beat just until blended. Stir in cabbage. To serve, drizzle with butter; top with parsley and bacon.

1 CUP: 168 cal., 5g fat (3g sat. fat), 14mg chol., 361mg sod., 27g carb. (6g sugars, 4g fiber), 4g pro. **DIABETIC EXCHANGES:** 2 starch, 1 fat.

SWISS BEER BREAD

This recipe is a favorite of my family because it isn't greasy like most of the other cheese breads I have tried. It will not last long!
—*Debi Wallace, Chestertown, NY*

Prep: 15 min. • **Bake:** 50 min. + cooling
Makes: 1 loaf (12 pieces)

- 4 oz. Jarlsberg or Swiss cheese
- 3 cups all-purpose flour
- 3 Tbsp. sugar
- 3 tsp. baking powder
- 1½ tsp. salt
- ½ tsp. pepper
- 1 bottle (12 oz.) beer or nonalcoholic beer
- 2 Tbsp. butter, melted

1. Preheat oven to 375°. Divide cheese in half. Cut half into ¼-in. cubes; shred remaining cheese. In a large bowl, combine next 5 ingredients. Stir beer into dry ingredients just until moistened. Fold in cubed and shredded cheese.

2. Transfer to a greased 8x4-in. loaf pan. Drizzle with butter. Bake until a toothpick inserted in center comes out clean, 50-60 minutes. Cool 10 minutes before removing from pan to a wire rack.
1 PIECE: 182 cal., 5g fat (3g sat. fat), 11mg chol., 453mg sod., 28g carb. (4g sugars, 1g fiber), 6g pro.

★ ★ ★ ★ ★ **READER REVIEW**

"If you have unexpected company, it's easy to put together and serve with fruit or a tray of summer sausage. While it's baking, you can converse with your company and *viola!*— homemade goodness."

DRAGONSLAYERSROSEBUD
TASTEOFHOME.COM

PEARL ONION BROCCOLI BAKE

With its creamy white cheese sauce and buttery crumb topping, this dish is pure comfort food. If you're looking for a mild way to dress up broccoli, this is the recipe.
—*Charles Keating, Manchester, MD*

Prep: 20 min. • **Bake:** 25 min.
Makes: 12 servings

- 2 pkg. (16 oz. each) frozen broccoli florets
- 1 pkg. (14.4 oz.) pearl onions
- ½ cup butter, divided
- ¼ cup all-purpose flour
- ¾ tsp. salt
- ⅛ tsp. pepper
- 2 cups 2% milk
- 6 oz. cream cheese, cubed
- 1 cup shredded cheddar cheese
- 2 cups soft bread crumbs

1. Preheat oven to 350°. Cook broccoli in 1 in. of water until almost tender; drain. Cook pearl onions in 1 in. of water until almost tender; drain. Transfer both to a greased 13x9-in. baking dish.
2. In a large saucepan, melt ¼ cup butter; whisk in flour, salt and pepper until smooth. Gradually whisk in milk. Bring to a boil; cook and stir until thickened, 1-2 minutes. Reduce heat; stir in cream cheese until blended. Add to vegetables; stir gently to coat. Sprinkle with cheddar cheese.
3. Melt remaining butter; toss with bread crumbs. Sprinkle over casserole. Bake, uncovered, until topping is golden brown, 25-30 minutes.
NOTE: To make soft bread crumbs, tear bread into pieces and place in a food processor or blender. Cover and pulse until crumbs form. One slice of bread yields ½-¾ cup crumbs.
¾ CUP: 241 cal., 17g fat (10g sat. fat), 46mg chol., 389mg sod., 15g carb. (5g sugars, 3g fiber), 7g pro.

OLD-FASHIONED
POOR MAN'S STEAK,
PAGE 161

Slow Cooker

When it comes to make-and-take ease, nothing spells success like a slow-cooked specialty. After all, these comfy favorites simmer on their own, travel well and keep warm on any buffet. What could be better?

SLAW-TOPPED BEEF SLIDERS

When I was working full time, I would rely on these delicious, fast-to-fix beef sliders for simple meals. To ease prep time and avoid extra clean-up, I used bagged coleslaw mix and bottled slaw dressing.
—*Jane Whittaker, Pensacola, FL*

Prep: 20 min. • **Cook:** 6 hours
Makes: 1 dozen

- 3 cups coleslaw mix
- ½ medium red onion, chopped (about ⅔ cup)
- ⅛ tsp. celery seed
- ¼ tsp. pepper
- ⅓ cup coleslaw salad dressing

SANDWICHES
- 1 boneless beef chuck roast (2 lbs.)
- 1 tsp. salt
- ½ tsp. pepper
- 1 can (6 oz.) tomato paste
- ¼ cup water
- 1 tsp. Worcestershire sauce
- 1 small onion, diced
- 1 cup barbecue sauce
- 12 slider buns or dinner rolls, split

1. Combine coleslaw, onion, celery seed and pepper. Add salad dressing; toss to coat. Refrigerate until serving.
2. Sprinkle roast with salt and pepper; transfer roast to a 5-qt. slow cooker. Mix tomato paste, water and Worcestershire sauce; pour over roast. Top with onion. Cook, covered, on low 6-8 hours or until meat is tender.
3. Shred meat with 2 forks; return to the slow cooker. Stir in barbecue sauce; heat through. Place the beef on buns; top with coleslaw. Replace bun tops.
1 SLIDER: 322 cal., 12g fat (4g sat. fat), 67mg chol., 726mg sod., 34g carb. (13g sugars, 3g fiber), 20g pro.

SLOW-COOKED REUBEN SPREAD

I'm a big fan of Reuben sandwiches and anything with that flavor combination. For an appetizer, I blend corned beef with Swiss and a few other items to make a spread for rye bread or crackers.
—*June Herke, Watertown, SD*

- -

Prep: 10 min. • **Cook:** 4 hours
Makes: 3¾ cups

- 2 pkg. (8 oz. each) cream cheese, cubed
- 4 cups shredded Swiss cheese
- 1 can (14 oz.) sauerkraut, rinsed and well drained
- 4 pkg. (2 oz. each) thinly sliced deli corned beef, chopped
- ½ cup Thousand Island salad dressing
   Snack rye bread or rye crackers

1. Place the first 5 ingredients in a 3-qt. slow cooker; stir to combine. Cook, covered, on low 4-4½ hours or until heated through.
2. Stir to blend. Serve spread with rye bread or crackers.
2 TBSP.: 137 cal., 12g fat (6g sat. fat), 33mg chol., 285mg sod., 2g carb. (1g sugars, 0 fiber), 6g pro.

BRING IT
This marvelous spread is perfect for football parties, tailgates, Oktoberfest and more. To make it more satisfying, serve it with rye bakery bagels, halved and sliced, or homemade pretzels. It pairs well when cold beer is on the menu.

SLOW-COOKER PIZZA

Always a hit at our church dinners, this hearty casserole keeps folks coming back for more. You can't lose with pizza fixings.
—*Julie Sterchi, Campbellsville, KY*

Prep: 20 min. • **Cook:** 2 hours
Makes: 8 servings

- 1 pkg. (16 oz.) wide egg noodles
- 1½ lbs. ground beef or turkey
- ¼ cup chopped onion
- 1 jar (26 oz.) spaghetti sauce
- 1 jar (4½ oz.) sliced mushrooms, drained
- 1½ tsp. Italian seasoning
- 1 pkg. (3½ oz.) sliced pepperoni, halved
- 3 cups shredded cheddar cheese
- 3 cups shredded part-skim mozzarella cheese

1. Cook noodles according to package directions. Meanwhile, in a large skillet, cook beef and onion over medium heat until meat is no longer pink, breaking it into crumbles; drain. Stir in the spaghetti sauce, sliced mushrooms and Italian seasoning. Drain noodles.
2. In a 5-qt. slow cooker coated with cooking spray, spread a third of the meat sauce. Cover with a third each of the noodles and pepperoni. Sprinkle with a third of the cheeses. Repeat layers twice. Press down to compact.
3. Cover; cook on low 2-3 hours or until heated through and the cheese is melted.
1½ CUPS: 780 cal., 41g fat (21g sat. fat), 192mg chol., 1262mg sod., 53g carb. (9g sugars, 4g fiber), 49g pro.

★ ★ ★ ★ ★ **READER REVIEW**
"Excellent flavor ... great hit with the kids."
MTJOHNSON025 TASTEOFHOME.COM

ITALIAN POT ROAST

This delicious pot roast is a favorite of my husband's. You'll love the tender beef seasoned with Italian herbs. I'm always asked for the recipe.
—*Debbie Daly, Buckingham, IL*

Prep: 20 min. • **Cook:** 5 hours
Makes: 8 servings

- 1 boneless beef chuck roast (3 to 4 lbs.)
- 1 can (28 oz.) diced tomatoes, drained
- ¾ cup chopped onion
- ¾ cup Burgundy wine or beef broth
- 1½ tsp. salt
- 1 tsp. dried basil
- ½ tsp. dried oregano
- 1 garlic clove, minced
- ¼ tsp. pepper
- ¼ cup cornstarch
- ½ cup cold water

1. Cut roast in half. Place in a 5-qt. slow cooker. Add the tomatoes, onion, wine, salt, basil, oregano, garlic and pepper. Cover and cook on low for 5-6 hours or until meat is tender.
2. Remove meat to a serving platter; keep warm. Skim fat from cooking juices; transfer to a small saucepan. Combine cornstarch and water until smooth. Gradually stir into pan. Bring to a boil; cook and stir until thickened, about 2 minutes. Serve with meat.
5 OZ. COOKED BEEF: 345 cal., 16g fat (6g sat. fat), 111mg chol., 641mg sod., 10g carb. (4g sugars, 2g fiber), 34g pro.

BARBECUED PARTY STARTERS

These sweet and tangy bites are sure to tide everyone over until dinner. At the buffet, set out some fun toothpicks to make for easy nibbling.
—*Anastasia Weiss, Punxsutawney, PA*

Prep: 30 min. • **Cook:** 2¼ hours
Makes: 16 servings

- 1 lb. ground beef
- ¼ cup finely chopped onion
- 1 pkg. (16 oz.) miniature hot dogs, drained
- 1 jar (12 oz.) apricot preserves
- 1 cup barbecue sauce
- 1 can (20 oz.) pineapple chunks, drained

1. In a bowl, combine the beef and onion, mixing lightly but thoroughly. Shape into 1-in. balls. In a large skillet over medium heat, cook meatballs in 2 batches until cooked through, turning occasionally.
2. Using a slotted spoon, transfer the meatballs to a 3-qt. slow cooker. Add the hot dogs; stir in the preserves and barbecue sauce. Cook, covered, on high or until heated through, 2-3 hours.
3. Stir in pineapple; cook, covered, until heated through, 15-20 minutes longer.
⅓ CUP: 237 cal., 11g fat (4g sat. fat), 36mg chol., 491mg sod., 26g carb. (20g sugars, 0 fiber), 9g pro.

MAKE AHEAD
BACK PORCH MEATBALLS

This idea came to me while sitting on my back porch. You'll love these meatballs!
—*Justin Boudreaux, Walker, LA*

Prep: 30 min. • **Cook:** 3 hours
Makes: 6 dozen

- 2 large eggs, lightly beaten
- 2 cups seasoned bread crumbs
- 2 cups salsa
- ½ cup grated onion
- ⅔ lb. ground turkey
- ⅔ lb. ground pork
- ⅔ lb. ground beef

SAUCE
- 3 cups tomato sauce
- 1 medium onion, grated
- 1 cup beef stock
- 1 cup mixed fruit jelly
- 1 cup molasses
- ½ cup packed brown sugar
- ½ cup canola oil
- ½ cup red wine vinegar
- ⅓ cup prepared mustard
- ⅓ cup Worcestershire sauce
- 1 tsp. salt

1. Preheat oven to 400°. In a large bowl, combine eggs, bread crumbs, salsa and onion. Add turkey, pork and beef; mix lightly but thoroughly. Shape into 1½-in. balls. Place meatballs on greased racks in two 15x10x1-in. baking pans. Bake until browned, 18-22 minutes.
2. In a 6-qt. slow cooker, combine sauce ingredients. Add meatballs; gently stir to coat. Cook, covered, on low 3-4 hours or until meatballs are cooked through.
FREEZE OPTION: Freeze cooled sauce and meatballs in freezer containers. To use, partially thaw in the refrigerator overnight. Microwave, covered, on high in a microwave-safe dish until heated through, gently stirring; add water if necessary.
1 MEATBALL: 87 cal., 3g fat (1g sat. fat), 13mg chol., 195mg sod., 11g carb. (8g sugars, 0 fiber), 3g pro.

SLOW-COOKER FRENCH DIP SANDWICHES

These sandwiches make a standout addition to any buffet line. Make sure to have plenty of small cups of broth for everyone to grab. Dipping perfection!
—*Holly Neuharth, Mesa, AZ*

- -

Prep: 15 min. • **Cook:** 8 hours
Makes: 12 servings

- 1 beef rump or bottom round roast (about 3 lbs.)
- 1½ tsp. onion powder
- 1½ tsp. garlic powder
- ½ tsp. Creole seasoning
- 1 carton (26 oz.) beef stock
- 12 whole wheat hoagie buns, split
- 6 oz. Havarti cheese, cut into 12 slices

1. Cut the roast in half. Mix onion powder, garlic powder and Creole seasoning; rub onto beef. Place in a 5-qt. slow cooker; add stock. Cook, covered, on low until meat is tender, 8-10 hours.
2. Remove beef; cool slightly. Skim fat from cooking juices. When cool enough to handle, shred beef with 2 forks and return to slow cooker.
3. Place the buns on ungreased baking sheets, cut side up. Using tongs, place beef on bun bottoms. Place cheese on bun tops. Broil 3-4 in. from heat until cheese is melted, 1-2 minutes. Close sandwiches; serve with cooking juices.
NOTE: If you don't have Creole seasoning in your cupboard, you can make your own using ¼ tsp. each salt, garlic powder and paprika; and a pinch each of dried thyme, ground cumin and cayenne pepper.
1 SANDWICH WITH ⅓ CUP JUICES: 456 cal., 14g fat (5g sat. fat), 81mg chol., 722mg sod., 50g carb. (9g sugars, 7g fiber), 35g pro.

SLOW-COOKED BAKED BEANS

My friend suggested this recipe when I needed a dish to bring to a barbecue. It was an incredible success, and I've been making it ever since.
—*Jodi Caple, Cortez, CO*

- -

Prep: 25 min. + soaking
Cook: 9 hours • **Makes:** 8 servings

- 1 lb. dried navy beans
- 2 cups water
- ½ cup dark molasses
- 5 slices salt pork belly (about 3 oz.), cut into ½-in. pieces
- 1 small onion, finely chopped
- 3 Tbsp. brown sugar
- 2 garlic cloves, minced
- 1 tsp. ground ginger
- ½ tsp. salt
- ½ tsp. ground mustard
- ½ tsp. pepper

1. Rinse and sort beans; soak according to package directions.
2. Drain and rinse beans, discarding liquid. Transfer beans to a 4-qt. slow cooker. Stir in remaining ingredients. Cook, covered, on low until beans are tender, 9-11 hours.
¾ CUP: 463 cal., 20g fat (7g sat. fat), 19mg chol., 1429mg sod., 56g carb. (23g sugars, 9g fiber), 15g pro.

BBQ BEEF SANDWICHES

After years of searching, I found a recipe for shredded barbecue beef that's a hit with all my family and friends. It's easy to freeze for future meals, if any is left over!
—*Rebecca Rohland, Medford, WI*

Prep: 15 min. • **Cook:** 8 hours
Makes: 14 servings

- 2 cups ketchup
- 1 medium onion, chopped
- ¼ cup cider vinegar
- ¼ cup molasses
- 2 Tbsp. Worcestershire sauce
- 2 garlic cloves, minced
- ½ tsp. salt
- ½ tsp. ground mustard
- ½ tsp. pepper
- ¼ tsp. garlic powder
- ¼ tsp. crushed red pepper flakes
- 1 boneless beef chuck roast (3 lbs.)
- 14 sesame seed hamburger buns, split

1. In a large bowl, combine the first 11 ingredients. Cut roast in half; place in a 5-qt. slow cooker. Pour ketchup mixture over roast. Cover and cook on low for 8-10 hours or until meat is tender.
2. Remove meat and shred with 2 forks. Skim fat from cooking juices. Return meat to slow cooker; heat through. Using a slotted spoon, serve beef on buns.
1 SERVING: 354 cal., 12g fat (5g sat. fat), 63mg chol., 805mg sod., 37g carb. (16g sugars, 1g fiber), 24g pro.

SLOW-COOKER SAUERKRAUT

This recipe was made by a special someone in my life. I was never a fan of sauerkraut until I tried this and fell in love. It's terrific as a side dish or on Reuben sandwiches.
—*Karen Tringali, Minooka, IL*

Prep: 20 min. • **Cook:** 1 hour
Makes: 10 servings

- ½ lb. bacon strips, chopped
- 1 medium onion, chopped
- ¾ cup white vinegar
- ¾ cup sugar
- 2 cans (14 oz. each) sauerkraut, rinsed and well drained
- ½ tsp. caraway seeds

In a large skillet, cook bacon and onions over medium heat until bacon is crisp and onions are just tender, 5-7 minutes. Add vinegar and sugar to skillet; cook and stir 5 minutes. Add sauerkraut and caraway seeds to skillet; stir to combine. Transfer mixture to a 4-qt. slow cooker. Cover and cook on low to allow flavors to blend, 1-2 hours.
½ CUP: 173 cal., 9g fat (3g sat. fat), 15mg chol., 675mg sod., 20g carb. (17g sugars, 2g fiber), 4g pro.

QUICK FIX
If the sauerkraut gets too dry, simply add a little water.

CARNITAS HUEVOS RANCHEROS

When I was in college, I was a church counselor in Colorado and had my first taste of Mexican food. Recently, I've learned to make more authentic dishes. These are a favorite to serve for dinner.
—*Lonnie Hartstack, Clarinda, IA*

Prep: 35 min. • **Cook:** 7 hours
Makes: 12 servings

- 1 boneless pork shoulder butt roast (3 lbs.), halved
- 2 tsp. olive oil
- 3 garlic cloves, thinly sliced
- ½ tsp. salt
- ½ tsp. pepper
- 1 medium onion, chopped
- 2 cans (4 oz. each) chopped green chiles
- 1 cup salsa
- ½ cup minced fresh cilantro
- ½ cup chicken broth
- ½ cup tequila or additional chicken broth
- 1 can (15 oz.) black beans, rinsed and drained

ASSEMBLY
- 12 large eggs
- 1 jar (16 oz.) salsa
- 4 medium ripe avocados, peeled and sliced
- 12 flour tortillas (6 in.), warmed and quartered
  Additional minced fresh cilantro

1. Rub the roast with oil, garlic, salt and pepper. Place in a 5-qt. slow cooker. Top with onion, green chiles, salsa, cilantro, broth and tequila. Cook, covered, on low 7-8 hours or until meat is tender.

2. Remove the roast; shred with 2 forks. Discard cooking juices, reserving 1 cup. Return cooking juices and meat to slow cooker. Stir in beans; heat through.

3. Meanwhile, coat a large skillet with cooking spray; place over medium-high heat. Working in batches, break eggs, 1 at a time, into pan; reduce heat to low. Cook until whites are set and yolks begin to thicken, turning once if desired. Divide pork mixture among 12 serving bowls. Top with eggs, salsa, avocados and additional cilantro. Serve with tortillas.

FREEZE OPTION: Freeze cooled meat mixture and juices in freezer containers. To use, partially thaw in the refrigerator overnight. Heat through in a saucepan, stirring occasionally; add water or broth if necessary.

1 SERVING: 509 cal., 27g fat (8g sat. fat), 254mg chol., 858mg sod., 32g carb. (3g sugars, 7g fiber), 31g pro.

BREAKFAST APPLES

I have given people this recipe more than any other. It has a delicious nutty flavor. Use it to top waffles or pancakes. Or mix it with vanilla or plain yogurt for a light and quick dessert.
—*Rosemary Franta, New Ulm, MN*

Prep: 5 min. • **Cook:** 3 hours
Makes: 5 cups

- 8 baking apples (about 3½ lbs.), peeled and sliced
- ½ to 1 cup chopped pecans
- ¾ cup raisins
- ½ cup butter, melted
- ⅓ cup sugar
- ¼ cup old-fashioned oats
- 2 Tbsp. lemon juice
- ¼ tsp. ground cinnamon

Combine all ingredients in a 1½-qt. slow cooker. Cook on high heat for 3 hours, stirring occasionally. Serve warm with waffles, pancakes or yogurt.

¼ CUP: 133 cal., 7g fat (3g sat. fat), 12mg chol., 47mg sod., 19g carb. (15g sugars, 2g fiber), 1g pro.

MAKE AHEAD
TEX-MEX CHILI

Need to satisfy big, hearty appetites? Look no further than a chili brimming with beef stew meat, plenty of beans and tasty spices.
—*Eric Hayes, Antioch, CA*

Prep: 20 min. • **Cook:** 6 hours
Makes: 12 servings (about 4 qt.)

- 3 lbs. beef stew meat
- 1 Tbsp. canola oil
- 3 garlic cloves, minced
- 3 cans (16 oz. each) kidney beans, rinsed and drained
- 3 cans (15 oz. each) tomato sauce
- 1 can (14½ oz.) diced tomatoes, undrained
- 1 cup water
- 1 can (6 oz.) tomato paste
- ¾ cup salsa verde
- 1 envelope chili seasoning
- 2 tsp. dried minced onion
- 1 tsp. chili powder
- ½ tsp. crushed red pepper flakes
- ½ tsp. ground cumin
- ½ tsp. cayenne pepper

Optional toppings: Shredded cheddar cheese, minced fresh cilantro, sour cream, sliced jalapeno or fresno peppers and additional salsa verde

1. In a large skillet, brown beef in oil in batches. Add garlic; cook 1 minute longer. Transfer to a 6-qt. slow cooker.
2. Stir in beans, tomato sauce, tomatoes, water, tomato paste, salsa verde and seasonings. Cover and cook on low for 6-8 hours or until meat is tender. Garnish each serving with toppings as desired.
FREEZE OPTION: Before adding toppings, cool chili. Freeze the chili in freezer containers. To use, partially thaw in refrigerator overnight. Heat through in a saucepan, stirring occasionally and adding broth or water if necessary. Garnish with toppings as desired.

1⅓ CUPS: 334 cal., 9g fat (3g sat. fat), 70mg chol., 1030mg sod., 31g carb. (7g sugars, 8g fiber), 32g pro. **DIABETIC EXCHANGES:** 3 lean meat, 1 starch, 1 vegetable.

SHREDDED BEEF BURRITO FILLING

Make your next office party a taco bar or burrito bar! Set out the beef in the slow cooker on warm, along with tortillas, bowls of shredded cheese, salsa, sour cream, and chopped lettuce, jalapenos, onions and tomatoes.

—Hope Wasylenki, Gahanna, OH

Prep: 20 min. • **Cook:** 7 hours
Makes: 12 servings

- 5 lbs. boneless beef chuck roast, cut into 4 pieces
- ½ cup beef broth
- 2 Tbsp. canola oil
- 1 medium onion, finely chopped
- 2 jalapeno peppers, seeded and finely chopped
- 2 garlic cloves, minced
- 2 Tbsp. chili powder
- 1 Tbsp. ground cumin
- ⅛ tsp. salt
- 1 can (28 oz.) crushed tomatoes in puree
- 1 jar (16 oz.) salsa verde
  Optional toppings: Tortillas, shredded cheddar cheese, sour cream, guacamole, salsa, cooked rice and fresh cilantro leaves

1. In a 6-qt. slow cooker, combine beef and broth. Cook, covered, on low until meat is tender, 6-8 hours. Remove the meat; discard juices. When cool enough to handle, shred with 2 forks. Return to slow cooker.

2. In a large skillet, heat oil over medium heat. Add onion and jalapenos; cook and stir until softened, 3-4 minutes. Add the garlic and seasonings; cook 1 minute longer. Stir in the crushed tomatoes and salsa; bring to a boil. Pour mixture over shredded beef; stir to combine. Cook, covered, on high until heated through, about 1 hour.

3. If desired, serve filling (using tongs) on tortillas for burritos or tacos and add toppings. To make a burrito bowl, place beef on top of hot cooked rice and add topping as desired.

FREEZE OPTION: Freeze the cooled meat mixture in freezer containers. To use, partially thaw in refrigerator overnight. Heat through in a saucepan, stirring occasionally.

1 SERVING: 379 cal., 21g fat (7g sat. fat), 123mg chol., 509mg sod., 9g carb. (5g sugars, 2g fiber), 39g pro.

★★★★★ **READER REVIEW**

"Oh my! I made this in the slow cooker last night, and we awoke this morning to the most tempting, tantalizing aromas. We had to sample it before storing it in the fridge for dinner."

VICKI DARNELL TASTEOFHOME.COM

OLD-FASHIONED POOR MAN'S STEAK

These flavorful steaks fit into everybody's budget. A special friend shared the recipe, and I think of her each time I make this.
—*Susan Wright, Mineral Wells, WV*

Prep: 25 min. + chilling
Cook: 4 hours • **Makes:** 9 servings

- 1 cup crushed saltine crackers (about 30 crackers)
- ⅓ cup water
  Salt and pepper to taste
- 2 lbs. ground beef
- ¼ cup all-purpose flour
- 2 Tbsp. canola oil
- 2 cans (10¾ oz. each) condensed cream of mushroom soup, undiluted
  Hot mashed potatoes or noodles
  Minced fresh parsley, optional

1. In a large bowl, combine the cracker crumbs, water, salt and pepper. Crumble beef over mixture and mix lightly but thoroughly. Press into an ungreased 9-in. square pan. Cover and refrigerate for at least 3 hours.
2. Cut into 3-in. squares; dredge in flour. In a large skillet, heat oil over medium heat; add beef and cook until browned on both sides, 2-3 minutes on each side.
3. Transfer to a 3-qt. slow cooker with a slotted spatula or spoon. Add soup.
4. Cover and cook on high until meat is no longer pink, about 4 hours. Serve with mashed potatoes or noodles. If desired, top with minced parsley.
1 SERVING: 292 cal., 18g fat (6g sat. fat), 68mg chol., 372mg sod., 10g carb. (1g sugars, 1g fiber), 22g pro.

HONEY-GLAZED HAM

Here's an easy solution for feeding a large group. The simple ham is perfect for dinners where time in the kitchen is as valuable as space in the oven.
—*Jacquie Stolz, Little Sioux, IA*

Prep: 10 min. • **Cook:** 4½ hours
Makes: 14 servings

- 1 boneless fully cooked ham (4 lbs.)
- 1½ cups ginger ale
- ¼ cup honey
- ½ tsp. ground mustard
- ½ tsp. ground cloves
- ¼ tsp. ground cinnamon

1. Cut ham in half; place in a 5-qt. slow cooker. Pour ginger ale over ham. Cover and cook on low until heated through, 4-5 hours.
2. Combine the honey, mustard, cloves and cinnamon; stir until smooth. Spread over ham; cook 30 minutes longer.
3 OZ. COOKED HAM: 165 cal., 5g fat (2g sat. fat), 66mg chol., 1348mg sod., 8g carb. (7g sugars, 0 fiber), 24g pro.

SIMPLE SODA SWAP
Don't have ginger ale on hand? Use any other white soda instead.

EASY ITALIAN BEEF SANDWICHES

These party-sized sandwiches make the meal! Just add your favorite Italian salad on the side. If you like, top the sandwiches with some sliced provolone.
—*Troy Parkos, Verona, WI*

Prep: 20 min. • **Cook:** 5 hours
Makes: 12 servings

- 1 boneless beef chuck roast (3 lbs.)
- 1 tsp. Italian seasoning
- ¼ tsp. cayenne pepper
- ¼ tsp. pepper
- ¼ cup water
- 1 jar (16 oz.) sliced pepperoncini, undrained
- 1 medium sweet red pepper, julienned
- 1 medium green pepper, julienned
- 1 garlic clove, minced
- 1 envelope reduced-sodium onion soup mix
- 2 Tbsp. Worcestershire sauce
- 2 loaves (1 lb. each) Italian bread, split

1. Cut roast in half; place in a 5-qt. slow cooker. Sprinkle with Italian seasoning, cayenne and pepper. Add water. Cover and cook on high for 4 hours or until meat is tender.
2. Remove the roast; shred meat with 2 forks and return to the slow cooker. In a large bowl, combine pepperoncini, peppers, garlic, onion soup mix and Worcestershire sauce; pour over meat. Cover and cook on high for 1 hour or until peppers are tender.
3. Spoon beef mixture over the bottom halves of bread; replace bread tops. Cut each loaf into 6 sandwiches.
1 SERVING: 428 cal., 14g fat (5g sat. fat), 74mg chol., 661mg sod., 43g carb. (2g sugars, 3g fiber), 29g pro.

SLOW-COOKER BACON MAC & CHEESE

I'm all about easy slow-cooker meals. Using more cheese than ever, I developed an addictive spin on this casserole favorite.
—*Kristen Heigl, Staten Island, NY*

Prep: 20 min. • **Cook:** 3 hours + standing
Makes: 18 servings

- 2 large eggs, lightly beaten
- 4 cups whole milk
- 1 can (12 oz.) evaporated milk
- ¼ cup butter, melted
- 1 Tbsp. all-purpose flour
- 1 tsp. salt
- 1 pkg. (16 oz.) small pasta shells
- 1 cup shredded provolone cheese
- 1 cup shredded Manchego or Monterey Jack cheese
- 1 cup shredded white cheddar cheese
- 8 bacon strips, cooked and crumbled

1. In a bowl, whisk the first 6 ingredients until blended. Stir in pasta and cheeses; transfer to a 4- or 5-qt. slow cooker.
2. Cook, covered, on low until the pasta is tender, 3-3½ hours. Turn off slow cooker; remove insert. Let stand, uncovered, 15 minutes before serving. Top with bacon.
½ CUP: 272 cal., 14g fat (8g sat. fat), 59mg chol., 400mg sod., 24g carb. (5g sugars, 1g fiber), 13g pro.

★ ★ ★ ★ ★ **READER REVIEW**

"This was so delicious! If you like a little spice in your sandwich, this is the recipe for you."

JENCORDES TASTEOFHOME.COM

PERUVIAN POTATO SOUP

This Peruvian soup (known there as locro de papa) has the comfort of potatoes and the warming spiciness of chiles.
—Taste of Home *Test Kitchen*

Prep: 35 min. • **Cook:** 4 hours
Makes: 8 servings (2 qt.)

- 1 Tbsp. olive oil
- 1 medium onion, chopped
- 1 medium sweet red pepper, cut into 1-in. pieces
- 3 garlic cloves, minced
- 1 carton (32 oz.) chicken stock
- 2 large Yukon Gold potatoes, peeled and cut into 1-in. cubes
- 1 can (4 oz.) chopped green chiles
- ½ cup minced fresh cilantro, divided
- ½ to 1 serrano pepper, seeded and finely chopped
- 2 tsp. ground cumin
- 1 tsp. dried oregano
- ¼ tsp. salt
- ¼ tsp. pepper
- 1 fully cooked Spanish chorizo link (3 oz.), chopped
  Optional toppings: Sour cream and cubed avocado

1. In a large skillet, heat oil over medium-high heat. Add onion and sweet pepper; cook and stir for 6-8 minutes or until crisp-tender. Add garlic; cook 1 minute longer. Transfer to a 4- or 5-qt. slow cooker. Add the chicken stock, potatoes, chiles, ¼ cup cilantro, serrano pepper and seasonings. Cook, covered, on low 4-6 hours, until potatoes are tender.
2. Remove soup from heat; cool slightly. Process in batches in a blender until smooth. Return to slow cooker. Stir in chorizo and remaining ¼ cup cilantro; heat through. If desired, serve with sour cream and avocado.
1 CUP: 153 cal., 5g fat (1g sat. fat), 7mg chol., 472mg sod., 23g carb. (3g sugars, 2g fiber), 6g pro. **DIABETIC EXCHANGES:** 1½ starch, 1 fat.

APRICOT-APPLE CIDER

Dried apricots give this comforting cider a delicious twist. Add cranberries, cinnamon, allspice and cloves, and you've got the perfect hot drink to sip on cool nights.
—*Ginnie Busam, Pewee Valley, KY*

Prep: 20 min. • **Cook:** 3 hours
Makes: 13 servings (2½ qt.)

- 8 cups unsweetened apple juice
- 1 can (12 oz.) ginger ale
- ½ cup dried apricots, halved
- ½ cup dried cranberries
- 2 cinnamon sticks (3 in. each)
- 1 Tbsp. whole allspice
- 1 Tbsp. whole cloves

1. In a 5-qt. slow cooker, combine apple juice and ginger ale. Place the apricots, cranberries, cinnamon sticks, allspice and cloves on a double thickness of cheesecloth; bring up corners of cloth and tie with string to form a bag. Place in slow cooker; cover.
2. Cook on high until heated through, 3-4 hours. Discard spice bag.
¾ CUP: 79 cal., 0 fat (0 sat. fat), 0 chol., 8mg sod., 20g carb. (17g sugars, 0 fiber), 0 pro. **DIABETIC EXCHANGES:** 2 fruit.

ARTICHOKE SPREAD WITH GARLIC BREAD

I've tried several different artichoke dip recipes, but this one is the absolute best! I serve it at nearly every family gathering, and there are never any leftovers. This is probably my most-requested recipe.
—*Heidi Iacovetto, Phippsburg, CO*

- -

Prep: 10 min. • **Cook:** 2 hours
Makes: 16 servings

- 2 pkg. (8 oz. each) cream cheese, cubed
- 1 can (14 oz.) water-packed artichoke hearts, drained and quartered
- 1 cup fresh spinach, torn
- ¾ cup shredded Parmesan cheese
- 2 green onions, chopped
- 1 loaf (16 oz.) frozen garlic bread

Combine first 5 ingredients in a bowl; transfer to a 1½-qt. slow cooker. Cook, covered, on low, until cheese is melted, 2-3 hours. Meanwhile, prepare garlic bread according to package directions. Slice and serve with hot dip.

¼ CUP DIP WITH 2 SLICES GARLIC BREAD: 222 cal., 15g fat (8g sat. fat), 35mg chol., 395mg sod., 15g carb. (2g sugars, 1g fiber), 7g pro.

SPREAD IT ON THICK

This is a thick, spreadable mixture. If you'd like it thinner so that it's easier for dipping, stir in milk a tablespoon at a time.

MAKE AHEAD
BONNIE'S CHILI

This chili is incredibly easy to make and has a surprising depth of flavor— it tastes like chilis that take all day to create! I can make this for people who like it hot or mild just by changing the salsa. You can make it really spicy if you add hot peppers and hot salsa.
—*Bonnie Altig, North Pole, AK*

- -

Prep: 25 min. • **Cook:** 5 hours
Makes: 8 servings (2½ qt.)

- 2 lbs. lean ground beef (90% lean)
- 2 cans (16 oz. each) kidney beans, rinsed and drained
- 2 cans (15 oz. each) tomato sauce
- 1½ cups salsa
- ½ cup water or reduced-sodium beef broth
- 4½ tsp. chili powder
- ½ tsp. garlic powder
- ½ tsp. pepper
- ¼ tsp. salt
  Optional toppings: Corn chips, sliced jalapeno peppers and shredded cheddar cheese

In a Dutch oven, cook beef over medium heat until no longer pink, 8-10 minutes, breaking into crumbles; drain. Transfer to a 4- or 5-qt. slow cooker. Stir in the remaining ingredients. Cook, covered, on low until heated through, 5-6 hours. If desired, serve with optional toppings.
FREEZE OPTION: Freeze cooled chili in freezer containers. To use, partially thaw in refrigerator overnight. Heat through in a saucepan, stirring occasionally and adding a little water if necessary.

1¼ CUPS: 323 cal., 10g fat (4g sat. fat), 71mg chol., 1027mg sod., 27g carb. (5g sugars, 8g fiber), 31g pro.

STAMP-OF-APPROVAL SPAGHETTI SAUCE

My father is pretty opinionated—especially about food. This recipe received his nearly unattainable stamp of approval, and I have yet to hear any disagreement from anyone who has tried it!

—*Melissa Taylor, Higley, AZ*

Prep: 30 min.
Cook: 8 hours
Makes: 12 servings (3 qt.)

- 2 lbs. ground beef
- ¾ lb. bulk Italian sausage
- 4 medium onions, finely chopped
- 8 garlic cloves, minced
- 4 cans (14½ oz. each) diced tomatoes, undrained
- 4 cans (6 oz. each) tomato paste
- ½ cup water
- ¼ cup sugar
- ¼ cup Worcestershire sauce
- 1 Tbsp. canola oil
- ¼ cup minced fresh parsley
- 2 Tbsp. minced fresh basil or 2 tsp. dried basil
- 1 Tbsp. minced fresh oregano or 1 tsp. dried oregano
- 4 bay leaves
- 1 tsp. rubbed sage
- ½ tsp. salt
- ½ tsp. dried marjoram
- ½ tsp. pepper
   Hot cooked spaghetti

1. In a Dutch oven, cook beef, sausage, onions and garlic over medium heat until meat is no longer pink; drain.

2. Transfer to a 5- or 6-qt. slow cooker. Stir in the tomatoes, tomato paste, water, sugar, Worcestershire sauce, oil and seasonings.

3. Cook, covered, on low for 8-10 hours. Discard bay leaves. Serve with spaghetti.

FREEZE OPTION: Cool the sauce before placing in a freezer container. Cover and freeze for up to 3 months. Thaw in the refrigerator overnight. Place in a large saucepan; heat through, stirring occasionally. Serve with spaghetti.

1 CUP: 335 cal., 16g fat (5g sat. fat), 62mg chol., 622mg sod., 27g carb. (16g sugars, 5g fiber), 22g pro.

HOT SPICED CRANBERRY DRINK

I serve this rosy spiced beverage at parties and family gatherings during the winter. Friends like the tangy twist it gets from Red Hots.
—*Laura Burgess, Ballwin, MO*

Prep: 10 min. • **Cook:** 2 hours
Makes: 14 servings (3½ qt.)

- 8 cups hot water
- 1½ cups sugar
- 4 cups cranberry juice
- ¾ cup orange juice
- ¼ cup lemon juice
- 12 whole cloves, optional
- ½ cup Red Hot candies

In a 5-qt. slow cooker, combine water, sugar and juices; stir until sugar is dissolved. If desired, place cloves in a double thickness of cheesecloth; bring up corners of cloth and tie with string to form a bag. Add spice bag and Red Hots to slow cooker. Cover and cook on low until heated through, 2-3 hours. Before serving, discard spice bag and stir punch.

1 CUP: 155 cal., 0 fat (0 sat. fat), 0 chol., 2mg sod., 40g carb. (37g sugars, 0 fiber), 0 pro.

★ ★ ★ ★ ★ **READER REVIEW**

"I served this at a Christmas party and had recipe requests."

MISSSKARLA TASTEOFHOME.COM

GREEN CHILE SHREDDED PORK

Slow cooker pork with green chiles always makes my hungry family happy. Getting creative with the leftovers is part of the fun.
—*Mary Shivers, Ada, OK*

Prep: 10 min. • **Cook:** 6 hours
Makes: 8 servings

- 1 boneless pork loin roast (3 to 4 lbs.)
- 1½ cups apple cider or juice
- 1 can (4 oz.) chopped green chiles, drained
- 3 garlic cloves, minced
- 1½ tsp. salt
- 1½ tsp. hot pepper sauce
- 1 tsp. chili powder
- 1 tsp. pepper
- ½ tsp. ground cumin
- ½ tsp. dried oregano
- 16 flour tortillas (8 in.)
  Optional toppings: Chopped peeled mango, shredded lettuce, chopped fresh cilantro and lime wedges

1. Place pork in a 5- or 6-qt. slow cooker. In a small bowl, mix cider, green chiles, garlic, salt, pepper sauce, chili powder, pepper, cumin and oregano; pour over pork. Cook, covered, on low 6-8 hours or until meat is tender.

2. Remove the roast; cool slightly. Shred pork with 2 forks. Return to the slow cooker; heat through. Using tongs, serve pork in tortillas with toppings as desired.

FREEZE OPTION: Place the shredded pork in freezer containers; top with cooking juices. Cool and freeze. To use, partially thaw in the refrigerator. Heat through in a saucepan, stirring occasionally.

2 FILLED TORTILLAS: 559 cal., 15g fat (5g sat. fat), 85mg chol., 1032mg sod., 62g carb. (5g sugars, 4g fiber), 42g pro.

SLOW-COOKER CHEESY WHITE LASAGNA

Here's my best version of my favorite food—lasagna! The recipe is a winner, so it's worth the extra prep. You'll have plenty of time to plan side dishes while the main dish is cooking.
—*Suzanne Smith, Bluffton, IN*

Prep: 30 min. • **Cook:** 3 hours + standing
Makes: 8 servings

- 1 lb. ground chicken or beef
- 2 tsp. canola oil
- 1¾ cups sliced fresh mushrooms
- 1 medium onion, chopped
- 2 medium carrots, chopped
- 2 garlic cloves, minced
- 2 tsp. Italian seasoning
- ¾ tsp. salt
- ½ tsp. pepper
- ½ cup white wine or chicken broth
- 1 cup half-and-half cream
- 4 oz. cream cheese, softened
- 1 cup shredded white cheddar cheese
- 1 cup shredded Gouda cheese
- 1 large egg, beaten
- 1½ cups 2% cottage cheese
- ¼ cup minced fresh basil or 4 tsp. dried basil
- 9 no-cook lasagna noodles
- 4 cups shredded part-skim mozzarella cheese
  Additional minced fresh basil, optional

1. Fold two 18-in. square pieces of heavy-duty foil into thirds. Crisscross strips and place on bottom and up sides of a 6-qt. slow cooker. Coat strips with cooking spray.

2. In a 6-qt. stockpot, cook the chicken over medium heat until no longer pink, 6-8 minutes, breaking into crumbles; drain. Remove chicken from the pot and set aside.

3. In same pot, heat oil over medium-high heat. Add mushrooms, onion and carrots; cook and stir just until tender, 6-8 minutes. Add the garlic, Italian seasoning, salt and pepper; cook 1 minute longer. Stir in wine. Bring to a boil; cook until liquid is reduced by half, 4-5 minutes. Stir in cream, cream cheese, cheddar and Gouda cheeses. Return chicken to pot. In a large bowl, combine egg, cottage cheese and basil.

4. Spread 1 cup chicken mixture into slow cooker. Layer with 3 noodles (breaking noodles as necessary to fit), 1 cup chicken mixture, ½ cup cottage cheese mixture and 1 cup mozzarella cheese. Repeat layers twice. Top with remaining chicken mixture and mozzarella. Cook, covered, on low until noodles are tender, 3-4 hours. Remove slow cooker insert and let stand for 30 minutes. If desired, sprinkle with additional basil. Using foil strips as handles, remove lasagna to a cutting board or platter.

1 PIECE: 603 cal., 35g fat (19g sat. fat), 165mg chol., 1086mg sod., 28g carb. (7g sugars, 2g fiber), 40g pro.

TOMATO BASIL TORTELLINI SOUP

When my family first tried this soup, they all had seconds. My husband is happy anytime I put it on the table.
—*Christy Addison, Clarksville, OH*

Prep: 25 min. • **Cook:** 6¼ hours
Makes: 18 servings (4½ qt.)

- 2 **Tbsp. olive oil**
- 1 **medium onion, chopped**
- 3 **medium carrots, chopped**
- 5 **garlic cloves, minced**
- 3 **cans (28 oz. each) crushed tomatoes, undrained**
- 1 **carton (32 oz.) vegetable broth**
- 1 **Tbsp. sugar**
- 1 **tsp. dried basil**
- 1 **bay leaf**
- 3 **pkg. (9 oz. each) refrigerated cheese tortellini**
- ¾ **cup half-and-half cream**
  Optional: Grated Parmesan cheese and minced fresh basil

1. In a large skillet, heat oil over medium-high heat. Add onion and carrots; cook and stir until crisp-tender, 5-6 minutes. Add garlic; cook 1 minute longer. Transfer to a 6-qt. slow cooker. Add the tomatoes, broth, sugar, basil and bay leaf. Cook, covered, on low until the vegetables are tender, 6-7 hours.

2. Stir in tortellini. Cook, covered, on high 15 minutes. Reduce heat to low; stir in cream until heated through. Discard bay leaf. Serve topped with Parmesan cheese and basil, if desired.

FREEZE OPTION: Before stirring in the half-and-half, cool soup and freeze in freezer containers. To use, partially thaw in refrigerator overnight. Heat through in a saucepan, stirring occasionally; add half-and-half as directed.

1 CUP: 214 cal., 7g fat (3g sat. fat), 23mg chol., 569mg sod., 32g carb. (9g sugars, 4g fiber), 9g pro. **DIABETIC EXCHANGES:** 2 starch, 1 fat.

SWEET & SPICY SLOPPY JOES

These sandwiches have been the go-to meal for my son's basketball team. Turkey is a wonderful change from ground beef and really absorbs all the flavors. I have also used this for a Friday the 13th celebration at work, calling it 13-ingredient sloppy joes.
—*Karen Hildebrand, Labelle, FL*

Prep: 30 min. • **Cook:** 4 hours
Makes: 12 servings

- 2 tsp. canola oil
- 3 lbs. ground turkey
- 1 large onion, chopped
- ½ medium green pepper, chopped
- 3 garlic cloves, minced
- 2 Tbsp. Worcestershire sauce
- 1 tsp. crushed red pepper flakes
- 3 cups ketchup
- ⅔ cup water
- ⅓ cup packed brown sugar
- 3 Tbsp. spicy brown mustard
- ½ tsp. salt
- ¼ tsp. pepper
- 12 hamburger buns, split
  Optional: Coleslaw and dill pickle slices

1. Heat oil in a large nonstick skillet over medium-high heat. Cook the turkey in batches until no longer pink, breaking into crumbles, 8-10 minutes per batch. Transfer the meat to a 5- or 6-qt. slow cooker. In the same skillet, cook the onion and green pepper until tender, 2-3 minutes. Add garlic, Worcestershire and red pepper flakes; cook 1 minute longer. Transfer to slow cooker.
2. In a bowl, combine ketchup, water, brown sugar, mustard, salt and pepper; pour over meat. Cover and cook on low 4-5 hours or until flavors are blended. Serve on buns with toppings as desired.

1 SANDWICH: 390 cal., 11g fat (3g sat. fat), 75mg chol., 1206mg sod., 46g carb. (26g sugars, 1g fiber), 27g pro.

CRUNCH & MUNCH
Topping these sandwiches with coleslaw and dill pickles lends a little crunch. You could also use pickled jalapenos or fried onions.

CAROLINA-STYLE PORK BARBECUE

I am originally from North Carolina, and this recipe is a favorite. My husband swears my authentic Carolina 'cue is the best barbecue he's ever eaten!
—*Kathryn Ransom Williams, Sparks, NV*

Prep: 30 min. • **Cook:** 6 hours
Makes: 14 servings

- 1 boneless pork shoulder butt roast (4 to 5 lbs.)
- 2 Tbsp. brown sugar
- 2 tsp. salt
- 1 tsp. paprika
- ½ tsp. pepper
- 2 medium onions, quartered
- ¾ cup cider vinegar
- 4 tsp. Worcestershire sauce
- 1 Tbsp. sugar
- 1 Tbsp. crushed red pepper flakes
- 1 tsp. garlic salt
- 1 tsp. ground mustard
- ½ tsp. cayenne pepper
- 14 hamburger buns, split
- 1¾ lbs. deli coleslaw

1. Cut roast into quarters. Mix brown sugar, salt, paprika and pepper; rub over meat. Place meat and onions in a 5-qt. slow cooker.

2. In a small bowl, whisk the vinegar, Worcestershire sauce, sugar and seasonings; pour over roast. Cook, covered, on low 6-8 hours or until meat is tender.

3. Remove the roast and cool slightly. Reserve 1½ cups cooking juices; discard remaining juices. Skim the fat from the reserved juices. Shred the pork with 2 forks. Return pork and reserved juices to slow cooker; heat through. Serve on buns with coleslaw.

1 SANDWICH: 453 cal., 22g fat (6g sat. fat), 85mg chol., 889mg sod., 35g carb. (14g sugars, 3g fiber), 27g pro.

TURN DOWN THE HEAT
Some like it hot, but if you're not one of those people, consider reducing the crushed red pepper flakes and cayenne pepper in the sauce by half.

MIXED VEGGIES & RICE

To add variety to sides for those who don't care for potatoes, I came up with this colorful dish. It's an easy slow-cooker recipe that you can put right onto the buffet table.
—*Judy Batson, Tampa, FL*

- -

Prep: 5 min. • **Cook:** 3 hours
Makes: 8 servings

- 4 pkg. (10 oz. each) frozen long grain white rice with mixed vegetables
- 12 oz. frozen mixed vegetables
- ½ cup vegetable broth or light beer
- 1 tsp. onion powder
- 1 tsp. garlic powder
- 1 tsp. seasoned salt
  Butter, optional

In a 5-qt. slow cooker, combine first 6 ingredients. Cook, covered, on low 3-4 hours or until heated through. If desired, serve with butter.
¾ CUP: 120 cal., 0 fat (0 sat. fat), 0 chol., 254mg sod., 26g carb. (3g sugars, 3g fiber), 3g pro. **DIABETIC EXCHANGES:** 1½ starch.

SAUCY COCKTAIL MEATBALLS

My grandmother shared this recipe with me many years ago. She would serve it every year at Christmastime while I was growing up. Now I serve it every year.
—*Susie Snyder, Bowling Green, OH*

- -

Prep: 10 min. • **Cook:** 3 hours
Makes: about 5 dozen

- 1 pkg. (32 oz.) frozen fully cooked homestyle meatballs, thawed
- 1 can (10¾ oz.) condensed tomato soup, undiluted
- ⅓ cup chopped onion
- ⅓ cup chopped green pepper
- 2 Tbsp. brown sugar
- 4 tsp. Worcestershire sauce
- 1 Tbsp. white vinegar
- 1 Tbsp. prepared mustard

1. Place meatballs in a 3-qt. slow cooker. In a small bowl, combine the remaining ingredients. Pour over meatballs.
2. Cover and cook on low for 3-4 hours or until heated through.
1 MEATBALL: 37 cal., 2g fat (1g sat. fat), 12mg chol., 49mg sod., 2g carb. (1g sugars, 0g fiber), 3g pro. **DIABETIC EXCHANGES:** ½ lean meat.

SWEET & SPICY PEANUTS

With a caramel-like coating and a touch of heat from the hot sauce, these crunchy peanuts make a tasty anytime snack.
—*Taste of Home Test Kitchen*

- -

Prep: 10 min. • **Cook:** 1½ hours + cooling
Makes: 4 cups

- 3 cups salted peanuts
- ½ cup sugar
- ⅓ cup packed brown sugar
- 2 Tbsp. hot water
- 2 Tbsp. butter, melted
- 1 Tbsp. Sriracha chili sauce or hot pepper sauce
- 1 tsp. chili powder

1. Place peanuts in a greased 1½-qt. slow cooker. In a small bowl, combine sugars, water, butter, chili sauce and chili powder. Pour over peanuts. Cover and cook on high for 1½ hours, stirring once.
2. Spread on nonstick aluminum foil to cool. Store in an airtight container.
⅓ CUP: 284 cal., 20g fat (4g sat. fat), 5mg chol., 214mg sod., 22g carb. (16g sugars, 3g fiber), 10g pro.

BEER BRAT CHILI

My husband and I love this chili because it smells so good as it simmers in the slow cooker all day. I can't think of a better way to use up leftover brats. He can't think of a better way to eat them!
—*Katrina Krumm, Apple Valley, MN*

Prep: 10 min. • **Cook:** 5 hours
Makes: 8 servings (2½ qt.)

- 1 can (15 oz.) cannellini beans, rinsed and drained
- 1 can (15 oz.) pinto beans, rinsed and drained
- 1 can (15 oz.) Southwest or seasoned recipe black beans, undrained
- 1 can (14½ oz.) Italian diced tomatoes, undrained
- 1 can (10 oz.) diced tomatoes and green chiles, undrained
- 1 pkg. (14 oz.) fully cooked beer bratwurst links, sliced
- 1½ cups frozen corn
- 1 medium sweet red pepper, chopped
- 1 medium onion, finely chopped
- ¼ cup chili seasoning mix
- 1 garlic clove, minced

In a 5- or 6-qt. slow cooker, combine all the ingredients. Cook, covered, on low 5-6 hours.

1¼ CUPS: 383 cal., 16g fat (5g sat. fat), 34mg chol., 1256mg sod., 42g carb. (7g sugars, 10g fiber), 17g pro.

MAKE AHEAD
KALUA PORK

A Hawaiian friend shared this recipe with me while I was stationed in Pearl Harbor several years ago. It's the perfect main dish for any get-together. It will feed a crowd, it's easy to prepare and everyone loves it. Cleanup is a breeze, too!
—*Becky Friedman, Hammond, LA*

Prep: 10 min. • **Cook:** 8 hours
Makes: 18 servings

- 1 boneless pork shoulder roast (5 to 6 lbs.)
- 1 Tbsp. liquid smoke
- 4 tsp. sea salt (preferably Hawaiian red sea salt)
  Hot cooked rice, optional

1. Pierce pork with a fork; rub with liquid smoke and salt. Place the pork in a 6-qt. slow cooker. Cook, covered, on low, for 8-10 hours or until pork is tender.
2. Remove the roast; shred with 2 forks. Strain cooking juices; skim fat. Return pork to the slow cooker. Stir in enough cooking juices to moisten; heat through. If desired, serve with rice.
FREEZE OPTION: Freeze the cooled shredded pork and juices in freezer containers. To use, partially thaw in refrigerator overnight. Heat through in a saucepan, stirring occasionally; add broth if necessary.
3 OZ. COOKED PORK: 205 cal., 13g fat (5g sat. fat), 75mg chol., 504mg sod., 0 carb. (0 sugars, 0 fiber), 21g pro. **DIABETIC EXCHANGES:** 3 medium-fat meat.

SLOW-COOKER SPUMONI CAKE

I created this cake for a holiday potluck one year. It has become one of my most requested desserts. If you prefer, you can use all semisweet chips instead of a mix.
—*Lisa Renshaw, Kansas City, MO*

- -

Prep: 10 min. • **Cook:** 4 hours + standing
Makes: 10 servings

- 3 cups cold 2% milk
- 1 pkg. (3.4 oz.) instant pistachio pudding mix
- 1 pkg. white cake mix (regular size)
- ¾ cup chopped maraschino cherries
- 1 cup white baking chips
- 1 cup semisweet chocolate chips
- 1 cup pistachios, chopped

1. In a large bowl, whisk the milk and pudding mix for 2 minutes. Transfer to a greased 5-qt. slow cooker. Prepare cake mix batter according to package directions, folding cherries into batter. Pour into slow cooker.
2. Cook, covered, on low about 4 hours, until edges of cake are golden brown.
3. Remove slow-cooker insert; sprinkle cake with baking chips and chocolate chips. Let the cake stand, uncovered, 10 minutes. Sprinkle with pistachios before serving.
1 SERVING: 588 cal., 27g fat (9g sat. fat), 9mg chol., 594mg sod., 79g carb. (54g sugars, 3g fiber), 10g pro.

SLOW-COOKER BARBECUE BEEF

This juicy shredded beef is so popular at summer gatherings. The tender meat is slow-cooked in a savory sauce that includes tomato paste, brown sugar, molasses and chili powder. It makes a big batch—enough for seconds.
—*Colleen Nelson, Mandan, ND*

- -

Prep: 15 min. • **Cook:** 8 hours
Makes: 8-10 servings

- 1 beef sirloin tip roast (3 lbs.), cut into large chunks
- 3 celery ribs, chopped
- 1 large onion, chopped
- 1 medium green pepper, chopped
- 1 cup ketchup
- 1 can (6 oz.) tomato paste
- ½ cup packed brown sugar
- ¼ cup cider vinegar
- 3 Tbsp. chili powder
- 2 Tbsp. lemon juice
- 2 Tbsp. molasses
- 2 tsp. salt
- 2 tsp. Worcestershire sauce
- 1 tsp. ground mustard
- 8 to 10 sandwich rolls, split

1. Place beef in a 5-qt. slow cooker. Add celery, onion and green pepper. In a bowl, combine ketchup, tomato paste, brown sugar, vinegar, chili powder, lemon juice, molasses, salt, Worcestershire sauce and mustard. Pour over the beef mixture. Cover and cook on low 8-9 hours or until meat is tender.
2. Skim fat from cooking juices if necessary. Shred beef. Toast rolls if desired. Use a slotted spoon to serve beef on rolls.
1 SERVING: 413 cal., 9g fat (3g sat. fat), 72mg chol., 1127mg sod., 52g carb. (23g sugars, 4g fiber), 32g pro.

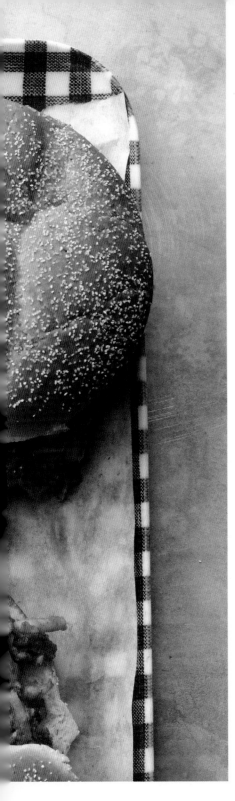

FALL VEGETABLE SLOPPY JOES

I make this dish in the fall and sneak grated vegetables into the sloppy joe mixture, which is especially good for children who don't like to eat their vegetables! Just walk away and let the slow cooker do all the work. Top the filling with a little shredded cheese before serving.

—*Nancy Heishman, Las Vegas, NV*

Prep: 30 min. • **Cook:** 4 hours
Makes: 18 servings

- 8 bacon strips, cut into 1-in. pieces
- 2 lbs. lean ground beef (90% lean)
- 1 medium onion, chopped
- 2 garlic cloves, minced
- 2 cups shredded peeled butternut squash
- 2 medium parsnips, peeled and shredded
- 2 medium carrots, peeled and shredded
- 1 can (12 oz.) cola
- 1 can (8 oz.) tomato paste
- 1 cup water
- ⅓ cup honey mustard
- 1½ tsp. ground cumin
- 1¼ tsp. salt
- 1 tsp. ground allspice
- ½ tsp. pepper
- 18 hamburger buns, split

1. In a skillet, cook bacon over medium heat until crisp, stirring occasionally. Remove with a slotted spoon; drain on paper towels. Discard drippings. In the same skillet, cook beef, onion and garlic over medium heat until beef is no longer pink and onion is tender, 10-12 minutes, breaking meat into crumbles; drain.

2. Transfer to a 5- or 6-qt. slow cooker. Stir in the squash, parsnips, carrots, cola, tomato paste, water, mustard and seasonings. Cook, covered, on low until vegetables are tender, 4-5 hours. Stir in bacon. Serve on buns.

FREEZE OPTION: Freeze cooled meat mixture in freezer containers. To use, partially thaw in refrigerator overnight. Heat through in a saucepan, stirring occasionally; add water if necessary.

1 SANDWICH: 275 cal., 8g fat (3g sat. fat), 35mg chol., 526mg sod., 35g carb. (9g sugars, 3g fiber), 17g pro. **DIABETIC EXCHANGES:** 2 starch, 2 lean meat.

NACHO SALSA DIP

This zesty dip is ideal for any get-together and allows me to spend more time with my guests. I always have requests to bring it when my husband and I attend parties.
—*Sally Hull, Homestead, FL*

Prep: 15 min. • **Cook:** 3 hours
Makes: 7 cups

- 1 lb. ground beef
- ⅓ cup chopped onion
- 2 lbs. Velveeta, cubed
- 1 jar (16 oz.) chunky salsa
- ¼ tsp. garlic powder
    Tortilla chips or cubed French bread

1. In a large skillet, cook beef and onion over medium heat until meat is no longer pink; drain well.

2. Transfer beef to a greased 3-qt. slow cooker; stir in the process cheese, salsa and garlic powder. Cover and cook on low for 3-4 hours or until heated through. Stir; serve warm with tortilla chips or cubed bread.

¼ CUP: 143 cal., 10g fat (6g sat. fat), 36mg chol., 484mg sod., 4g carb. (3g sugars, 0 fiber), 9g pro.

POTLUCK BEANS

It was the morning of our family potluck, and I still needed something to take. I threw together this recipe while drinking my morning coffee. By the end of the gathering, the beans were all gone, and someone had even washed the slow cooker for me!
—*Mary Anne Thygesen, Portland, OR*

Prep: 10 min. • **Cook:** 4 hours
Makes: 12 servings

- 1 cup brewed coffee
- ½ cup packed brown sugar
- ¼ cup spicy brown mustard
- 2 Tbsp. molasses
- 2 cans (16 oz. each) butter beans
- 2 cans (16 oz. each) kidney beans
- 2 cans (16 oz. each) navy beans

In a greased 3- or 4-qt. slow cooker, mix the first 4 ingredients. Rinse and drain beans; stir into coffee mixture. Cook, covered, on low until flavors are blended, 4-5 hours.

FREEZE OPTION: Freeze cooled beans in freezer containers. To use, partially thaw in refrigerator overnight. Heat through in a covered saucepan, stirring occasionally; add water if necessary.

½ CUP: 243 cal., 0 fat (0 sat. fat), 0 chol., 538mg sod., 50g carb. (13g sugars, 10g fiber), 14g pro.

SPICY HONEY SRIRACHA GAME-DAY DIP

You can easily whip up this creamy, spicy and salty dip. I love dips for parties in the slow cooker—just turn the slow cooker to low once it is cooked and let your guests help themselves. No need to worry about the dip getting cold and having to reheat it.
—*Julie Peterson, Crofton, MD*

Prep: 20 min. • **Cook:** 3 hours
Makes: 3 cups

- 1 lb. ground chicken
- 1 pkg. (8 oz.) cream cheese, cubed
- 1 cup shredded white cheddar cheese
- ¼ cup chicken broth
- 2 to 4 Tbsp. Sriracha chili sauce
- 2 Tbsp. honey
  Tortilla chips
  Chopped green onions, optional

1. In a large skillet, cook chicken over medium heat 6-8 minutes or until no longer pink, breaking it into crumbles; drain. Transfer to a greased 3-qt. slow cooker. Stir in cream cheese, cheddar cheese, broth, chili sauce and honey.
2. Cook, covered, on low for 3-4 hours, until cheese is melted, stirring every 30 minutes. Serve with tortilla chips. If desired, sprinkle with green onions.

¼ CUP: 168 cal., 13g fat (6g sat. fat), 54mg chol., 243mg sod., 5g carb. (4g sugars, 0 fiber), 9g pro.

★ ★ ★ ★ ★ **READER REVIEW**

"Very good. I subbed mozzarella for the white cheddar cheese."
MONA4EYES TASTEOFHOME.COM

BANANA FUDGE PIE,
PAGE 215

The Sweetest Treats

Time to celebrate the stars of the party: those beautiful sweets we always save room for! It won't be hard when these lovely desserts are on the menu.

LEMONADE ICEBOX PIE

You will detect a definite lemonade flavor in this refreshing pie. High and fluffy, this dessert has a creamy, smooth consistency that we really appreciate. It's the dessert that came immediately to mind when I put together my favorite summer meal.
—*Cheryl Wilt, Eglon, WV*

Prep: 15 min. + chilling
Makes: 8 servings

1 pkg. (8 oz.) cream cheese, softened
1 can (14 oz.) sweetened condensed milk
¾ cup thawed lemonade concentrate
1 carton (8 oz.) frozen whipped topping, thawed
Yellow food coloring, optional
1 graham cracker crust (9 in.)

In a large bowl, beat cream cheese and milk until smooth. Beat in lemonade concentrate. Fold in whipped topping and, if desired, food coloring. Pour into crust. Cover and refrigerate until set.

NOTE: Sweetened condensed milk is made with cow's milk from which water has been removed and to which sugar has been added, yielding a very thick, sweet canned product. It is used most often in candy and dessert recipes.

1 PIECE: 491 cal., 24g fat (15g sat. fat), 48mg chol., 269mg sod., 61g carb. (52g sugars, 0 fiber), 7g pro.

ORANGE ICEBOX PIE: Substitute ¾ cup thawed orange juice concentrate for the lemonade, add ½ tsp. grated orange peel and omit food coloring.

CREAMY PINEAPPLE PIE: Substitute 1 can (8 oz.) crushed, undrained pineapple and ¼ cup lemon juice for lemonade. Omit cream cheese and food coloring.

COOL LIME PIE: Substitute ¾ cup thawed limeade concentrate for lemonade and use green food coloring instead of yellow.

WHITE CHOCOLATE MACADAMIA COOKIES

White baking chips and macadamia nuts are a fantastic duo in these buttery cookies. They are a nice change from the classic chocolate chip ones.

—*Cathy Lennon, Newport, TN*

Prep: 15 min.
Bake: 10 min./batch + cooling
Makes: 2½ dozen

- ½ cup butter, softened
- ⅔ cup sugar
- 1 large egg, room temperature
- 1 tsp. vanilla extract
- 1 cup plus 2 Tbsp. all-purpose flour
- ½ tsp. baking soda
- 1 cup macadamia nuts, chopped
- 1 cup white baking chips

1. Preheat oven to 350°. In a large bowl, cream butter and sugar until light and fluffy, 5-7 minutes. Beat in egg and vanilla. In another bowl, whisk flour and baking soda; gradually beat into creamed mixture. Stir in nuts and baking chips.

2. Drop by tablespoonfuls 2 in. apart onto ungreased baking sheets. Bake 10-13 minutes or until golden brown. Cool on pans 1 minute. Remove to wire racks to cool completely.

1 COOKIE: 127 cal., 8g fat (4g sat. fat), 16mg chol., 69mg sod., 12g carb. (8g sugars, 1g fiber), 1g pro.

CREAMING KNOW-HOW

Many bakers underestimate the time it takes to cream butter and sugar; you want your mixture to be pale in color and fluffy, without obvious sugar crystals. The standard time needed to reach this stage is 5-7 minutes; with a more powerful mixer, it might require only 2-3 minutes. The truth is, you cannot over-cream the butter and sugar mixture. If you're using a stand mixer, a good timesaver is to start creaming the mixture while you prep and gather the other ingredients.

CHOCOLATE THUMBPRINT COOKIES

My group of friends had a weekly movie night during winters on Martha's Vineyard, and we'd take turns making a chocolate treat to share. These terrific cookies were an instant success. Once they debuted, I had to make them many more times.
—*Laura Bryant German, West Warren, MA*

Prep: 25 min. + chilling
Bake: 10 min. + cooling
Makes: about 2½ dozen

- ½ cup butter, softened
- ⅔ cup sugar
- 1 large egg, separated, room temperature
- 2 Tbsp. 2% milk
- 1 tsp. vanilla extract
- 1 cup all-purpose flour
- ⅓ cup baking cocoa
- ¼ tsp. salt
- 1 cup finely chopped walnuts

FILLING

- ½ cup confectioners' sugar
- 1 Tbsp. butter, softened
- 2 tsp. 2% milk
- ¼ tsp. vanilla extract
- 24 milk chocolate kisses

1. In a large bowl, cream butter and sugar until light and fluffy, 5-7 minutes. Beat in the egg yolk, milk and vanilla. Combine the flour, cocoa and salt; gradually add to creamed mixture and mix well. Cover and refrigerate until easy to handle, about 1 hour.

2. Preheat oven to 350°. In a small bowl, whisk egg white until foamy. Shape dough into 1-in. balls; dip in egg white, then roll in nuts. Place on greased baking sheets. Using a wooden spoon handle, make an indentation in center of each cookie. Bake until center is set, 10-12 minutes.

3. For filling, combine the confectioners' sugar, butter, milk and vanilla; stir until smooth. Spoon or pipe ¼ tsp. into each warm cookie; gently press a chocolate kiss in the center. Carefully remove from pans to wire racks to cool.

1 COOKIE: 117 cal., 7g fat (3g sat. fat), 16mg chol., 52mg sod., 13g carb. (8g sugars, 1g fiber), 2g pro.

CRACK-FREE COOKIES
Use a gentle touch when imprinting the cookies with your thumb or a spoon to prevent the dough from cracking. If you still get a crack, gently reshape the dough by pressing it toward the center. Because these cookies get a coating of chopped nuts, most cracks will likely go unnoticed.

RHUBARB CRUMBLE

To tell you the truth, I'm not sure how well my crumble keeps—we usually eat it all in a day! You can make this with all rhubarb, but the apples and strawberries make this dessert extra good.
—*Linda Enslen, Schuler, AB*

Prep: 20 min. • **Bake:** 40 min.
Makes: 8 servings

    3 cups sliced fresh or frozen rhubarb
       (½-in. pieces)
    1 cup diced peeled apples
    ½ to 1 cup sliced strawberries
    ⅓ cup sugar
    ½ tsp. ground cinnamon
    ½ cup all-purpose flour
    1 tsp. baking powder
    ¼ tsp. salt
    4 Tbsp. cold butter
    ⅔ cup packed brown sugar
    ⅔ cup quick-cooking oats
       Vanilla ice cream, optional

1. Preheat oven to 350°. Combine rhubarb, apples and strawberries; spoon into a greased 8-in. square baking dish. Combine sugar and cinnamon; sprinkle over rhubarb mixture. Set aside.
2. In a bowl, combine flour, baking powder and salt. Cut in butter until mixture resembles coarse crumbs. Stir in brown sugar and oats. Sprinkle over rhubarb mixture.
3. Bake at 350° for 40-50 minutes or until lightly browned. Serve warm or cold, with a scoop of ice cream if desired.
1 SERVING: 227 cal., 6g fat (4g sat. fat), 15mg chol., 191mg sod., 41g carb. (29g sugars, 2g fiber), 2g pro.

DIPPED CHERRY COOKIES

Our children and grandchildren declared this festive, flavorful cookie a keeper. We gave a batch to our mail carrier to thank her for trudging through so much snow, and she requested the recipe.
—*Ruth Anne Dale, Titusville, PA*

Prep: 30 min.
Bake: 10 min./batch + standing
Makes: about 4 dozen

    2½ cups all-purpose flour
    ¾ cup sugar, divided
    1 cup cold butter, cubed
    ½ cup finely chopped maraschino
       cherries, patted dry
    12 oz. white baking chocolate,
       finely chopped, divided
    ½ tsp. almond extract
    2 tsp. shortening
       Coarse clear and red sugars

1. In a large bowl, combine flour and ½ cup sugar; cut in butter until crumbly. Knead in cherries, ⅔ cup white chocolate and the extract until dough forms a ball.
2. Shape into ¾-in. balls. Place 2 in. apart on ungreased baking sheets. Flatten slightly with a glass dipped in remaining ¼ cup sugar. Bake at 325° for 10-12 minutes or until edges are lightly browned. Remove to wire racks to cool completely.
3. In a microwave, melt shortening and the remaining white chocolate; stir until smooth.
4. Dip half of each cookie into chocolate; allow excess to drip off. Place on waxed paper; sprinkle with coarse sugar and edible glitter. Let stand until set. Store in an airtight container.
1 COOKIE: 108 cal., 6g fat (4g sat. fat), 11mg chol., 34mg sod., 12g carb. (7g sugars, 0 fiber), 1g pro.

KEY LIME CREAM PIE

I am very proud of this luscious no-bake beauty. It's so cool and refreshing—perfect for any summer potluck or get-together. Wherever I take this pie, it quickly disappears, with everyone asking for the recipe.
—*Shirley Rickis, The Villages, FL*

Prep: 40 min. + chilling
Makes: 12 servings

- 1 pkg. (11.3 oz.) pecan shortbread cookies, crushed (about 2 cups)
- ⅓ cup butter, melted
- 4 cups heavy whipping cream
- ¼ cup confectioners' sugar
- 1 tsp. coconut extract
- 1 pkg. (8 oz.) cream cheese, softened
- 1 can (14 oz.) sweetened condensed milk
- ½ cup Key lime juice
- ¼ cup sweetened shredded coconut, toasted
   Sliced Key limes, optional

1. In a small bowl, mix crushed cookies and butter. Press onto bottom and up side of a greased 9-in. deep-dish pie plate. In a large bowl, beat cream until it begins to thicken. Add confectioners' sugar and extract; beat until stiff peaks form. In another large bowl, beat cream cheese, condensed milk and lime juice until blended. Fold in 2 cups whipped cream. Spoon into prepared crust.
2. Top with remaining whipped cream and toasted coconut. Refrigerate until serving, at least 4 hours. If desired, garnish with sliced Key limes.
1 PIECE: 646 cal., 52g fat (30g sat. fat), 143mg chol., 252mg sod., 41g carb. (29g sugars, 0 fiber), 8g pro.

MILE-HIGH PIE
If you're looking for a gorgeous bakery-level pie for a special occasion, this is the one.

FLUFFY RAISIN PUMPKIN BARS

Chocolate-covered raisins are a fun surprise inside these pumpkin bars.
—*Margaret Wilson, San Bernardino, CA*

Prep: 20 min. • **Bake:** 25 min. + cooling
Makes: 4 dozen

- 2 cups sugar
- ¾ cup vegetable oil
- 4 large eggs, room temperature
- 2 cups canned pumpkin
- 2 cups all-purpose flour
- 2 tsp. baking powder
- 1 tsp. baking soda
- 1 tsp. ground cinnamon
- 1 tsp. ground nutmeg
- ½ tsp. ground ginger
- ¼ tsp. ground cloves
- 1 cup chopped walnuts
- 1 cup chocolate-covered raisins for baking

FROSTING
- ⅓ cup butter, softened
- 3 oz. cream cheese, softened
- 2 cups confectioners' sugar
- 1 Tbsp. 2% milk
- 1 tsp. orange extract

1. In a large bowl, beat sugar and oil. Add eggs, 1 at a time, beating well after each addition. Add pumpkin; mix well. Combine the flour, baking powder, baking soda and spices; gradually add to the pumpkin mixture. Stir in walnuts and chocolate-covered raisins.
2. Pour into a greased 15x10x1-in. baking pan. Bake at 350° for 25-30 minutes or until a toothpick inserted in the center comes out clean. Cool on a wire rack.
3. For frosting, in a large bowl, cream the butter, cream cheese and confectioners' sugar. Add milk and orange extract; beat until smooth. Frost bars. Sprinkle with additional cinnamon if desired. Cut into bars. Store in the refrigerator.
1 PIECE: 162 cal., 8g fat (2g sat. fat), 23mg chol., 67mg sod., 21g carb. (15g sugars, 1g fiber), 2g pro.

MOIST CHOCOLATE CAKE

The cake reminds me of my grandma because it was her specialty. I bake it for family parties, and the fond memories come flooding back for everyone. This layered dessert is light and airy but with a decadent chocolate taste.
—*Patricia Kreitz, Richland, PA*

Prep: 15 min. • **Bake:** 25 min. + cooling
Makes: 16 servings

- 2 **cups all-purpose flour**
- 2 **cups sugar**
- 2 **tsp. baking soda**
- ¾ **cup baking cocoa**
- 1 **tsp. salt**
- 1 **tsp. baking powder**
- 1 **cup canola oil**
- 1 **cup brewed coffee**
- 1 **cup whole milk**
- 2 **large eggs, room temperature**
- 1 **tsp. vanilla extract**

FAVORITE ICING
- 5 **Tbsp. all-purpose flour**
- 1 **cup whole milk**
- ½ **cup butter, softened**
- ½ **cup shortening**
- 1 **cup sugar**
- 1 **tsp. vanilla extract**
- 2 **to 4 Tbsp. sprinkles, optional**

1. Preheat oven to 325°. Grease and flour two 9-in. round baking pans. Sift dry ingredients together into a large bowl. Add oil, coffee and milk; mix at medium speed 1 minute. Add eggs and vanilla; beat 2 minutes longer. (Batter will be thin.) Pour into prepared pans.
2. Bake until a toothpick inserted in the center comes out clean, 25-30 minutes. Cool in pans 10 minutes before removing to wire racks to cool completely.
3. Meanwhile, for icing, in a small saucepan, whisk flour and milk until smooth. Bring to a boil over medium heat; cook and stir until thickened, 1-2 minutes. Transfer to a small bowl. Cover and refrigerate until chilled.

4. In a large bowl, beat butter, shortening, sugar and vanilla until creamy, 3-4 minutes. Add chilled milk mixture and beat 10 minutes. Stir in sprinkles if desired. Spread frosting between layers and over the top and sides of cake.
1 PIECE: 482 cal., 28g fat (7g sat. fat), 42mg chol., 404mg sod., 55g carb. (39g sugars, 1g fiber), 4g pro.

MAKE AHEAD
BERRIES IN CHAMPAGNE JELLY

My sister gave me this recipe a few years back when I was looking for an elegant fruit dish to serve guests. A refreshing alternative to salad, it's also sparkly—and special enough to double as a light dessert.
—*Andrea Barnhoom, Scottsville, NY*

Prep: 40 min. • **Cook:** 10 min. + chilling
Makes: 12 servings

- 4 **envelopes unflavored gelatin**
- 2 **cups cold water**
- 1½ **cups sugar**
- 4 **cups champagne**
- 2 **cups sparkling grape juice**
- 3 **cups fresh raspberries**
- 3 **cups fresh blueberries**
- 2 **cups fresh blackberries**

1. In a large saucepan, sprinkle gelatin over cold water; let stand 2 minutes. Add sugar. Cook and stir over medium-low heat until gelatin and sugar are dissolved (do not boil). Remove from heat. Slowly stir in champagne and grape juice.
2. Transfer to a 13x9-in. dish coated with cooking spray. Refrigerate, covered, for 8 hours or overnight. Using a potato masher, gently break up champagne jelly. Layer jelly and berries in 12 dessert dishes. Refrigerate, covered, for at least 2 hours before serving.
1⅓ CUPS: 218 cal., 0 fat (0 sat. fat), 0 chol., 6mg sod., 44g carb. (38g sugars, 4g fiber), 2g pro.

PEACH BAVARIAN

Fruit molds are my specialty. This one, with its refreshing peach taste, makes a colorful dessert.
—*Adeline Piscitelli, Sayreville, NJ*

Prep: 15 min. + chilling
Makes: 8 servings

- 1   can (15¼ oz.) sliced peaches
- 2   pkg. (3 oz. each) peach or apricot gelatin
- ½   cup sugar
- 2   cups boiling water
- 1   tsp. almond extract
- 1   carton (8 oz.) frozen whipped topping, thawed
      Sliced fresh peaches, optional

1. Drain peaches, reserving ⅔ cup juice. Chop peaches into small pieces.
2. In a large bowl, dissolve gelatin and sugar in the boiling water. Stir in reserved juice. Chill until slightly thickened. Stir extract into whipped topping; gently fold into gelatin mixture. Fold in peaches.
3. Pour into an oiled 6-cup mold. Chill overnight. Unmold onto a serving platter; garnish with peaches if desired.
1 SERVING: 249 cal., 5g fat (5g sat. fat), 0 chol., 53mg sod., 47g carb. (47g sugars, 0 fiber), 2g pro.

PEANUT BUTTER COOKIES

These simple cookies have so much flavor. I make them often because I always have the ingredients on hand. It's nice that the recipe makes a little batch.
—*Maggie Schimmel, Wauwatosa, WI*

Takes: 30 min. • **Makes:** 2 dozen

- 1   large egg, room temperature, beaten
- 1   cup sugar
- 1   cup creamy peanut butter

1. In a large bowl, mix all ingredients. Scoop by level tablespoonfuls and roll into balls. Place on ungreased baking sheets and flatten with a fork.
2. Bake at 350° until set, about 18 minutes. Remove to wire racks to cool.
1 COOKIE: 99 cal., 6g fat (1g sat. fat), 8mg chol., 48mg sod., 11g carb. (10g sugars, 1g fiber), 3g pro.

NO-BAKE CEREAL BARS

With crisp rice cereal and peanut butter, these bars taste almost like candy.
—*Pauline Christiansen, Columbus, KS*

Takes: 20 min. • **Makes:** about 10 dozen

- 2   cups sugar
- 2   cups corn syrup
- 1   jar (40 oz.) chunky peanut butter
- 6   cups Cheerios oat cereal
- 6   cups Chex crisp rice cereal

In a large saucepan, cook and stir sugar and corn syrup until the sugar is dissolved. Remove from the heat. Add peanut butter; mix well. Stir in cereals. Spread quickly into 2 lightly greased 15x10x1-in. pans. Cut into bars while warm.
1 SERVING: 95 cal., 5g fat (1g sat. fat), 0 chol., 79mg sod., 12g carb. (7g sugars, 1g fiber), 3g pro.

ICE CREAM COOKIE DESSERT

Our family loves dessert, and this chocolaty, layered treat is one of Mom's most requested recipes and it's so easy to prepare.

—*Kimberly Laabs, Hartford, WI*

Prep: 15 min. + freezing
Makes: 12 servings

- 1 pkg. (15½ oz.) Oreo cookies, crushed, divided
- ¼ cup butter, melted
- ½ gallon vanilla ice cream, softened
- 1 jar (16 oz.) hot fudge ice cream topping, warmed
- 1 carton (8 oz.) frozen whipped topping, thawed

1. In a large bowl, combine 3¾ cups cookie crumbs and butter. Press into a greased 13x9-in. dish. Spread with ice cream; cover and freeze until set.
2. Drizzle fudge topping over ice cream; cover and freeze until set. Spread with whipped topping; sprinkle with the remaining cookie crumbs. Cover and freeze 2 hours or until firm. Remove from freezer 10 minutes before serving.
1 PIECE: 573 cal., 27g fat (14g sat. fat), 49mg chol., 353mg sod., 76g carb. (46g sugars, 2g fiber), 6g pro.

COCONUT EGG NESTS

Looking for an Easter treat that kids will devour? Try these sweet birds' nest cookies. They're a snap to make and call for just a few ingredients.
—*Tonya Hamrick, Wallace, WV*

Takes: 20 min. • **Makes:** 1 dozen

- 6 oz. white candy coating, coarsely chopped
- 6 drops green food coloring
- 1 drop yellow food coloring
- 1 cup sweetened shredded coconut
- 36 jelly beans

In a microwave, melt candy coating; stir in food coloring until blended. Stir in coconut. Drop by tablespoonfuls onto waxed paper into 12 mounds. Make an indentation in the center of each with the end of a wooden spoon handle. Fill each with 3 jelly beans. Let stand until set.

1 SERVING: 127 cal., 7g fat (6g sat. fat), 0 chol., 22mg sod., 17g carb. (15g sugars, 0 fiber), 0 pro.

★ ★ ★ ★ ★ **READER REVIEW**

"Fabulous tasting and incredibly easy. I used white chocolate chips in place of candy coating (couldn't find it) and Cadbury mini eggs instead of jelly beans. I will repeat this every year. Yum!"

SONGLOVER1 TASTEOFHOME.COM

APPLE PIE TARTLETS

Sweet and cinnamony, these apple-pie morsels are a delightful addition to a dessert buffet or snack tray. You can prebake the shells a day or two in advance.
—*Mary Kelley, Minneapolis, MN*

Prep: 35 min. + cooling
Makes: 20 servings

- 1 sheet refrigerated pie crust
- 1 Tbsp. sugar
  Dash ground cinnamon
  FILLING
- 2 tsp. butter
- 2 cups diced peeled tart apples
- 3 Tbsp. sugar
- 3 Tbsp. fat-free caramel ice cream topping
- 2 Tbsp. all-purpose flour
- ½ tsp. ground cinnamon
- ½ tsp. lemon juice
- ⅛ tsp. salt

1. Preheat oven to 350°. On a lightly floured surface, roll out crust; cut into twenty 2½-in. circles. Press onto the bottom and up the sides of miniature muffin cups coated with cooking spray. Prick crusts with a fork. Spray lightly with cooking spray. Combine sugar and cinnamon; sprinkle over crusts.
2. Bake until golden brown, 6-8 minutes. Cool for 5 minutes before removing from pans to wire racks.
3. In a large saucepan, melt butter. Add apples; cook and stir over medium heat until crisp-tender, 4-5 minutes. Stir in sugar, caramel topping, flour, cinnamon, lemon juice and salt. Bring to a boil; cook and stir until sauce is thickened and apples are tender, about 2 minutes. Cool for 5 minutes. Spoon into tart shells.
1 PIECE: 74 cal., 3g fat (1g sat. fat), 3mg chol., 62mg sod., 11g carb. (5g sugars, 0 fiber), 1g pro.

MAKE AHEAD
POTLUCK PUMPKIN TORTE

A local newspaper featured this potluck-friendly recipe years ago. A creamy alternative to pumpkin pie, it quickly became one of my favorites.
—*Peggy Shea, Lowell, IN*

Prep: 30 min. • **Bake:** 25 min. + chilling
Makes: 15 servings

- 1⅔ cups graham cracker crumbs
- ⅓ cup sugar
- ½ cup butter, melted
  CREAM CHEESE FILLING
- 2 pkg. (8 oz. each) cream cheese, softened
- ¾ cup sugar
- 2 large eggs
  PUMPKIN FILLING
- 2 envelopes unflavored gelatin
- ½ cup cold water
- 1 can (30 oz.) pumpkin pie filling
- 1 can (5½ oz.) evaporated milk
- 2 large eggs, lightly beaten
  TOPPING
- 1 carton (12 oz.) frozen whipped topping, thawed

1. Preheat oven to 350°. In a small bowl, combine the crumbs, sugar and butter. Press onto the bottom of an ungreased 13x9-in. baking dish; set aside. In a large bowl, beat cream cheese and sugar until smooth. Add eggs; beat on low speed just until combined. Pour over crust. Bake until the center is almost set, 25-30 minutes.
2. Meanwhile, in a small bowl, sprinkle gelatin over cold water; let stand for 1 minute. In a large saucepan, combine pie filling and evaporated milk. Bring to a boil. Add gelatin; stir until dissolved. Whisk a small amount of hot mixture into the eggs. Return all to the pan, whisking constantly.
3. Cook and stir over low heat until mixture is thickened and coats the back of a spoon. Cool for 10 minutes. Spread over cream cheese layer. Spread whipped topping over top. Cover and refrigerate overnight.
1 PIECE: 413 cal., 24g fat (15g sat. fat), 109mg chol., 296mg sod., 42g carb. (32g sugars, 2g fiber), 7g pro.

CHOCOLATE-COVERED STRAWBERRY COBBLER

This cobbler came about because I love chocolate-covered strawberries. Top it with whipped cream, either plain or with a little chocolate syrup stirred in.
—*Andrea Bolden, Unionville, TN*

Prep: 15 min. • **Bake:** 35 min. + standing
Makes: 12 servings

- 1 cup butter, cubed
- 1½ cups self-rising flour
- 2¼ cups sugar, divided
- ¾ cup 2% milk
- 1 tsp. vanilla extract
- ⅓ cup baking cocoa
- 4 cups fresh strawberries, quartered
- 2 cups boiling water
  Whipped cream and additional strawberries

1. Preheat oven to 350°. Place butter in a 13x9-in. baking pan; heat pan in oven 3-5 minutes or until butter is melted. Meanwhile, in a large bowl, combine flour, 1¼ cups sugar, milk and vanilla until well blended. In a small bowl, mix cocoa and remaining sugar.
2. Remove baking pan from oven; add batter. Sprinkle with strawberries and cocoa mixture; pour boiling water evenly over top (do not stir). Bake 35-40 minutes or until a toothpick inserted into cake portion comes out clean. Let stand for 10 minutes. Serve warm, with whipped cream and additional strawberries.
1 SERVING: 368 cal., 16g fat (10g sat. fat), 42mg chol., 316mg sod., 55g carb. (41g sugars, 2g fiber), 3g pro.

CHOCOLATE ZUCCHINI BREAD

I shred and freeze zucchini from my garden each summer so that I can make this bread all winter long. Our family loves this chocolaty treat.
—*Shari McKinney, Birney, MT*

Prep: 15 min. • **Bake:** 50 min. + cooling
Makes: 2 loaves (12 pieces each)

- 2 cups sugar
- 1 cup canola oil
- 3 large eggs, room temperature
- 3 tsp. vanilla extract
- 2½ cups all-purpose flour
- ½ cup baking cocoa
- 1 tsp. salt
- 1 tsp. baking soda
- 1 tsp. ground cinnamon
- ¼ tsp. baking powder
- 2 cups shredded peeled zucchini

1. In a large bowl, beat the sugar, oil, eggs and vanilla until well blended. Combine the flour, cocoa, salt, baking soda, cinnamon and baking powder; gradually beat into sugar mixture until blended. Stir in zucchini. Transfer to 2 greased 8x4-in. loaf pans.

2. Bake at 350° for 50-55 minutes or until a toothpick inserted in the center comes out clean. Cool for 10 minutes before removing from pans to wire racks to cool completely.

1 PIECE: 209 cal., 10g fat (1g sat. fat), 26mg chol., 165mg sod., 28g carb. (17g sugars, 1g fiber), 3g pro.

MINT SUNDAE BROWNIE SQUARES

I love brownies, and this recipe makes a luscious, after-dinner dessert that's so scrumptious.
—*Edie DeSpain, Logan, UT*

- -

Prep: 20 min. + freezing
Bake: 25 min. + cooling
Makes: 15 servings

- 1 pkg. fudge brownie mix (13x9-in. pan size)
- ¾ cup chopped walnuts
- 1 can (14 oz.) sweetened condensed milk
- 2 tsp. peppermint extract
- 4 drops green food coloring, optional
- 2 cups heavy whipping cream, whipped
- ½ cup miniature semisweet chocolate chips
- 1 jar (16 oz.) hot fudge ice cream topping, warmed
- ⅓ cup chopped salted peanuts

1. Prepare brownie mix according to package directions. Stir in walnuts.
2. Pour into a greased 13x9-in. baking pan. Bake at 325° for 23-27 minutes or until a toothpick inserted in the center comes out clean (do not overbake). Cool on a wire rack.
3. Meanwhile, in a large bowl, combine the milk, extract and food coloring if desired. Fold in whipped cream and chocolate chips. Spread over brownie layer. Cover and freeze for several hours or overnight.
4. Let stand at room temperature for 10 minutes before cutting. Drizzle with ice cream topping; sprinkle with peanuts.
1 PIECE: 579 cal., 31g fat (9g sat. fat), 60mg chol., 247mg sod., 68g carb. (47g sugars, 3g fiber), 9g pro.

MAGIC BARS

These rich bar cookies will melt in your mouth! They're ideal to have on hand for a snack.
—*Pauline Schrag, Theresa, NY*

- -

Prep: 15 min. • **Bake:** 30 min. + cooling
Makes: 16 bars

- ½ cup butter, cubed
- 1 cup graham cracker crumbs
- 1 cup sweetened shredded coconut
- 1 cup semisweet chocolate chips
- 1 cup chopped nuts
- 1 can (14 oz.) sweetened condensed milk

Preheat oven to 350°. Melt butter in a 9-in. square baking pan. On top of melted butter, sprinkle crumbs, then coconut, then chocolate chips, then nuts. Pour milk over all. Do not stir. Bake until a toothpick inserted in center comes out clean, about 30 minutes. Cool several hours before cutting.
1 BAR: 279 cal., 18g fat (9g sat. fat), 24mg chol., 138mg sod., 28g carb. (22g sugars, 1g fiber), 5g pro.

★ ★ ★ ★ ★ **READER REVIEW**

"These bars go over really well at potlucks, and I cut them into smaller bars so more people can try them. Always an empty pan to bring home."
CATHY143 TASTEOFHOME.COM

LUSCIOUS LIME ANGEL SQUARES

A creamy lime topping turns angel food cake into these yummy squares that are perfect for potlucks or picnics. You can eat a piece of this light and airy dessert without feeling one bit guilty. I adapted this luscious treat from another recipe. It is super easy to make.
—Beverly Marshall, Orting, WA

Prep: 15 min. + chilling
Makes: 15 servings

- 1 pkg. (3 oz.) lime gelatin
- 1 cup boiling water
- 1 prepared angel food cake (8 in.), cut into 1-in. cubes
- 1 pkg. (8 oz.) cream cheese, softened
- ½ cup sugar
- 2 tsp. lemon juice
- 1½ tsp. grated lemon zest
- 1 carton (8 oz.) frozen whipped topping, thawed (4½ cups)

1. In a small bowl, dissolve gelatin in boiling water. Refrigerate until mixture just begins to thicken, about 35 minutes. Place angel food cake cubes in a greased 13x9-in. dish.
2. In a small bowl, beat cream cheese until smooth. Beat in the sugar, lemon juice and zest. Add gelatin mixture; beat until combined. Fold in 1½ cups whipped topping.
3. Spread over top of cake, covering completely. Refrigerate for at least 2 hours or until firm. Cut into squares; top with remaining whipped topping.
1 PIECE: 147 cal., 8g fat (6g sat. fat), 15mg chol., 74mg sod., 17g carb. (16g sugars, 0 fiber), 2g pro.

MAKE AHEAD
CREAMY CARAMEL FLAN

A small slice of this impressively rich, creamy treat goes a long way. What a delightful finish for a special meal or holiday celebration.
—Pat Forete, Miami, FL

Prep: 25 min. + standing
Bake: 50 min. + chilling
Makes: 10 servings

- ¾ cup sugar
- ¼ cup water
- 1 pkg. (8 oz.) cream cheese, softened
- 5 large eggs, room temperature
- 1 can (14 oz.) sweetened condensed milk
- 1 can (12 oz.) evaporated milk
- 1 tsp. vanilla extract

1. In a heavy saucepan, cook sugar and water over medium-low heat until melted and golden, about 15 minutes. Brush down crystals on the side of the pan with additional water as necessary. Quickly pour into an ungreased 2-qt. round baking or souffle dish, tilting to coat the bottom; let stand for 10 minutes.
2. Preheat oven to 350°. In a bowl, beat the cream cheese until smooth. Beat in eggs, 1 at a time, until thoroughly combined. Add remaining ingredients; mix well. Pour over caramelized sugar.
3. Place the dish in a larger baking pan. Pour boiling water into larger pan to a depth of 1 in. Bake until the center is just set (mixture will jiggle), 50-60 minutes.
4. Remove dish from a larger pan to a wire rack; cool for 1 hour. Refrigerate overnight.
5. To unmold, run a knife around edge and invert onto a large rimmed serving platter. Cut into wedges or spoon onto dessert plates; spoon the sauce over each serving.
1 PIECE: 345 cal., 16g fat (9g sat. fat), 140mg chol., 189mg sod., 41g carb. (41g sugars, 0 fiber), 10g pro.

BRING IT
Don't take chances! To ensure this gorgeous flan arrives intact, transport it in its baking dish along with a serving platter, knife, paper towels and pie server. Unmold the flan on-site, then cut. Wipe the knife with paper towels as you go for clean, pretty slices. Then hide the dishes away until it's time to retrieve your pie server and empty platter.

HEAVENLY FILLED STRAWBERRIES

These luscious stuffed berries are the perfect bite-sized dessert.
—Stephen Munro, Beaverbank, NS

Takes: 20 min. • Makes: 3 dozen

- 3 dozen large fresh strawberries
- 11 oz. cream cheese, softened
- ½ cup confectioners' sugar
- ¼ tsp. almond extract
  Grated chocolate, optional

1. Remove stems from strawberries; cut a deep "X" in the tip of each berry. Gently spread berries open.

2. In a small bowl, beat the cream cheese, confectioners' sugar and extract until light and fluffy. Pipe or spoon about 2 tsp. into each berry; if desired, sprinkle with chocolate. Chill until serving.

1 SERVING: 41 cal., 3g fat (2g sat. fat), 10mg chol., 26mg sod., 3g carb. (2g sugars, 0 fiber), 1g pro.

★ ★ ★ ★ ★ READER REVIEW

"A delightful dessert for a warm summer day. Cool and refreshing end to a meal. Not overly sweet."

GRACIE56 TASTEOFHOME.COM

POTLUCK BANANA CAKE

I found this recipe more than five years ago and have been making it for family gatherings ever since. The coffee-flavored frosting complements the moist banana cake.
—Kathy Hoffman, Topton, PA

Prep: 25 min. • Bake: 35 min. + cooling
Makes: 15 servings

- ½ cup butter, softened
- 1 cup sugar
- 2 large eggs, room temperature
- 1 tsp. vanilla extract
- 2 cups all-purpose flour
- 2 tsp. baking soda
- ½ tsp. salt
- 1½ cups mashed ripe bananas (about 3 medium)
- 1 cup sour cream

COFFEE FROSTING
- ⅓ cup butter, softened
- 2½ cups confectioners' sugar
- 2 tsp. instant coffee granules
- 2 to 3 Tbsp. 2% milk

1. Preheat oven to 350°. In a large bowl, cream butter and sugar until light and fluffy, 5-7 minutes. Add eggs, 1 at a time, beating well after each addition. Stir in vanilla. Combine flour, baking soda and salt; add to creamed mixture alternately with bananas and sour cream, beating well after each addition.

2. Pour into a greased 13x9-in. baking dish. Bake until a toothpick inserted in center comes out clean, 35-40 minutes. Cool completely on a wire rack.

3. For frosting, in a small bowl, beat butter and confectioners' sugar until smooth. Dissolve coffee granules in milk; add to butter mixture and beat until smooth. Spread over cake. Sprinkle with additional instant coffee, if desired.

1 PIECE: 344 cal., 14g fat (8g sat. fat), 67mg chol., 368mg sod., 52g carb. (37g sugars, 1g fiber), 4g pro.

GLAZED APPLE PIE BARS

This is only one of many wonderful recipes that my mother handed down to me. With their flaky crust and scrumptious fruit filling, these delicious bars are the perfect way to serve apple pie to a crowd.

—*Janet English, Pittsburgh, PA*

Prep: 30 min. • **Bake:** 45 min. + cooling
Makes: 2 dozen

- 4 cups all-purpose flour
- 1 tsp. salt
- 1 tsp. baking powder
- 1 cup shortening
- 4 large egg yolks
- 2 Tbsp. lemon juice
- 8 to 10 Tbsp. cold water

FILLING
- 7 cups finely chopped peeled apples
- 2 cups sugar
- ¼ cup all-purpose flour
- 2 tsp. ground cinnamon
  Dash ground nutmeg

GLAZE
- 1 cup confectioners' sugar
- 1 Tbsp. 2% milk
- 1 Tbsp. lemon juice

1. In a large bowl, combine flour, salt and baking powder. Cut in shortening until mixture resembles coarse crumbs. In a small bowl, whisk egg yolks, lemon juice and water; gradually add to flour mixture, tossing with a fork until dough forms a ball. Divide in half. Chill for 30 minutes.

2. Roll out 1 portion of dough between 2 large sheets of waxed paper into a 17x12-in. rectangle. Transfer to an ungreased 15x10x1-in. baking pan. Press dough onto bottom and up sides of pan; trim even with top edge.

3. In a large bowl, toss the apples, sugar, flour, cinnamon and nutmeg; spread into crust. Roll out remaining dough to fit top of pan; place over filling. Brush edges with water or milk; pinch to seal. Cut slits in top.

4. Bake at 375° for 45-50 minutes or until golden brown. Cool on a wire rack. Combine glaze ingredients until smooth; drizzle over bars.

1 BAR: 264 cal., 9g fat (2g sat. fat), 31mg chol., 121mg sod., 43g carb. (25g sugars, 1g fiber), 3g pro.

ROSE WATER RICE PUDDING

Rose water rice pudding is a popular Middle Eastern treat. Pomegranate seeds and chopped pistachios add a simple yet elegant touch to this floral Lebanese specialty.
—*Michael & Mathil Chebat, Lake Ridge, VA*

Prep: 10 min. • **Cook:** 45 min. + chilling
Makes: 14 servings

- 4 cups water
- 2 cups uncooked long grain rice
- 4 cups half-and-half cream
- 1½ cups sugar
- 1 to 2 tsp. rose water
  Optional: Pomegranate seeds and chopped pistachios

In a heavy saucepan, combine water and rice; bring to a boil over medium heat. Reduce heat; cover and simmer until water is absorbed, about 15 minutes. Add cream and sugar; bring to a boil. Reduce heat; simmer, uncovered, until slightly thickened, 30-40 minutes. Stir in rose water. Refrigerate until chilled, at least 2 hours. Stir in additional cream to reach desired consistency. If desired, top with pomegranate seeds and pistachios.
½ CUP: 281 cal., 7g fat (5g sat. fat), 34mg chol., 35mg sod., 47g carb. (24g sugars, 0 fiber), 4g pro.

BEST DATE BARS

These wholesome bar cookies freeze well. Simply cool them in the pan, cut them into squares and then store them in freezer containers.
—*Dorothy DeLeske, Scottsdale, AZ*

Prep: 25 min. • **Bake:** 35 min.
Makes: 40 bars

- 2½ cups pitted dates, cut up
- ¼ cup sugar
- 1½ cups water
- ⅓ cup coarsely chopped walnuts, optional
- 1¼ cups all-purpose flour
- ½ tsp. salt
- ½ tsp. baking soda
- 1½ cups quick-cooking oats
- 1 cup packed brown sugar
- ½ cup butter, softened
- 1 Tbsp. water

1. In a saucepan, combine the dates, sugar and water. Cook, stirring frequently, until very thick. Stir in walnuts, if desired; cool.
2. Sift the flour, salt and baking soda together in a large bowl; add oats and brown sugar. Cut in butter until mixture is crumbly. Sprinkle water over mixture; stir lightly. Pat half into a greased 13x9-in. baking pan. Spread with date mixture; cover with remaining oat mixture and pat lightly.
3. Bake at 350° for 35-40 minutes or until lightly browned. Cool on a wire rack. Cut into bars.
1 BAR: 97 cal., 3g fat (2g sat. fat), 6mg chol., 65mg sod., 19g carb. (12g sugars, 1g fiber), 1g pro.

TRADITIONAL CHEESECAKE

Here's a basic cheesecake that tastes great alone or with any number of toppings.
—Taste of Home *Test Kitchen*

Prep: 20 min. • **Bake:** 55 min. + chilling
Makes: 12 servings

- 1 cup graham cracker crumbs
- 1 Tbsp. sugar
- 3 Tbsp. cold butter

FILLING
- 4 pkg. (8 oz. each) cream cheese, softened
- 1¼ cups sugar
- 1 Tbsp. lemon juice
- 2 tsp. vanilla extract
- 3 large eggs, room temperature, lightly beaten
  Raspberry sauce and fresh raspberries, optional

1. In a small bowl, combine cracker crumbs and sugar; cut in butter until crumbly. Grease the sides only of a 9-in. springform pan; press crumb mixture onto bottom of pan. Place on a baking sheet. Bake at 350° for 10 minutes. Cool on a wire rack.

2. In a large bowl, beat cream cheese and sugar until smooth. Beat in lemon juice and vanilla. Add eggs; beat on low speed just until combined. Pour filling onto crust. Return pan to baking sheet.

3. Bake at 350° until center is almost set, 45-55 minutes. Cool on a wire rack for 10 minutes. Carefully run a knife around the inside edge of pan to loosen; cool 1 hour longer.

4. Refrigerate overnight. Serve with raspberry sauce and fresh raspberries if desired. Refrigerate leftovers.

1 PIECE: 424 cal., 31g fat (19g sat. fat), 144mg chol., 311mg sod., 30g carb. (24g sugars, 0 fiber), 8g pro.

EASY BLUEBERRY PIE

I've been making this dessert for decades since blueberries are readily available in Michigan. Nothing says summer like a piece of fresh blueberry pie!
—Linda Kernan, Mason, MI

Prep: 15 min. + cooling
Makes: 6-8 servings

- 1 sheet refrigerated pie crust
- ¾ cup sugar
- 3 Tbsp. cornstarch
- ⅛ tsp. salt
- ¼ cup cold water
- 5 cups fresh blueberries, divided
- 1 Tbsp. butter
- 1 Tbsp. lemon juice

1. Preheat oven to 425°. On a floured surface, roll dough to fit a 9-in. pie plate. Trim and flute edge. Refrigerate 30 minutes. Line crust with a double thickness of foil. Fill with pie weights. Bake on a lower oven rack until golden brown, 20-25 minutes. Remove foil and weights; bake until bottom is golden brown, 3-6 minutes. Cool on a wire rack.

2. In a saucepan over medium heat, combine sugar, cornstarch, salt and water until smooth. Add 3 cups blueberries. Bring to a boil; cook and stir for 2 minutes or until thickened and bubbly.

3. Remove from the heat. Add butter, lemon juice and remaining 2 cups berries; stir until butter is melted. Cool. Pour into crust. Refrigerate until serving.

1 PIECE: 269 cal., 9g fat (4g sat. fat), 9mg chol., 150mg sod., 48g carb. (29g sugars, 2g fiber), 2g pro.

WATCH THE TIME
Cornstarch needs to boil just a few minutes to thicken the pie filling. If it cooks too long, the cornstarch will lose its thickening power. Carefully follow the recipe for the best results.

CHOCOLATE CHIP COOKIE DELIGHT

This is a simple chocolate dessert recipe for any type of potluck occasion, and the pan always comes home empty.
—*Diane Windley, Grace, ID*

Prep: 35 min. + chilling
Makes: 15 servings

- 1 tube (16½ oz.) refrigerated chocolate chip cookie dough
- 1 pkg. (8 oz.) cream cheese, softened
- 1 cup confectioners' sugar
- 1 carton (12 oz.) frozen whipped topping, thawed, divided
- 3 cups cold 2% milk
- 1 pkg. (3.9 oz.) instant chocolate pudding mix
- 1 pkg. (3.4 oz.) instant vanilla pudding mix
  Optional: Chopped nuts and miniature semisweet chocolate chips or chocolate curls

1. Let cookie dough stand at room temperature for 5-10 minutes to soften. Press into an ungreased 13x9-in. baking pan. Bake at 350° until golden brown, 14-16 minutes. Cool on a wire rack.
2. In a large bowl, beat cream cheese and confectioners' sugar until smooth. Fold in 1¾ cups whipped topping. Spread over crust.
3. In a large bowl, whisk milk and pudding mixes for 2 minutes. Spread over cream cheese layer. Top with remaining whipped topping. Sprinkle with nuts and miniature semisweet chocolate chips if desired.
4. Cover and refrigerate until firm, 8 hours or overnight.
1 PIECE: 365 cal., 17g fat (10g sat. fat), 29mg chol., 329mg sod., 47g carb. (22g sugars, 1g fiber), 4g pro.

CARAMEL HEAVENLIES

Before I cut these bars into triangles, I usually trim the edges so all the cookies look the same. My husband and daughter love this part because they get to eat the scraps.
—*Dawn Burns, Lake St. Louis, MO*

Prep: 20 min. • **Bake:** 15 min. + cooling
Makes: 3 dozen

- 12 whole graham crackers
- 2 cups miniature marshmallows
- ¾ cup butter, cubed
- ¾ cup packed brown sugar
- 1 tsp. ground cinnamon
- 1 tsp. vanilla extract
- 1 cup sliced almonds
- 1 cup sweetened shredded coconut

1. Preheat oven to 350°. Line a 15x10x1-in. baking pan with foil, letting foil extend over sides by 1 in.; lightly coat foil with cooking spray. Arrange the graham crackers in prepared pan; sprinkle with marshmallows.
2. In a small saucepan, combine butter, brown sugar and cinnamon; cook and stir over medium heat until butter is melted and sugar is dissolved. Remove from heat; stir in vanilla.
3. Spoon the butter mixture over marshmallows. Sprinkle with almonds and coconut. Bake until browned, 14-16 minutes. Cool completely in pan on a wire rack.
4. Using foil, lift out of pan. Cut into triangles; discard foil.
1 PIECE: 110 cal., 7g fat (3g sat. fat), 10mg chol., 68mg sod., 13g carb. (8g sugars, 1g fiber), 1g pro.

CLASSIC LEMON BARS

These bars are simple enough for no-fuss dinners yet elegant enough for special celebrations.
—*Melissa Mosness, Loveland, CO*

- -

Prep: 15 min. • **Bake:** 25 min. + cooling
Makes: 9 servings

- ½   cup butter, softened
- ¼   cup sugar
- 1   cup all-purpose flour

FILLING
- ¾   cup sugar
- 2   large eggs
- 3   Tbsp. lemon juice
- 2   Tbsp. all-purpose flour
- 1   tsp. grated lemon zest
- ¼   tsp. baking powder
   Confectioners' sugar

1. Preheat oven to 350°. In a small bowl, cream butter and sugar until light and fluffy, 5-7 minutes; gradually beat in flour until blended.
2. Press into an ungreased 8-in. square baking dish. Bake for 15-20 minutes or until edges are lightly browned.
3. For filling, in a small bowl, beat the sugar, eggs, lemon juice, flour, lemon zest and baking powder until frothy. Pour over crust.
4. Bake 10-15 minutes longer or until set and lightly browned. Cool on a wire rack. Sprinkle with confectioners' sugar. Cut into squares.
1 PIECE: 250 cal., 11g fat (7g sat. fat), 74mg chol., 99mg sod., 35g carb. (23g sugars, 0 fiber), 3g pro.

★ ★ ★ ★ ★ **READER REVIEW**

"Great bright, lemony taste, perfect filling-to-crust ratio, and not too sweet nor too tart. I did add a few drops of yellow food coloring to amp up the color."
KM1995 TASTEOFHOME.COM

CHERRY RHUBARB CRUNCH

My husband's grandmother gave me this recipe, along with a bundle of rhubarb, when we were first married. I had never cared for rhubarb, but after trying this dessert, I changed my mind. Now my children dig in, too!
—*Sharon Wasikowski, Middleville, MI*

- -

Prep: 20 min. • **Bake:** 40 min.
Makes: 15 servings

- 1   cup rolled oats
- 1   cup packed brown sugar
- 1   cup all-purpose flour
- ¼   tsp. salt
- ½   cup cold butter, cubed
- 4   cups diced rhubarb
- 1   cup sugar
- 2   Tbsp. cornstarch
- 1   cup water
- 1   tsp. almond extract
- 1   can (21 oz.) cherry pie filling
- ½   cup finely chopped walnuts
   Vanilla ice cream, optional

1. Preheat oven to 350°. In a large bowl, combine oats, brown sugar, flour and salt; stir well. Cut in butter until crumbly. Pat 2 cups mixture into a greased 13x9-in. baking dish; cover with rhubarb. Set aside remaining crumb mixture.
2. In a saucepan, combine sugar and cornstarch. Stir in water; cook until mixture is thickened and clear. Stir in extract and cherry filling; spoon over rhubarb. Combine nuts with reserved crumb mixture; sprinkle over cherries. Bake until filling is bubbly and topping is lightly browned, 40-45 minutes. If desired, serve with ice cream.
1 PIECE: 294 cal., 9g fat (4g sat. fat), 16mg chol., 116mg sod., 52g carb. (38g sugars, 2g fiber), 3g pro.

FUDGY BROWNIES WITH PEANUT BUTTER PUDDING FROSTING

Rich brownies are topped with a peanut butter pudding frosting to make this a recipe the whole family will love. These are perfect for a potluck, bake sale or yummy after-dinner treat.
—*Amy Crook, Syracuse, UT*

Prep: 20 min. • **Bake:** 25 min. + chilling
Makes: 2½ dozen

- 1 pkg. fudge brownie mix (13x9-in. pan size)
- 1½ cups confectioners' sugar
- ½ cup butter, softened
- 2 to 3 Tbsp. peanut butter
- 2 Tbsp. cold 2% milk
- 4½ tsp. instant vanilla pudding mix
- 1 can (16 oz.) chocolate fudge frosting

1. Prepare and bake the brownies according to package directions. Cool on a wire rack.
2. Meanwhile, in a small bowl, beat the confectioners' sugar, butter, peanut butter, milk and pudding mix until smooth. Spread over the brownies. Refrigerate for 30 minutes or until firm. Frost with chocolate frosting just before cutting.

1 BROWNIE: 236 cal., 12g fat (4g sat. fat), 23mg chol., 145mg sod., 31g carb. (23g sugars, 1g fiber), 2g pro.

★ ★ ★ ★ ★ **READER REVIEW**

"Chocolate and peanut butter—what's not to love! The recipe is so easy to make since it starts with a brownie mix and ends with a can of frosting."

TNBLUFFBAKER TASTEOFHOME.COM

OATMEAL CHOCOLATE CHIP PEANUT BUTTER BARS

Oatmeal, peanut butter and chocolate chips make these bars a big hit. Because I always have these basic ingredients on hand, I can whip up a batch anytime.
—*Patricia Staudt, Marble Rock, IA*

Prep: 15 min. • **Bake:** 20 min. + cooling
Makes: 4 dozen

- ½ cup butter, softened
- ½ cup sugar
- ½ cup packed brown sugar
- ½ cup creamy peanut butter
- 1 large egg, room temperature
- 1 tsp. vanilla extract
- 1 cup all-purpose flour
- ½ cup quick-cooking oats
- 1 tsp. baking soda
- ¼ tsp. salt
- 1 cup semisweet chocolate chips

ICING
- ½ cup confectioners' sugar
- 2 Tbsp. creamy peanut butter
- 2 Tbsp. milk

1. In a large bowl, cream the butter, sugars and peanut butter until light and fluffy. Beat in egg and vanilla. Combine the flour, oats, baking soda and salt; gradually beat into creamed mixture and mix well. Spread into a greased 13x9-in. baking pan. Sprinkle with chocolate chips.
2. Bake at 350° for 20-25 minutes or until lightly browned. Cool on a wire rack for 10 minutes.
3. Combine icing ingredients; drizzle over the top. Cool completely. Cut into bars.
1 BAR: 90 cal., 5g fat (2g sat. fat), 9mg chol., 71mg sod., 11g carb. (8g sugars, 1g fiber), 1g pro.

HOLIDAY CORNFLAKE COOKIES

I can't seem to make enough of these cornflake wreaths around the holidays. The cookies firm up quickly, so you'll need to place the Red Hots right away.
—*Kathleen Hedger, Godfrey, IL*

- -

Takes: 15 min. • **Makes:** 16 cookies

½ cup butter, cubed
40 large marshmallows
4 cups frosted cornflakes
 Red Hots
 Assorted sprinkles

1. In a 6-qt. stockpot, melt butter over medium heat. Add marshmallows; cook and stir until melted. Remove from heat.
2. Fold in cornflakes. Working quickly, fill 16 greased muffin cups two-thirds full. Using the end of a wooden spoon, make holes in centers to resemble wreaths. Decorate immediately with Red Hots and sprinkles.
1 COOKIE: 147 cal., 6g fat (4g sat. fat), 15mg chol., 109mg sod., 24g carb. (14g sugars, 0 fiber), 1g pro.

MAKE AHEAD

SHORTCUT TRES LECHES CAKE

My mom's favorite cake is tres leches, a butter cake soaked in three kinds of milk. I developed a no-fuss version that's rich and tender.
—*Marina Castle-Kelley, Canyon Country, CA*

- -

Prep: 20 min. + chilling
Bake: 30 min. + cooling
Makes: 20 servings

1 pkg. butter recipe golden cake or yellow cake mix (regular size)
3 large eggs, room temperature
⅔ cup 2% milk
½ cup butter, softened
1 tsp. vanilla extract
TOPPING
1 can (14 oz.) sweetened condensed milk
1 can (12 oz.) evaporated milk
1 cup heavy whipping cream
WHIPPED CREAM
1 cup heavy whipping cream
3 Tbsp. confectioners' sugar
1 tsp. vanilla extract

1. Preheat oven to 350°. Grease a 13x9-in. baking pan.
2. In a large bowl, combine cake mix, eggs, milk, softened butter and vanilla; beat on low speed 30 seconds. Beat on medium 2 minutes. Transfer to prepared pan. Bake 30-35 minutes or until a toothpick inserted in center comes out clean. Cool in pan on a wire rack 20 minutes.
3. In a 4-cup measuring cup, whisk topping ingredients until blended. Using a skewer, generously poke holes in top of warm cake. Pour milk mixture slowly over cake, filling holes. Cool 30 minutes longer. Refrigerate, covered, at least 4 hours or overnight.
4. In a bowl, beat cream until it begins to thicken. Add confectioners' sugar and vanilla; beat until soft peaks form. Spread over cake.
1 PIECE: 343 cal., 20g fat (12g sat. fat), 89mg chol., 257mg sod., 36g carb. (28g sugars, 0 fiber), 6g pro.

2. Preheat oven to 400°. Drain peaches, reserving juice. In a small saucepan, combine cornstarch, nutmeg, cinnamon and salt; gradually stir in the reserved juice. Bring to a boil; cook and stir until thickened, about 2 minutes. Remove from the heat; stir in lemon juice and butter. Gently fold in peaches. Pour into crust.

3. Roll remaining dough to a ⅛-in.-thick circle; cut into 1½-in.-wide strips. Arrange over filling in a lattice pattern. Trim and seal strips to edge of bottom crust; flute edge. Cover edge loosely with foil. Bake 40 minutes; remove foil. Bake until the crust is golden brown and filling is bubbly, 10-20 minutes longer. Cool on a wire rack. If desired, serve with ice cream.

DOUGH FOR DOUBLE-CRUST PIE: Combine 2½ cups all-purpose flour and ½ tsp. salt; cut in 1 cup cold butter until crumbly. Gradually add ⅓ to ⅔ cup ice water, tossing with a fork until dough holds together when pressed. Divide dough in half. Shape each portion into a disk; wrap and refrigerate 1 hour.

1 PIECE: 380 cal., 16g fat (7g sat. fat), 14mg chol., 254mg sod., 59g carb. (29g sugars, 2g fiber), 3g pro.

HOW TO PEEL PEACHES

Place peaches in a large pot of boiling water until the skins begin to split, 10-20 seconds. Remove with a slotted spoon and immediately place in ice water bath to cool peaches and stop their cooking. Use a paring knife to peel the skin, which should come right off. If stubborn spots remain, return fruit to the boiling water for a few more seconds.

PEACH PIE

I acquired this delicious peach pie filling recipe some 40 years ago, when my husband and I first moved to southern Iowa and had peach trees growing in our backyard. It's been a family favorite since then and it always brings back memories of both summer and those happy early years.
—June Mueller, Sioux City, IA

Prep: 35 min. + standing
Bake: 50 min. + cooling
Makes: 8 servings

½ cup sugar
¼ cup packed brown sugar
4½ cups sliced peeled peaches
   Dough for double-crust pie
3 Tbsp. cornstarch
¼ tsp. ground nutmeg
¼ tsp. ground cinnamon
⅛ tsp. salt
2 tsp. lemon juice
1 Tbsp. butter
   Vanilla ice cream, optional

1. In a large bowl, combine sugars; add peaches and toss gently. Cover and let stand for 1 hour. On a lightly floured surface, roll 1 half of dough to a ⅛-in.-thick circle; transfer to a 9-in. pie plate or iron skillet. Trim even with rim. Refrigerate while preparing filling.

BANANA FUDGE PIE

This dessert, which is like a banana sundae, is both light and delicious. I make it often.
—*Myra Innes, Auburn, KS*

- -

Prep: 20 min. • **Bake:** 30 min. + chilling
Makes: 8 servings

- 1   sheet refrigerated pie crust
- ½ cup miniature semisweet chocolate chips, melted
- 3   cups whipped topping, divided
- 2   large eggs
- ¼ cup sugar
- 2   to 3 bananas, sliced
    Additional miniature chocolate chips, optional

1. Preheat oven to 350°. Unroll crust into a 9-in. pie plate; flute edge. In a large bowl, combine melted chocolate, 1 cup whipped topping, eggs and sugar. Mix well. Pour into crust. Bake until center is set, about 30 minutes. Cool 10 minutes, then refrigerate for 1 hour.
2. Layer sliced bananas over pie and top with remaining whipped topping. Sprinkle miniature chocolate chips on top if desired. Chill until serving.
1 PIECE: 317 cal., 16g fat (10g sat. fat), 58mg chol., 117mg sod., 39g carb. (22g sugars, 1g fiber), 3g pro.

★ ★ ★ ★ ★ **READER REVIEW**

"I made this for Pi Day. I am not an expert pie maker, but this pie turned out well for me. I recommend it for beginners. My husband and I enjoyed it."

TGI TASTEOFHOME.COM

SNICKERDOODLE BLONDIE BARS

When asked to bring a dessert for my boys' football team to share, I whipped up these unique blondies and was instantly named the greatest mom by all.
—*Valonda Seward, Coarsegold, CA*

- -

Prep: 15 min. • **Bake:** 35 min. + cooling
Makes: 20 bars

- 1   cup butter, softened
- 2   cups packed brown sugar
- 3   tsp. vanilla extract
- 2   large eggs, room temperature
- 2⅔ cups all-purpose flour
- 2   tsp. baking powder
- 1   tsp. ground cinnamon
- ¼ tsp. ground nutmeg
- ½ tsp. salt

TOPPING
- 1½ tsp. sugar
- ½ tsp. ground cinnamon

1. Preheat oven to 350°. Cream butter and brown sugar until light and fluffy, 3-4 minutes. Beat in the vanilla. Beat in the eggs, 1 at a time, beating well after each addition. In another bowl, whisk together flour, baking powder, spices and salt; gradually beat into creamed mixture. Spread into a greased 9-in. square baking pan.
2. Mix topping ingredients; sprinkle over top. Bake until set and golden brown, 35-40 minutes. Cool completely in pan on a wire rack. Cut into bars.
1 BAR: 235 cal., 10g fat (6g sat. fat), 45mg chol., 180mg sod., 35g carb. (22g sugars, 1g fiber), 2g pro.

MOVIE-NIGHT
SNACK BOARD,
PAGE 225

Boards

Sweet or savory, snack boards are all the rage.
And they're easy to create with the inspirational
photos and detailed styling tips provided here.
Time to let your creativity blossom!

HOW TO BUILD A...
BASIC CHARCUTERIE BOARD
Follow these steps when putting together a board or platter of your own.

EASY ASSEMBLY

Step 1: Pull the cheeses out of the refrigerator about an hour before assembling your board. Cheese is at its fullest flavor when it's at room temperature.

If you're using several different types of cheese, set the cheese on the board first. Always pre-cut a few slices or crumble a corner of a wedge to let guests know how each cheese is supposed to be consumed. Crumble a corner of blue cheese, for instance, slice a bit of mimolette and add a wheel of Boursin.

Step 2: Add small bowls to the board. (If you're using several bowls on your board, you might want to start with those instead of the cheeses.) Bowls of different sizes and colors will add visual interest.

If you want to use decorative elements to elevate your charcuterie board, place them next so you won't have to tuck them under foods later. For example, you might add a few clusters of food-safe greenery such as lemon leaves, fig leaves or grape leaves.

Step 3: Add the meats. Fold slices of meat in different ways to add visual interest, texture and height. For example, arrange slices of soppressata in an S shape. Fold calabrese slices in half and fan them out. Fold prosciutto and mortadella into quarters. Keep meats of similar colors apart from one another on the board.

Step 4: Distribute any crackers and condiments around the board, thinking about which items pair best and placing them near one another. This helps your guests enjoy the best flavor combinations.

Pile the thyme-flavored crackers near the prosciutto, keep the honey near the blue cheese and set the mustard near the smoky Gouda.

Step 5: Fill in some of the gaps on the board with grapes and dried fruits.

Step 6: Fill in the very last open spaces of the board with the nuts and pickles.

Step 7: Add mini utensils to the board, including cheese knives and spoons for condiments. Set out extra cheese knives, appetizer plates and napkins.

Next, grab a plate and start noshing! Guests may feel shy about digging into your perfectly arranged charcuterie board. When you start eating, you're letting them know that everything is ready for them to pile on their plates and enjoy the wonderful board.

Do you have to make homemade recipes for a charcuterie board?
Absolutely not! That's the beauty of a board! Even though this book includes more than 200 potluck-perfect recipes, this bonus Boards chapter calls for store-bought items such as crackers, veggies, marshmallows and candy. You'll be amazed at all of the impressive boards you can build with convenience items.

Can you make a charcuterie board ahead of time?
Even though it's best to take cheese out of the refrigerator about an hour ahead of time, you should assemble a board as close to the serving time as possible.

How do I store the leftovers on a charcuterie board after the party?
You can wrap a board tightly and store it in the fridge for next-day snacking, but it's best to remove groupings of like items, storing each appropriately. (Wrap the cheese and set it in the fridge, put crackers in a resealable bag and store in the pantry, etc.)

What else can you put on a charcuterie board?
Variety is key when selecting ingredients for a board, and no food is off-limits. Hummus, pretzels, pita wedges, potato chips and even sweets such as truffles or chocolate-covered nuts work well on a traditional meat-and-cheese charcuterie board. Jazz things up with sliced donut peaches in late spring, figs in early summer or late fall, and pomegranates in winter.

HOMEMADE HONEY-MUSTARD DRESSING

This creamy dressing is a fantastic way to top off a green salad tossed with grapes or grapefruit segments. Dijon mustard provides the lively taste.
—*Carol Severson, Shelton, WA*

Takes: 15 min. • **Makes:** 2 cups

- ⅓ cup honey
- ¼ cup Dijon mustard
- ¼ cup white wine vinegar
- 2 Tbsp. lemon juice
- 1 garlic clove, minced
- 1 cup vegetable oil

In a blender, combine first 5 ingredients. While processing, gradually add oil in a steady stream until smooth and creamy. Store in the refrigerator.

2 TBSP.: 148 cal., 14g fat (2g sat. fat), 0 chol., 95mg sod., 7g carb. (6g sugars, 0 fiber), 0 pro.

HOW TO BUILD A...
RAINBOW SNACK PLATTER

Everyone will want to eat their veggies when this pretty rainbow makes an appearance. The idea is pure snacking gold.

ITEMS TO INCLUDE
- Red bell pepper strips
- Halved cherry tomatoes
- Halved orange mini peppers
- Cubed cheddar cheese
- Cucumber slices
- Snap peas, trimmed
- Colored goldfish crackers
- Cauliflower florets
- Homemade Honey-Mustard Dressing or hummus

EASY ASSEMBLY
Step 1: Arrange multicolored snacks—including raw vegetables, cheese cubes and crackers—in a rainbow pattern on a serving tray.

Step 2: Fill out the scene with caulifloweret clouds.

Step 3: Put a small bowl of honey-mustard dressing or hummus at the end of the rainbow for dipping.

GO FOR THE GOLD
Rainbow-themed boards are a low-fuss choice for anyone new to charcuterie. You can even have the kids assemble them. Simply group together foods of similar colors for an oh-so easy yet very impressive presentation.

MARSHMALLOW FRUIT DIP
You can whip up this sweet and creamy dip in just 10 minutes. I like to serve it in a bowl surrounded by fresh-picked strawberries at spring brunches or luncheons.
—Cindy Steffen, Cedarburg, WI

- -

Takes: 10 min.
Makes: 5 cups (40 servings)

1	pkg. (8 oz.) cream cheese, softened
¾	cup cherry yogurt
1	carton (8 oz.) frozen whipped topping, thawed
1	jar (7 oz.) marshmallow creme
	Assorted fresh fruit

In a large bowl, beat cream cheese and yogurt until blended. Fold in whipped topping and marshmallow creme. Serve with fruit.
2 TBSP.: 56 cal., 3g fat (2g sat. fat), 7mg chol., 24mg sod., 6g carb. (5g sugars, 0 fiber), 1g pro.

GOURMET BAGEL SPREADS

Choose your favorite flavor combo to create your own specialty.

1. ORANGE MARMALADE

Combine 1 cup softened cream cheese with ⅓ cup orange marmalade.

2. MEDITERRANEAN GOAT CHEESE

Combine 1 cup softened cream cheese, ⅓ cup goat cheese, ¼ cup chopped olives, ¼ cup chopped roasted red peppers and 2 tsp. grated lemon peel. Season with salt and pepper to taste.

3. "EVERYTHING" SEASONING

Combine 1 cup cream cheese, 1 Tbsp. each poppy seeds and sesame seeds, 2 tsp. each dried minced garlic and dried minced onion, and 1 tsp. Worcestershire sauce. Season with salt and pepper to taste.

4. BEER CHEESE

Combine 1 cup softened cream cheese, ½ cup shredded cheddar cheese, 3 Tbsp. beer and ½ envelope ranch dressing mix. Add salt and pepper to taste.

5. PECAN PIE

Combine 1 cup softened cream cheese, ½ cup toasted chopped pecans and ¼ cup caramel sauce.

6. GARLIC & HERB (FACING PAGE)

Combine 3 oz. softened cream cheese, ⅓ cup sour cream, ⅓ cup crumbled feta cheese, 2 garlic gloves and ½ tsp. each of garlic powder, dried oregano and basil.

HOW TO CUT BAGELS FOR LOW COMMITMENT

Order bagels uncut so you can thinly slice them vertically at home. This makes for easy sampling.

HOW TO BUILD A...
CONTINENTAL BREAKFAST BOARD

Rise and shine! A quick breakfast board is perfect when hosting a few overnight guests. Surprise them with this simply eye-opening presentation.

ITEMS TO INCLUDE
- Bagel spread(s) of your choice
- Avocado, diced
- Egg bread, sliced
- Bacon, cooked
- Everything bagel seasoning
- Honey
- Tangerine segments
- Green grapes

EASY ASSEMBLY

Step 1: Place bagel spread in a small serving bowl; add to board.

Step 2: Place avocado in a separate small serving bowl; add to board.

Step 3: Add bread slices to board in 2 groupings.

Step 4: Group slices of bacon in center of board.

Step 5: Set bagel seasoning and honey on opposite ends of board.

Step 6: Fill in gaps with tangerines and grapes. Add serving utensils and a bread knife.

BACON BUFFER
Before arranging the breakfast items, consider covering your board with parchment paper to protect it from any bacon grease.

6

SNACK TACTICS
Try unwrapping distinctly shaped candies and setting them on the tray. Smaller items that might get lost, such as the Raisinets, are best kept in their small movie-theater-like boxes or served in bowls.

HOW TO BUILD A ...
MOVIE-NIGHT SNACK BOARD

Dim the lights, grab a blanket and settle in with family, friends and your favorite flick. Top off your cozy night in with this fun assortment of concession-stand favorites.

ITEMS TO INCLUDE
- Parmesan Ranch Popcorn
- Good & Plenty
- M&Ms
- Milk Duds
- Cheddar popcorn
- Snow Caps
- Raisinets
- Caramel popcorn
- Red Vines
- Peanut butter cups
- Gummy bears
- Sour Patch Kids
- Kit Kats
- Mini pretzels
- Skittles

EASY ASSEMBLY
Step 1: Set the Parmesan Ranch Popcorn in the center of a rimmed tray or platter.

Step 2: Fill small bowls with Good & Plenty, M&Ms, Milk Duds, cheddar popcorn, Snow Caps or whatever snacks you feel work best served in bowls. Scatter bowls on and around tray.

Step 3: Fill in any gaps with the remaining items.

PARMESAN RANCH POPCORN
Make ho-hum popcorn worthy of a carnival with a savory seasoning blend.
—Taste of Home *Test Kitchen*

- -

Prep: 10 min. • **Makes:** 3½ qt.

- ¼ cup grated Parmesan cheese
- 2 Tbsp. ranch salad dressing mix
- 1 tsp. dried parsley flakes
- ¼ tsp. onion powder
- ⅓ cup butter, melted
- 3½ qt. popped popcorn

Mix first 4 ingredients. Drizzle butter over popcorn; toss with cheese mixture. Store in airtight containers.
1 CUP: 112 cal., 10g fat (4g sat. fat), 13mg chol., 243mg sod., 6g carb. (0 sugars, 1g fiber), 1g pro.

HOW TO BUILD A ...
S'MORES BOARD

Get ready for fun when guests gather around the fire and you set out this sweet assortment of s'more fixings.

ITEMS TO INCLUDE
- Nutella
- Peanut butter
- Chocolate chip cookies
- Homemade Honey Grahams
- White chocolate-covered pretzels
- Peanut butter cups
- White chocolate squares
- Marshmallows
- Chocolate bars
- Strawberries, halved
- Oreo cookies
- Miniature marshmallows

EASY ASSEMBLY

Step 1: Spoon Nutella and peanut butter into small bowls and set on opposite ends of board.

Step 2: Line chocolate chip cookies and graham crackers in groupings on board.

Step 3: Add groupings of white chocolate-covered pretzels, peanut butter cups, white chocolate squares, marshmallows, chocolate bars, strawberries and Oreo cookies.

Step 4: Fill in gaps with miniature marshmallows.

Step 5: Add serving utensils.

HOW TO BUILD A ...
FRUIT & CHEESE BOARD

ITEMS TO INCLUDE
- Cream Cheese Fruit Dip
- Honey
- Brie cheese
- Medium mango, halved and scored
- Large kiwifruit, peeled, halved and thinly sliced
- Seedless watermelon, sliced
- Seedless red grapes
- Fresh or dried figs, halved
- Small navel oranges, thinly sliced
- Dried banana chips
- Unblanched almonds
- Blueberries
- Blackberries
- Strawberries, halved

EASY ASSEMBLY

Step 1: Spoon dip into a small serving bowl. Set bowl on board or platter with jar of honey and Brie.

Step 2: Add mango halves to board.

Step 3: Pile kiwi slices on the board in a circle as shown at left.

Step 4: Shingle watermelon slices in a grouping on the board.

Step 5: Fill in gaps on board with remaining items.

CREAM CHEESE FRUIT DIP
Color it Christmas with a platter of red and green apple slices piled 'round a bowl of this yummy no-fuss fruit dip! The dip also goes well with strawberries, grapes and kiwi.
—*Sheryl Renner, El Paso, TX*

- -

Takes: 5 min. • **Makes:** 1 cup

- 1   **pkg. (8 oz.) cream cheese, softened**
- ¾   **cup packed brown sugar**
- 1   **tsp. vanilla extract**
  Assorted fresh fruit

In a small bowl, beat cream cheese, brown sugar and vanilla until smooth. Serve with fresh fruit for dipping. Refrigerate leftovers.
2 TBSP.: 179 cal., 10g fat (6g sat. fat), 29mg chol., 95mg sod., 22g carb. (21g sugars, 0 fiber), 2g pro.

FRUIT & CHEESE BOARD TIPS
How do I store leftovers from this fruit charcuterie board?
Fresh fruit and cheese can be thrown into airtight containers or zip-top bags and stored in the refrigerator. Keep in mind that your charcuterie board's fixings will hold better if they've been sitting out for less than an hour. If it's been longer than that, you may want to toss them. You can always put out less food on your board initially, then add to it if you're worried about food waste.

What other types of fruit and cheese can I add to this charcuterie board?
Have fun playing around with your favorite types of cheese and fruit. For cheese, try goat or gouda. As for fruit, consider apricots, pears, apples or even star fruit.

HAM PICKLE PINWHEELS

My mom introduced me to these little appetizers many years ago, and I've been making them for parties ever since.
—*Gloria Jarrett, Loveland, OH*

- -

Prep: 15 min. + chilling • **Makes:** 3½ dozen

- 1 pkg. (8 oz.) cream cheese, cubed
- ¼ lb. sliced Genoa salami
- 1 Tbsp. prepared horseradish
- 7 slices deli ham
- 14 to 21 okra pickles or dill pickle spears

1. In a food processor, combine cream cheese, salami and horseradish; cover and process until blended. Spread over ham slices.

2. Remove stems and ends of okra pickles. Place 2 or 3 okra pickles or 1 dill pickle down the center of each ham slice. Roll up tightly and cover. Refrigerate for at least 2 hours. Cut into 1-in. pieces.

1 PIECE: 34 cal., 3g fat (1g sat. fat), 9mg chol., 105mg sod., 1g carb. (0 sugars, 0 fiber), 2g pro.

★ ★ ★ ★ ★ **READER REVIEW**

"This appetizer is so common where I live it's sometimes jokingly called 'Iowa Sushi.' I had never tried it with Genoa salami or okra pickles, but now that's a must! Also, some people prefer to use thinly sliced corned beef instead of ham."

KIMBERLYBEAM TASTEOFHOME.COM

HOW TO BUILD A ...
HEALTHY WHOLESOME SNACK BOARD

Surprise the kids with this eye-fetching selection of lighter bites, including berries, veggies and fruit.

ITEMS TO INCLUDE
- Ham Pickle Pinwheels
- Yogurt-covered raisins
- Animal crackers
- Blueberries
- Banana chips
- Goldfish crackers
- Cheddar cheese, sliced
- Mozzarella cheese, sliced
- Teddy grahams
- Grapes
- Mini pretzels
- Celery sticks
- Baby carrots
- Graham crackers
- Clementines

EASY ASSEMBLY

Step 1: Line the Ham Pickle Pinwheels across the board.

Step 2: Set yogurt-covered raisins, animal crackers, blueberries, banana chips and goldfish crackers in small serving bowls. Arrange bowls above and below the pinwheels.

Step 3: Using small cookie cutters, cut cheese slices into shapes. Arrange cheese in groupings on board.

Step 4: Fill in gaps on board with groupings of remaining ingredients.

PLATTER POINTER
When assembling any board, try to balance colors and shapes. For instance, avoid piling 2 or 3 orange foods too close to one another, and try to put some space between round items such as grapes, berries and banana chips.

HOW TO BUILD A ...
PATRIOTIC PLATTER

It's easy to fill a board with red, white and blue snacks that are sure to please. Consider this simple idea or give a nod to Old Glory with your own platter!

ITEMS TO INCLUDE
- Honey-Lime Yogurt Dip
- Blue M&M's
- Blackberries
- Figs, halved
- Red grapes
- Grape licorice
- Blueberries
- Chocolate candies with red, white and blue nonpareils or sprinkles
- Blueberry yogurt pretzels
- White cheddar
- Cranberry Stilton
- Star-shaped crackers
- Blue cheese
- Strawberries
- Watermelon, sliced
- Raspberries
- Strawberry licorice
- Maraschino cherries
- Wrapped mini peanut butter cups

EASY ASSEMBLY

Step 1: Visually divide your tray or board into thirds horizontally.

Step 2: Pour Honey-Lime Yogurt Dip into a serving bowl and set it in the middle of the tray.

Step 3: Fill in bottom third of tray with like groupings of M&M's, blackberries, figs, red grapes, grape licorice, blueberries, chocolates and pretzels.

Step 4: Working around the bowl of dip, fill center of board with like groupings of cheddar, cranberry Stilton, crackers and blue cheese.

Step 5: Fill the top third of tray with strawberries, watermelon and raspberries.

Step 6: Fill in any gaps with strawberry licorice, maraschino cherries and mini peanut butter cups.

HONEY-LIME YOGURT DIP

When it comes to this tangy fruit dip, I don't mind my kids playing with their food. We like to dip strawberries, but friends have reported happy results with pears, bananas and more.
—*Shelly Bevington, Hermiston, OR*

- -

Takes: 5 min. • **Makes:** 2 cups

- 2 cups plain yogurt
- ¼ cup honey
- 2 Tbsp. lime juice
- ½ tsp. grated lime zest
  Assorted fresh fruit

Whisk the yogurt, honey, lime juice and lime zest in a small bowl. Refrigerate until serving. Serve with fruit.
¼ CUP: 70 cal., 2g fat (1g sat. fat), 8mg chol., 29mg sod., 12g carb. (12g sugars, 0 fiber), 2g pro.

HALLOWEEN TREAT BOARD

The boo-board is more treats than tricks! It comes together easily with mini popcorn balls and the colorful candies everyone loves.

ITEMS TO INCLUDE

- Black jelly beans
- Black licorice cats
- Black licorice bites
- Eyeball gumballs
- Peanut Butter Popcorn Balls
- Pumpkin Halloween Peeps
- Cheez-It® Original Snack Crackers
- Fall gummy worms
- Oreos
- Hershey Kisses (Purple Foiled)
- Mellocreme pumpkins
- Orange M&Ms
- Candy corn
- Cheddar cheese balls
- Gummy peach rings
- Gummy teeth

EASY ASSEMBLY

Step 1: On a round board create 1 eye with jelly beans, second eye with licorice cats and the mouth with licorice bites. Use gumballs for eyeballs.

Step 2: Prepare Peanut Butter Popcorn Balls, leaving out sticks. Line balls on a curve along right side of board.

Step 3: Line Peeps on curve along left side of the board. Complete pumpkin outline with crackers and gummy worms. Add Oreos at top for stem.

Step 4: Fill in with remaining items as seen in photo. Add additional Oreo for the nose.

PEANUT BUTTER POPCORN BALLS

Friends and family are always happy to see these popcorn balls. I love making them just as much as eating them!
—*Betty Claycomb, Alverton, PA*

Prep: 20 min. + standing
Makes: 10 servings

- 5 **cups popped popcorn**
- 1 **cup dry roasted peanuts**
- ½ **cup sugar**
- ½ **cup light corn syrup**
- ½ **cup chunky peanut butter**
- ½ **tsp. vanilla extract**
- 10 **lollipop sticks**

1. Place popcorn and peanuts in a large bowl. In a large heavy saucepan over medium heat, bring sugar and corn syrup to a rolling boil, stirring occasionally. Remove from the heat; stir in peanut butter and vanilla. Quickly pour over popcorn mixture and mix well.

2. When cool enough to handle, quickly shape into ten 2½-in. balls; insert a lollipop stick into each ball. Let stand at room temperature until firm; wrap in plastic.

1 POPCORN BALL: 281 cal., 16g fat (2g sat. fat), 0 chol., 228mg sod., 32g carb. (25g sugars, 3g fiber), 7g pro.

HARDWORKING LAZY SUSAN
A tiered lazy Susan is the ultimate way to keep ice cream cones, sauces and toppings within reach of hungry partygoers.

HOW TO BUILD A ...
SUNDAE STATION

I scream, you scream, we all scream for ice cream! Invite the gang to build their own sundae or "scooper"-duper cone with this icy idea. We piled cones and toppings on a three-tiered serving piece—but feel free to use whatever platters, bowls and boards you happen to have on hand.

ITEMS TO INCLUDE
- Sugar cones
- Cake cones
- Waffle cones
- Peanuts
- Milk chocolate English toffee pieces
- Star-shaped sprinkles
- Mini marshmallows
- Jimmies
- Shredded coconut
- Maraschino cherries
- Fudge sauce
- Easy Strawberry Cheesecake Ice Cream or ice cream of your choice

EASY ASSEMBLY

Step 1: Pile ice cream cones onto a tray (or stand them in glasses).

Step 2: Spoon peanuts, toffee pieces, sprinkles, marshmallows, jimmies and coconut into small bowls. Set bowls on tray with jar of cherries.

Step 3: Set out the fudge sauce and a container of Chocolate Chip Strawberry Ice Cream.

Step 4: Add spoons, bowls, ice cream scoops and serving utensils.

EASY STRAWBERRY CHEESECAKE ICE CREAM

When I got my ice cream maker, a friend shared her dreamy freezy cheesecake recipe.
—*Joan Hallford, North Richland Hills, TX*

- -

Prep: 15 min.
Process: 25 min. + freezing
Makes: 1½ qt.

- 1 cup half-and-half cream
- 1 Tbsp. vanilla extract
- 2 tsp. grated lemon zest
- 2 tsp. lemon juice
- 1 cup sugar
- 1 pkg. (8 oz.) cream cheese, cubed and softened
- 1 cup heavy whipping cream
- 1½ cups fresh strawberries
   Sliced fresh strawberries or crushed graham crackers, optional

1. Place the first 6 ingredients in a blender; cover and process until smooth. Add whipping cream; cover and process until blended. Transfer to a large bowl.
2. Add 1½ cups strawberries to blender; cover and process until pureed. Stir into cream mixture.

3. Fill cylinder of ice cream maker no more than two-thirds full; freeze according to manufacturer's directions. (Refrigerate any remaining mixture until ready to freeze.)
4. Transfer ice cream to freezer containers, allowing headspace for expansion. Freeze 4-6 hours or until firm. If desired, serve with crushed graham crackers and additional strawberries, sliced.
½ CUP: 234 cal., 16g fat (10g sat. fat), 58mg chol., 87mg sod., 20g carb. (20g sugars, 0 fiber), 2g pro.

BRING IT
A sundae bar is a blast for kids of all ages, and it's economical if each attendee brings a different sprinkle, sauce or topping. Consider halved bananas, sliced fresh strawberries, Skittles, chocolate chips, M&Ms, whipped cream and caramel sauce. Go crazy!

Recipe Index

la courte échelle

Dominique Demers

Dominique Demers a une maîtrise en littérature jeunesse et elle prépare un doctorat sur le même sujet. Bien connue pour ses reportages dans *Châtelaine* et dans *L'Actualité*, elle est aussi, depuis une dizaine d'années, critique de littérature jeunesse au *Devoir*. Elle a reçu de nombreux prix de journalisme. Elle a également publié *La bibliothèque des enfants*.

Dominique Demers est une auteure un peu bizarre, elle ne lit que des romans pour les jeunes. Elle a été très émue en écrivant l'histoire de Marie-Lune, puisqu'elle-même a vécu un drame semblable quand elle était adolescente. À son avis, l'adolescence n'est pas toujours rose. Elle croit que les jeunes vivent, eux aussi, toutes sortes de drames et que ça peut les réconforter un peu d'être témoins de ceux des autres.

Un hiver de tourmente est le deuxième roman qu'elle publie à la courte échelle.

De la même auteure, à la courte échelle

Collection Premier Roman
Valentine Picotée

Dominique Demers

Un hiver
de tourmente

la courte échelle

Les éditions de la courte échelle inc.

Les éditions de la courte échelle inc.
5243, boul. Saint-Laurent
Montréal (Québec) H2T 1S4

Illustration de la couverture:
Louis Montpetit

Conception graphique:
Derome design inc.

Révision des textes:
Odette Lord

Dépôt légal, 1er trimestre 1992
Bibliothèque nationale du Québec

Données de catalogage avant publication (Canada)

Demers, Dominique

    Un hiver de tourmente   '

    (Roman+; R+21)

    ISBN 2-89021-171-1

    I. Titre.

PS8557.E4683H58 1992   jC843'.54   C91-096934-5
PS9557.E4683H58 1992
PZ23.D45Hi 1992

À Jeannine et à Michel

Chapitre 1

Vert forêt et bleu électrique

Ma mère a les cheveux bleus. Elle n'est pas complètement marteau, ni même un peu Martienne, mais simplement coloriste, au Salon Charmante, rue Principale à Saint-Jovite. La semaine dernière, ses cheveux étaient «or cuivré». Le flacon 57, sur l'étagère du haut.

Derrière les séchoirs, tout au fond du salon, ma mère mélange des couleurs. Mèches, teintures, balayages, reflets... Il y a des peintres en bâtiment, d'autres en chevelure.

Le bleu, normalement, n'est qu'un reflet. Mais Fernande n'a pas eu le temps de revenir à sa couleur naturelle — noir corbeau sans numéro — avant de l'essayer. Elle sait maintenant que le nouveau «bleu nuit 13» fait un peu psychédélique lorsqu'on l'applique sur un fond «or cuivré 57».

Moi, je rêve d'une mèche bleu électrique. Juste une, presque discrète, qui se tiendrait bravement debout sur le dessus de ma tête. Mais pas question! La petite Marie-Lune de Fernande et Léandre n'a pas le droit d'être punk. Je me contente d'une coupe légèrement étagée et terriblement ordinaire, signée Gaëtanne, l'amie de ma mère, propriétaire du Salon Charmante.

Ce n'est pas très sophistiqué, mais c'est un peu ébouriffé, ce qui me convient. Avant, j'étais plutôt du genre coupe champignon. Un bol de cheveux renversé sur le crâne. Une auréole de poils trop sages. Maintenant, c'est fini. Je m'appelle encore Marie-Lune, mais attention! Je suis plutôt une Marie-Éclipse, une Marie-Tonnerre, une Marie-Tremblement de terre.

C'est drôle! Les clientes de Fernande lui réclament les pires extravagances, et elle ne bronche pas. Maman peint en blond Barbie les cheveux roux de Mme Lalonde, étale du jaune carotte sur la tignasse noire de Mme Bélanger, teint en noir charbon les derniers poils blancs de Joséphine Lacasse et jure à ces épouvantails qu'elles sont ravissantes. Ces dames lui demanderaient une mèche vert limette, et ma mère brasserait les couleurs sans dire un mot.

Moi? Voyons donc! C'est différent.

J'ai déjà été la gloire de Fernande. Sa fille unique. Belle et brillante. Belle, dans la langue de ma mère, ça veut dire propre, bien mise et en bonne santé. Et brillante? Des «A» partout, en français comme en chimie.

Depuis l'an dernier, ma mère me trouve moins belle et brillante, et beaucoup trop adolescente. Et depuis qu'Antoine est entré dans ma vie, je me suis métamorphosée en cauchemar ambulant. Je fais peur à mes parents. La nuit des vampires, c'est du chocolat à côté de moi.

Fernande a du mal à digérer la nouvelle Marie-Lune. Elle se ronge les sangs et elle s'arracherait aussi les cheveux si elle n'en avait pas déjà perdu autant. Elle fait des drames avec tout, pleure pour rien et souffre toujours de migraines.

Quant à mon père, journaliste sportif au *Clairon des Laurentides,* il lit plus d'articles sur l'adolescence que sur le hockey. Le pauvre a failli faire une syncope en apprenant que 50 % des adolescents ont fait l'amour avant la fin du cours secondaire.

Je suis devenue suspecte.

J'aime Antoine depuis le 27 octobre. Je l'aimais peut-être déjà auparavant, mais j'étais trop poire pour m'en apercevoir. L'année dernière, à la fête d'Halloween de la polyvalente, j'avais dansé avec Sylvie Brisebois.

Sylvie est ma meilleure amie. On se connaît depuis la pouponnière. Nos mères étaient enceintes en même temps. Et toutes les deux, on habite au bout du monde. À vingt minutes de Saint-Jovite, en plein bois, au bord du lac Supérieur. Il n'y a que cinq familles assez cinglées pour vivre là douze mois par année. Quand je pense qu'on pourrait avoir un appartement au coeur de Montréal, près des boutiques de la rue Sainte-Catherine, ça me rend complètement folle.

Tout ça pour dire que l'an dernier, au party d'Halloween, pas un traître gars ne nous avait invitées à danser. On buvait sagement nos Coke dans un coin en faisant attention de ne déranger personne et de ne pas trop attirer l'attention. Deux vraies dindes!

Il faut croire que le Coke nous était monté à la tête parce qu'on avait décidé de danser ensemble. Un slow. Quand j'y pense, j'ai tellement honte. Mais Sylvie et moi, on fait toujours tout ensemble. Sylvie, c'est presque une soeur. On trouvait la musique belle, on était de bonne humeur et on avait envie de danser. C'est tout. Quand Claude Dubé et sa bande nous ont vues, ils se sont mis à hurler.

— Hé! Allez-y, embrassez-vous, les lesbiennes! Dérangez-vous surtout pas pour nous.

Notre soirée avait fini là. Sylvie et moi, on était rentrées au lac sans parler.

Cette année, Sylvie n'est pas venue au party d'Halloween. Et ça n'avait rien à voir avec les moqueries de la bande à Dubé. Ses parents descendaient passer la fin de semaine à Montréal. Pas question de manquer ça.

J'avais enfilé mon plus beau jean et la chemise bleu ciel du père de Sylvie. C'est elle qui me l'avait prêtée. Je n'avais pas osé emprunter celle de mon père: il aurait fait tout un plat.

Je me sentais drôle, ce soir-là. Triste et heureuse en même temps. Pour rien. Ça m'arrive parfois. J'ai les émotions de travers. Comme si on les avait passées au malaxeur.

Je regardais Nathalie Gadouas danser avec Antoine Fournier et je les trouvais terriblement romantiques. Antoine est grand et beau. Ses cheveux blonds sautillent sur son front et courent un peu sur sa nuque. Ses yeux verts sont immenses et ils brillent comme la forêt autour du lac, les matins d'été.

— Tu danses?

J'ai changé de galaxie. J'étais loin dans mes songeries. Je ne l'avais pas vu approcher. Antoine était là, devant moi. Gauche et sérieux. Il avait l'air trop grand. Et gêné de l'être.

Je n'ai pas répondu. Je l'ai suivi. Ce n'était pas un noeud que j'avais dans la gorge, mais un troupeau d'éléphants. En avançant, je lui ai écrasé un pied — le droit, je crois — avec mes bottes western à bout métallique. Il était aussi gauche que moi. En voulant me prendre le bras, il a failli s'enfuir avec mon chandail.

On n'a rien dit. On était encore un peu à l'écart du peloton de danseurs quand il m'a enlacée. Ça m'a donné un grand coup au coeur. Il faisait chaud et doux dans ses bras. Son chandail sentait l'automne, la terre noire et les feuilles mouillées.

J'ai toujours aimé l'automne. À cause des grands vents qui hurlent et qui secouent tout. L'automne n'est pas une saison morte. C'est plein de vie, de furie. Mais c'est aussi une saison qui nous berce pendant de longs moments. Au ralenti. En silence. Quand la pluie cesse et que les vents s'apaisent.

Je pensais à tout ça. Et au nom d'Antoine, pas très loin d'automne. Du bout de mon nez, je touchais son cou. Mes lèvres étaient toutes proches. J'aurais voulu l'embrasser. Tout de suite. J'avais envie de passer les trois prochains siècles, enveloppée dans ses bras et portée par la musique.

Peut-être m'a-t-il entendue penser? Il s'est détaché lentement. J'ai décollé mon nez de son cou. On s'est regardés. Ses paupières se sont abaissées. La grande forêt verte a disparu, et il m'a embrassée. Sur les lèvres. Tout doucement. Tellement doucement que, si ses lèvres n'avaient pas été aussi chaudes, je me serais demandé si c'était vraiment arrivé.

Les musiciens ont annoncé une pause. J'ai pensé à Cendrillon. Mon père venait me chercher à vingt-trois heures. Le métro ne passe pas souvent à Saint-Jovite, surtout à destination du lac Supérieur.

— Il faut que je parte...

J'espérais qu'il comprendrait. Il n'a rien dit. Mais il a attrapé mes mains et les a serrées entre les siennes. Puis il est parti.

À la maison, Fernande m'attendait. Tant mieux! J'habite à deux heures de Montréal, au bord d'un lac où il y a plus de canards que de jeunes de mon âge. Ma mère a toujours été mon amie. Un peu comme Sylvie. L'année dernière, après la danse, j'avais tout raconté à Fernande. Ma gêne, ma rage, mon désespoir. Cette fois, il m'arrivait quelque chose d'extraordinaire. Et je ne pouvais quand même pas aller le crier aux canards.

Je m'étais assise sur le bord du lit de ma mère. Et je lui avais encore une fois tout raconté. Depuis l'apparition d'Antoine jusqu'au baiser.

J'avais oublié qu'elle avait changé depuis quelques mois. Un vrai porc-épic. Je suis tombée de mon nuage. Une bonne débarque.

— Je n'en reviens pas! Mon Dieu, que tu es naïve! Réveille-toi, Marie-Lune! Tu joues avec le feu. Si tu continues, tu vas te réveiller enceinte à quinze ans.

Ah bon! Et moi qui croyais que pour faire des bébés, il fallait faire l'amour, pas juste s'embrasser. Ma mère gâchait tout. Je n'avais pas envie de faire l'amour avec Antoine.

Pas tout de suite, en tout cas. Je n'ai jamais fait l'amour, moi. Et je ne suis pas certaine du tout d'aimer ça. Des pénis, je n'en ai pas vu des tonnes.

La soeur de Sylvie a déjà fait l'amour. Elle dit qu'on transpire tellement qu'on dégoutte partout. J'imagine des flaques dans le lit et sur le plancher. Ce n'est pas très romantique. Elle dit aussi que la première fois, ça fait mal. Terriblement mal.

Ça fait rire Sylvie.

— Ma soeur aime faire du théâtre. Si c'était tellement horrible et effrayant, penses-tu qu'elle avalerait une pilule tous les matins?

J'avais claqué la porte de la chambre de ma mère et j'étais allée me réfugier dans mon lit. Là, bien au chaud, j'avais fermé les yeux et je m'étais remise à danser.

Chapitre 2

Souvenir bleu ciel
et contrat bidon

— Veux-tu des oeufs, du gruau ou du pain trempé dans le sirop? Dépêche-toi de manger... Ah non! On ne se déguise pas pour aller à l'école.

La voilà repartie. Drame numéro mille. Tout ça parce que j'ai enfilé la chemise bleu ciel du père de Sylvie. Gaston Boisvert a sûrement plusieurs chemises de la même couleur: il n'a pas encore remarqué la disparition.

Ça fait deux semaines et cinq jours que je n'ai pas vu Antoine. Enfin, c'est une façon de parler. À l'école, le matin, avant le début des cours, il m'attend. Il s'installe toujours sous le gros tilleul, au fond de la cour. Même les jours de pluie. On dirait qu'Antoine ne remarque pas le temps qu'il fait. Il porte toujours son blouson bleu-vert.

— Salut!

C'est tout ce qu'il m'avait dit le premier lundi matin après la danse d'Halloween. Je lui avais répondu, et la conversation s'était arrêtée là. Deux mots en tout. Il n'y avait pas de quoi écrire un roman.

J'étais gênée et j'avais peur. À peine descendue de l'autobus, je l'avais cherché des yeux. En l'apercevant, sous son parapluie de feuilles, je m'étais demandé si je devais le rejoindre. D'accord, on avait dansé et il m'avait embrassée. Mais la moitié des jeunes à la danse en avaient fait au moins autant. Comme le dit Sylvie, ça ne voulait rien dire.

J'étais adossée au tilleul. L'écorce est vieille et toute crevassée. Je sentais les bosses dans mon dos. J'avais froid. Il pleuvait bêtement. Des gouttelettes éparpillées, fines et froides. J'avais envie de disparaître. Je pensais que Sylvie avait probablement raison.

Sylvie croit que tous les gars sont comme Thierry Lamothe. L'été dernier, elle était allée au cinéma avec lui. Au moment où

Indiana Jones échouait dans un marais infesté de crocodiles, Thierry avait plongé sa main sous la jupe de Sylvie. Elle avait crié, mais personne ne s'était retourné. La moitié des spectateurs avaient hurlé en même temps: un gros croco fonçait sur le héros.

Sylvie avait vidé son panier de pop-corn sur les cuisses de Thierry. Il avait déjà retiré sa main, à son cri. Au coup du pop-corn, il était parti. Sylvie était restée. Mais elle était furieuse. Et triste.

Tous les garçons ne sont pas comme Thierry. Le premier matin, pendant que je grelottais sous le tilleul en me tracassant, Antoine m'a entendue penser. Comme à la danse. On aurait dit qu'il avait deviné ce qui me trottait dans la tête. Il m'a regardée et il a pris ma main.

C'est tout. Ensuite, le temps a filé. On croirait qu'il fait exprès pour sprinter quand quelqu'un vous prend la main. La sonnerie du début des cours nous a surpris aussi trempés qu'heureux.

Depuis deux semaines, on se tient par la main le matin, et c'est tout. Parfois, il parle un peu. De la saison de hockey ou du cours d'anglais. Il adore le hockey et déteste Joan Cartner, la prof d'*english*.

Le midi, Antoine travaille à la cafétéria. On ne le voit pas. Il lave les chaudrons. Sylvie était tout étonnée quand je lui ai raconté ça.

— Ouache! Dégueulasse! Tu imagines le fond des plats de spaghetti et de pâté chinois. Le dessus est dégoûtant, alors le dessous...

C'est vrai que la cafétéria de la polyvalente n'a pas très bonne réputation. Mario Levert jure que tous les plats du jour, pâté chinois, chili ou sauce à spaghetti, sont cuisinés avec du rat. Tous les midis, il achète trois hot-dogs. Il dit que les saucisses fumées sont faites de tripes, d'os et de toutes sortes de vieux restes: yeux, oreilles, queues, mettez-en! Et il ajoute que c'est cent fois meilleur pour la santé que du pâté de rat.

Antoine a besoin d'argent. Son père est «ébéniste de métier, mais ivrogne de profession». C'est Léandre, mon père, qui a déjà dit ça. Ça m'avait frappée, même si je ne connaissais pas vraiment Antoine dans ce temps-là. Le père d'Antoine est comme la cafétéria: il a mauvaise réputation. Tout le monde sait qu'il boit. Et la mère d'Antoine n'existe pas. Il n'en parle jamais. Elle est peut-être morte.

L'après-midi, entre la fin du dernier cours et l'arrivée de l'autobus, j'ai exactement huit minutes pour voir Antoine. Ça devrait rassurer ma mère: huit minutes, c'est un peu court pour faire l'amour.

Depuis l'Halloween, mes parents s'arrangent pour remplir mes week-ends. Ça fait deux semaines d'affilée qu'on va à Montréal. Ma mère a des rendez-vous avec un grand médecin spécialiste. Si je comprends bien, sa ménopause fait des siennes. C'est peut-être un prétexte pour m'empêcher de voir Antoine. Pendant que mes parents s'éclipsent, je magasine au Carrefour Angrignon près de chez Flavi, ma grand-mère.

Flavi était étrange, dimanche. La semaine précédente, je lui avais parlé d'Antoine. Elle avait été chouette. Comme d'habitude. Pas de question, pas de sermon. Cette fois, j'avais envie de la mettre dans le coup. Si seulement Flavi pouvait expliquer à sa fille et à son gendre que ce n'est pas bon pour une adolescente de passer ses soirées à compter les canards. J'allais lui parler quand Flavi a fermé la radio.

— Marie, il faut que je te parle.

Flavi ne m'appelle jamais Marie-Lune. Elle trouve mon nom un peu trop astrologique. Elle préfère Marie tout court. C'est plus terre à terre.

— Ta mère ne va pas très bien, Marie... Elle est un peu malade... Et tes amours l'inquiètent...

— Flavi! Tu te ranges de leur côté maintenant?

— Mais non!

Elle était pâle. Je ne l'avais jamais vue aussi triste. Elle avait peut-être honte d'être prise en flagrant délit de trahison. Nous avons toujours été complices.

— Bon! Oublie tout ça...

Flavi avait souri. Ce n'était pas très convaincant, mais c'était mieux que son air d'enterrement. N'empêche que le petit discours de Flavi m'avait coupé le mien.

Heureusement, j'ai Sylvie.

— Tu veux voir Antoine? Pas de problème!

Sylvie adore jouer la marraine de Cendrillon. Elle aime secourir les âmes en peine et exaucer les voeux compliqués. En plus, elle est douée.

Demain soir, je garde deux petits monstres. Jacynthe et Clothilde. Des jumelles.

Mais elles ne me verront même pas. Ce n'est qu'un alibi. Sylvie s'occupera des petites pestes pendant que je serai chez Antoine, à deux rues de là.

J'ai raconté à Fernande et à Léandre que Sylvie m'avait décroché un contrat de gardienne. Je ne pourrais malheureusement pas veiller au lac vendredi soir.

— Papa n'aura pas à faire le taxi, je filerai droit chez les Dumoulin après l'école.

Léandre a promis de venir me chercher à vingt-deux heures trente, devant la maison des Dumoulin. Sylvie était fière de son coup.

— Penses-y! Une soirée à bécoter ton Antoine. Si tes parents téléphonent, je dirai que je te tiens compagnie. J'ajouterai que les deux petits monstres t'en font voir de toutes les couleurs et qu'en bonne gardienne tu leur racontes une centième histoire. Si Fernande et Léandre tiennent à tout prix à te parler, je t'appelle chez Antoine, et tu laisses ton Roméo deux secondes pour donner un coup de fil à tes parents.

Le plan est génial, et je meurs d'envie de passer une soirée seule avec Antoine. Mais en même temps, je me sens un peu triste.

Quelque part en moi, un continent vient

d'être inondé. Une grosse tempête et pouf!, disparu de la carte. Avant, je n'avais pas de chum, mais j'avais deux amies. Ma mère et Sylvie. J'ai gagné un chum, mais je pense que j'ai perdu une amie.

Chapitre 3

Seule avec Antoine

Je me suis réveillée ce matin avec un bébé bouton éléphantesque sous le nez. Les boutons, c'est comme les embryons. Ça enfle tranquillement. Au début, notre face ne sait pas qu'elle est enceinte. Dans mon cas, l'accouchement ne devrait pas tarder.

Il est arrivé quelque chose d'étrange ce matin. Fernande avait la voix rauque, les yeux pochés, le visage pâle et les gestes lourds. On aurait dit que tous ses membres pesaient trois tonnes. Elle a encore téléphoné à Gaëtanne pour annoncer qu'elle serait en retard. Ma mère sirotait lentement son café quand une mésange a piqué dans la fenêtre de la cuisine.

Fernande s'est mise à hurler comme un chien blessé en voyant le petit paquet de plume inerte. Rien ne semblait pouvoir l'arrêter. Léandre l'a entraînée dans leur chambre à coucher.

Avant de quitter la maison, je suis allée l'embrasser. Elle était étendue sur son lit mais ne pleurait plus.

— Tu te souviens que je garde ce soir?

— Oui? Oui, oui... Bonne chance! Et n'oublie pas que les enfants doivent se brosser les dents avant d'aller se coucher.

Non mais faut le faire! Ma mère a le don de se concentrer sur des insignifiances. Elle a l'air complètement lessivée et elle se fait du souci pour les caries de deux petits inconnus.

Ça me rappelle l'année dernière. Fernande avait passé deux semaines à l'hôpital. Une tumeur au sein. Rien d'inquiétant: c'était bénin. Une bosse stupide avait poussé là sans raison. Comme mon bouton. Fernande a sûrement eu peur quand même, car le contraire de bénin, c'est malin et ça, c'est un cancer. Moi, je n'ai pas eu le temps de m'inquiéter. Avant même de connaître le résultat des examens, Léandre m'avait juré que la tumeur n'était pas cancéreuse.

À l'hôpital, ma mère se tracassait à propos du *Guide alimentaire canadien,* l'évangile, selon quelques diététiciens à la noix persuadés que notre corps et notre cervelle vont se détraquer s'ils ne carburent pas midi et soir aux légumes verts et au pain à neuf grains. Tous les matins, ma mère téléphonait pour savoir ce que j'allais mettre dans mon sac à lunch.

— As-tu pensé à un petit morceau de fromage? N'oublie pas ta pomme...

Ça m'étonne que l'hôpital ne lui ait pas offert un poste d'inspectrice des plateaux. J'imagine bien ma mère faisant le tour des civières pour sermonner des mourants parce qu'ils ont oublié trois petits pois dans leur assiette.

En sortant de la maison, ce matin, j'ai oublié ma mère et mon bouton. Antoine était dans l'air. On aurait dit que l'été des Indiens était revenu. Il faisait doux, et le soleil brillait comme un fou. Ça sentait presque le printemps. Au risque de rater l'autobus, j'ai descendu la côte jusqu'au lac. Ça ne m'arrive pas souvent, et je n'en parle jamais. Fernande et Léandre pourraient s'imaginer que j'aime vivre dans notre jungle glacée au bout du monde.

Le lac était beau. Des taches de soleil flottaient sur les vagues. Derrière, tout au loin, les pistes du Mont-Tremblant étaient presque blondes. La neige allait bientôt les envahir. Au pied de la montagne, les falaises noires forment un mur. On dirait qu'elles nous isolent du reste de la planète. Mais ce matin, ça ne m'embêtait pas. Il y a des jours où j'ai l'impression de posséder le lac au lieu d'en être prisonnière.

Un geai a crié. J'ai couru en pensant à l'autobus. Mais, à mi-chemin sur le sentier, je me suis retournée, j'ai regardé le lac une dernière fois, et j'ai crié, moi aussi. Pour me souhaiter bonne chance et bonne journée.

J'ai cherché Antoine toute la journée. Il n'était pas planté sous son arbre ce matin et il n'était pas à la cafétéria ce midi. J'ai téléphoné plusieurs fois chez lui, mais personne n'a répondu. J'étais prête à alerter les policiers quand Sylvie a fourré un billet dans la poche arrière de mon jean, en plein corridor, entre le cours de gym et le cours de maths. Elle s'est sauvée en riant.

J'ai attendu d'être assise, bien tranquille, au fond de la classe avant de défroisser le bout de papier. Même si Antoine est très grand, il écrit en lettres naines. Des pattes de mouches fines et minuscules, perdues sur la page:

À ce soir, beauté! J'ai congé d'école aujourd'hui. Je suis peut-être malade d'amour. J'espère que c'est contagieu_. Es-tu prête à l'attrapé_?

XXXXXXXXXXXXXXXXXXXXXXXXX

Antoine

Sylvie l'avait lu. C'est pour ça qu'elle riait. Elle avait même souligné les fautes d'orthographe. Un peu plus et elle gardait le message pour elle. Elle n'est vraiment pas gênée!

Moi, je n'ai pas ri. J'avais le coeur en jello. Antoine parle peu. Il écoute. Il rit. Il m'ébouriffe les cheveux. Il prend ma main. La caresse ou la presse. Parfois, il me serre très fort dans ses bras et il me soulève pour me faire danser dans les airs. Ça veut dire qu'il est heureux. Moi, je parle pour deux.

Alors sa lettre, quand on le connaît, c'est la débâcle, le déluge, une véritable inondation de mots. Une grande déclaration d'amour.

Il s'était passé quelque chose. Quoi? Je

ne savais pas. Mais c'était pour ça qu'il n'était pas à l'école. Sinon, il serait venu. Même s'il n'en avait pas envie. Parce qu'il savait bien que je le chercherais sous le tilleul.

Il s'était passé quelque chose, mais ce n'était pas la fin du monde.

Puisqu'il m'aimait.

J'avais envie d'envoyer promener Betterave, la prof de maths, et de courir tout de suite chez Antoine. Au diable Miss Mathématiques!

Betterave a les cheveux presque mauves, striés de mèches aux reflets rouges, et elle porte toujours des robes d'une autre époque aux couleurs mal assorties à sa tignasse. Sur une autre silhouette, ça ferait psychédélique et plutôt cool, mais dans son cas, c'est strictement inesthétique.

J'ai attendu patiemment la fin du cours. Ce n'était pas le temps d'être doublement délinquante. Le plan de ce soir suffisait pour aujourd'hui. La cloche a finalement sonné.

J'étais libre. Enfin! Pas d'autobus, pas de parents. Et Antoine qui m'attendait...

Je ne sais pas ce qui m'a pris. Cinq minutes plus tard, j'étais devant le Salon Charmante. J'avais envie de voir ma mère avant.

Sans raison. C'était fou, mais je n'y pouvais rien.

Fernande ne m'a pas vue tout de suite. Mme Laprise m'a souri dans le miroir. Maman me tournait le dos. Elle aspergeait d'un liquide brun les cheveux d'une Mme Laprise déguisée en extra-terrestre.

C'est comme ça, les mèches! Il faut mettre un casque de caoutchouc troué et faire sortir de petites touffes de cheveux en les tirant à l'aide d'un crochet. J'avais cinq ans la première fois que j'ai vu ça. Mon père m'avait emmenée au salon voir maman, et je m'étais mise à crier en baragouinant une histoire à propos d'une Mme Monstre. Ma mère et Gaëtanne étaient mortes de honte.

— Salut!

Ma mère s'est retournée. Elle a dû imaginer une catastrophe, car elle s'est renfrognée.

— Que fais-tu ici, Marie-Lune? Il est arrivé quelque chose? Tu devais être chez les Dumoulin!

— Tu paniques pour rien. Tout est parfait. Mme Dumoulin ne part pas avant dix-sept heures. J'ai le temps de flâner un peu. Je venais juste te dire bonjour.

Son visage s'est illuminé. Elle avait l'air franchement ravie.

— J'en ai pour cinq minutes. On pourrait boire un Coke ensemble... Veux-tu?

Je ne pensais pas rester, mais je n'arrivais pas à dire non.

Je me suis assise devant le miroir. Et j'ai vu mon bouton. L'horreur! Je l'ai tâté un peu pour mieux l'examiner. Évidemment, il avait grossi. J'ai sans doute fait une grimace. Ma mère devait m'épier. Elle a éclaté de rire. Un bon rire. Vrai. Franc. Ça faisait des siècles qu'elle n'avait pas ri comme ça.

— Tu es belle quand même, tu sais.

Ça aussi, on aurait dit que ça venait du fond du coeur.

Finalement, on n'a rien bu. Une cliente sans rendez-vous est arrivée à la dernière minute. J'ai embrassé ma mère à la sauvette et je suis sortie.

Antoine habite une rue presque déserte, sans arbres. C'est près de chez les Dumoulin, mais sur une autre planète. La maison des Dumoulin a trois étages, cinq chambres à coucher, un jardin immense, une piscine creusée et des tas de plantes toujours bien taillées. La maison d'Antoine est petite et laide. La peinture pèle sur les vieilles planches de bois, et les carreaux des fenêtres sont crottés. La maison semble fragile et terriblement fatiguée.

Ça m'a donné un coup. Antoine a l'air fort et solide. Comme les sapins géants au bord du lac. Les tempêtes s'abattent, le froid grignote tout, le vent fouette les bouleaux et tord dangereusement leurs branches, mais les sapins bougent à peine.

Je ne m'étais jamais demandé où Antoine pouvait habiter. Sa maison ne lui ressemble pas.

J'avais imaginé qu'à mon arrivée, Antoine me soulèverait en me serrant dans ses bras. Mais on s'est simplement regardés comme deux imbéciles, et il m'a dit d'entrer.

On s'est écrasés sur le divan fané. La télé était allumée. Un jeu stupide. Une grosse madame venait de gagner une petite voiture rouge tomate. Elle sautillait sur place en battant des mains comme une enfant. J'ai ri. Ça allait mieux. Tout dans cette maison respirait la misère, mais Antoine sentait encore l'automne. C'était rassurant. Il portait sa chemise à carreaux. Celle que j'aime.

Du coin de l'oeil, je l'ai observé. Il était

soucieux. Ou fatigué. Ou les deux. Son regard était triste derrière le voile d'indifférence.

J'aime ses yeux. On y plonge comme dans une forêt. Secrète et silencieuse. Vaste et enveloppante. Terriblement vivante.

Je me suis rapprochée de lui tout doucement. Comme si je pouvais l'effrayer. Et je l'ai embrassé délicatement. Sur la joue.

Il m'a regardée. J'ai vu les larmes immobiles dans ses yeux. Prêtes à couler. Il m'a entourée de ses grands bras, et tout est redevenu comme avant.

Pendant qu'on préparait des sandwiches au similipoulet, Antoine m'a tout raconté. Hier, son père est rentré. Il était parti depuis lundi. Quatre jours sans donner signe de vie. Pierre Fournier sentait le gros gin et il avait les yeux vitreux, à son retour. D'habitude, l'alcool le rend seulement idiot. Il dit des sottises, rit pour rien, pleure aussi facilement et s'endort n'importe où en ronflant comme un moteur de Boeing 747. Cette fois, il était furieux.

Pierre Fournier gueulait contre le monde entier. Antoine n'a pas été épargné. Son père l'a traité de tous les noms, de «grand insignifiant» à «christ de débile» en passant par tout ce qu'on peut imaginer. Antoine a encaissé pendant un bout de temps. Puis il s'est levé et il a frappé son père.

— C'est arrivé tout seul. C'est la première fois que je fais ça. Même si j'ai souvent eu envie... Je ne l'ai pas frappé fort. Un coup de poing sur l'épaule. Mais il était tellement soûl... Il est tombé à terre. J'ai voulu l'aider. Il s'est vite relevé. Comme si, d'un coup, il était dégrisé. Il n'avait plus l'air fâché. Il avait l'air seul au monde. Perdu. Il est parti.

Je n'ai rien dit. Je ne savais pas quoi dire. Antoine n'avait pas dormi de la nuit. Ce matin, il m'avait écrit le message et l'avait donné à Jacques Ledoux qui l'avait remis à Sylvie. Puis il s'était couché. Nos sandwiches au similipoulet, c'était son premier repas de la journée.

On était presque joyeux. Ça faisait drôle d'être seuls dans une maison. Comme un vrai couple. Antoine a engouffré trois énormes sandwiches et bu autant de verres de lait. Ensuite, on est sortis marcher. L'air était doux, et le ciel peuplé de milliards d'étoiles. C'est romantique, les étoiles. On n'y peut rien.

Au retour, avant d'ouvrir la porte, Antoine m'a soulevée et il m'a portée dans ses bras jusqu'au salon. Les nouveaux mariés font toujours ça dans les anciens films.

J'ai ri. Lui aussi. Il a failli m'échapper.

J'ai échoué un peu brutalement sur le vieux sofa. Le pauvre a grincé. J'étais allongée, je ne riais plus, et mon chemisier était tout de travers. Antoine regardait la dentelle de ma camisole et la bretelle fine sur mon épaule. J'aurais pu tirer sur mon chemisier, mais j'étais hypnotisée.

J'avais peur et en même temps, j'aurais donné la lune pour qu'il m'embrasse. Partout. Sur la bouche. Dans le cou. Sur l'épaule. Sur un sein peut-être...

Antoine devine toujours... Ses lèvres ont effleuré ma bouche. À peine. Un bec de papillon. Puis elles ont couru sur mon cou, glissé jusqu'à l'épaule. J'ai eu un grand frisson. Dans mon corps, la terre a tremblé. Parfois le plaisir et la peur se ressemblent. Antoine s'est arrêté. Je ne savais plus si j'étais déçue ou soulagée.

— Je t'aime.

C'est lui qui l'a dit.

— Moi aussi.

J'avais la gorge nouée, les jambes molles. Envie de rire et de pleurer. J'avais peur de bouger. Comme si je risquais de me réveiller.

Il m'a embrassée. Longtemps. Longtemps.

Je courais dans sa forêt. À toute vitesse. Du plus vite que je pouvais. J'étais étourdie, essoufflée. J'avais envie de me noyer dans sa forêt. C'était chaud et humide. L'air était grisant. J'entendais son coeur battre comme un fou. Il courait, lui aussi. Aussi vite que moi.

Ses mains se sont mises à danser sur mon corps. Des caresses d'oiseau. Légères comme l'air. C'était tellement bon. Mon chemisier était ouvert. Antoine a descendu doucement les bretelles de ma camisole.

— Non! Je ne veux pas!

C'est sorti comme un cri. J'étais déjà debout. J'étais fâchée, sans trop savoir contre qui ni pourquoi.

On avait couru trop vite. Ou trop longtemps. Je ne savais plus où j'étais.

Quelques minutes plus tard, j'étais dehors. L'air était glacé. J'ai couru jusque chez les Dumoulin.

Mon père était là. Dans sa vieille Plymouth. Il attendait. Il était furieux.

Chapitre 4

Le cri du pélican

— Je ne comprends toujours pas.

— Il n'y a rien à comprendre!

— Bon... Mais il a dit quoi, Antoine, quand tu es partie?

— Il n'a pas eu le temps de parler. Je suis partie trop vite. Il faut que je raccroche, Sylvie. Mon père est déjà fâché parce que sa lasagne refroidit. Je te rappelle plus tard. Si je peux...

Le mercredi soir, Léandre prépare le repas. Et on sait 2000 ans d'avance ce qu'on va manger. La lasagne suit le pâté chinois et les petites boulettes. Une semaine avant le spaghetti, sauce à la viande. Mon père n'a jamais compris que les bouchers vendent autre chose que du boeuf haché.

Et Sylvie, elle, n'a pas compris qu'il vaut parfois mieux se taire. Depuis cinq jours, elle pose sans arrêt les mêmes questions. Je serais ravie de lui retirer ses piles.

Depuis vendredi, tout va mal. Du village jusqu'au lac, Léandre n'avait rien dit. Il avait garé l'auto derrière la maison, coupé le moteur et s'était retourné vers moi. Si j'avais tué ma mère, ses yeux n'auraient pas lancé plus d'éclairs.

— Tu as menti!

C'était vrai, et je n'étais pas à un mensonge près.

— Non... Je devais garder avec Sylvie. Si vous m'aviez laissée garder à partir de treize ans comme elle, j'aurais des contrats, moi aussi. Antoine a téléphoné pour que je l'aide dans ses mathématiques, et je n'ai pas eu envie de refuser.

— Je ne suis pas né de la dernière pluie!

Quand mon père dit ça, c'est mauvais signe. Ç'a l'air poétique, mais ça signifie simplement: «Ne me prends pas pour un idiot!»

— Ta mère a téléphoné à dix-neuf heures. Sylvie prétendait que tu étais occupée. Ta mère a insisté pour que tu donnes signe de vie. Une heure plus tard, pas de nouvelles. J'ai rappelé. Sylvie s'est excusée. Elle avait oublié de faire le message, et tu étais partie prendre un peu d'air. Mon oeil! J'ai pris mes clés et je suis allé te chercher.

Notre plan n'était pas parfait. Pendant notre promenade, Sylvie ne pouvait plus m'alerter.

Maman était couchée quand on est arrivés. Je savais qu'elle ne dormait pas. Le lendemain, notre maison était gaie comme un salon funéraire. Je n'ai pas fait de plans pour la soirée. Même si c'était samedi.

Léandre aurait refusé de jouer au chauffeur de taxi. De toute façon, je serais sortie avec qui? Antoine était sûrement fâché. Avec raison. J'étais partie en furie trois minutes après qu'il m'eut dit: «Je t'aime.»

Je ne sais pas ce qui m'a pris. Je ne pensais pas qu'on irait aussi loin. Qu'on se toucherait. Qu'on se déshabillerait. Qu'on ferait l'amour, peut-être...

Enfin, j'y avais pensé... J'ai souvent essayé d'imaginer Antoine sans vêtements. Et chaque fois, je me dis que je le trouverais beau.

Mais dans ma tête, on faisait l'amour beaucoup plus tard. Un futur vague et éloigné. Chez lui, d'un coup, j'ai senti que c'était terriblement facile.

J'avais tellement envie qu'on ne s'arrête pas. Soudain, j'ai eu peur. Et honte. C'est bête, mais c'est vrai.

Antoine l'avait-il planifié? Sur une porte des toilettes des filles à l'école quelqu'un a écrit, ou plutôt égratigné: «Les gars sont tous des cochons». Ça m'agace chaque fois que je lis ça. Léandre et Fernande pensent un peu la même chose. Tous les adolescents seraient des loups affamés de sexe et prêts à bondir pour m'avaler tout rond.

Antoine, un loup! Qui serait assez fou pour penser ça?

J'ai revécu au moins mille fois la soirée de vendredi dans ma tête. Et une fois sur deux — ce qui donne quand même cinq cents fois! — on faisait l'amour. À ce rythme-là, je pourrais donner des cours dans quelques jours.

Les premières fois, on faisait l'amour comme des fous. Vers la cinquantième reprise, j'ai pensé aux pilules et aux condoms. J'avais eu le temps de faire assez de bébés pour fonder un village.

Avec les pilules, le problème c'est qu'on ne peut pas en traîner une dans sa poche en cas d'urgence. Il faut en prendre tous les jours et y penser d'avance. Les condoms, ça paraît bien dans les annonces à la télévision. Mais quand tu ne sais pas trop comment on fait l'amour, la scène du condom en plus, c'est presque héroïque.

Lundi matin, Antoine n'était pas sous le tilleul. Je m'y attendais, mais ça m'a quand même donné un coup.

En arrivant à la maison, en fin d'après-midi, je me sentais lourde comme un ciel d'orage. L'auto de Léandre était là. Pourtant, il n'était que seize heures. Maman travaille jusqu'à dix-sept heures et d'habitude, Léandre la prend au salon en passant.

Avant même d'ouvrir la porte, j'ai senti l'électricité dans l'air. J'ai tourné la poignée très lentement. Il y a eu un grand bruit de vitre fracassée. Et j'ai entendu Fernande crier:

— Je n'en peux plus! Endormez-moi! Tuez-moi! Faites quelque chose. Je ne veux plus continuer. J'ai mal, Léandre. Je suis fatiguée. Tellement, tellement fatiguée.

Sa voix était écorchée. Forte, mais brisée. La porte de la salle de bains était fermée. J'ai reconnu les pas pesants de Léandre. Il était là, lui aussi. Puis il y a eu des sanglots. Étouffés. Comme lorsqu'on pleure la tête enfouie dans les mains ou au creux de l'épaule de quelqu'un.

J'ai filé vers ma chambre. Deux minutes plus tard, Léandre cognait à ma porte.

— Ta mère est simplement fatiguée...

Je n'ai rien dit. J'étais un peu soulagée. Au moins, il ne disait pas que tout était à cause de moi.

— C'est sûrement la ménopause. Tu sais à l'âge de ta mère, les femmes...

— Oui, oui. Je comprends.

J'avais surtout hâte qu'il disparaisse. Mon père n'est pas très doué pour jouer les psychologues, et c'est terriblement gênant pour tout le monde.

J'avais un devoir de français qui risquait de me coûter la soirée au complet. Vendredi, il faut remettre le résumé critique d'un livre.

En plus de résumer l'histoire, il faut dire ce qu'on en pense. Ce qu'on aime et ce qu'on n'aime pas. Ce qu'il faudrait changer. C'est quand même drôle! Colombe, notre prof, répète sans cesse qu'on ne sait pas écrire, et voilà qu'il faut expliquer ce que les grands auteurs auraient dû faire.

Samedi, j'ai choisi un livre pour adolescents de 408 pages à la bibliothèque municipale du lac Supérieur. *Le héron bleu*. J'ai pensé que ça meublerait mon week-end.

Je l'ai lu en deux jours et une demi-nuit! C'est un très beau livre. Étrange et envoûtant. Il y a un passage où Jeff, le héros, se sauve sur une île. Tout va mal dans sa vie. Il est chaviré. Soudain, il aperçoit un héron bleu. C'est un grand oiseau, mince et magnifique. Bizarre aussi... Ça lui donne un coup au coeur! L'oiseau semble seul au monde. Comme lui. Perdu dans un pays immense.

Après avoir lu ce passage, des images et des mots se sont mis à me trotter dans la tête. On aurait dit que j'avais déjà vu cet oiseau. Avant même d'ouvrir ce livre. Je connaissais un oiseau étrange et beau. Grand et émouvant. Mais ce n'était pas un héron.

J'ai compris tout à coup. Mon oiseau à moi, c'était un pélican. Et je ne l'avais jamais vu. Sauf dessiné par des mots.

Je l'avais trouvé dans la cave. Pas l'oiseau, mais le vieux recueil de poèmes de ma mère. Elle l'avait reçu à l'école. Le nom de Fernande était écrit à l'encre verte sur la première page. J'avais mis presque une heure avant de tomber sur la bonne page.

Quand j'étais petite, ma mère me lisait des poèmes dans ce livre-là, le soir, au lieu de me raconter *La Belle au bois dormant*. Fernande a toujours adoré les mots. Elle aurait aimé étudier la littérature ou quelque chose comme ça. Mais Max est mort, et Flavi a eu besoin d'aide au dépanneur.

Il y avait des tas de poèmes plutôt ennuyeux dans le vieux livre de Fernande. Mais l'un d'eux était très beau. Le héron bleu a réveillé des mots dans ma mémoire.

Lorsque le pélican, lassé d'un long voyage
Dans les brouillards du soir retourne à ses roseaux
Ses petits affamés courent sur le rivage

Après, je ne savais plus. Je n'étais même pas sûre que ce soit le début. Le poème raconte que le pélican va chercher de la nourriture pour ses enfants et revient blessé, sans rien à manger. Je me souvenais aussi de quelques mots éparpillés. *Aile au vent, cri sauvage, rivage...* Je les ai retrouvés, à la page 166.

Alors il se soulève, ouvre son aile au vent
Et, se frappant le coeur avec un cri sau-
vage,
Il pousse dans la nuit un si funèbre adieu,
Que les oiseaux des mers désertent le ri-
vage

Les mots dont je me souvenais sont les plus beaux. Mais j'ai lu tout le poème plusieurs fois. Il s'intitule: «Le pélican». C'est Alfred de Musset qui l'a écrit, il y a plus de cent ans.

Dans un court paragraphe au-dessus du poème, on raconte qu'Alfred de Musset était «le poète de l'amour». J'ai pensé arracher la page et l'envoyer à Antoine. Mais il ne comprendrait pas, et j'aurais l'air idiote. De toute façon, il ne m'aime peut-être plus. Déjà.

Chapitre 5

Je t'aime encore plus qu'avant

C'est arrivé cette nuit. Il a neigé pendant six heures. Sans arrêt.

En me réveillant, j'ai tout de suite deviné. Une lumière blanche, toute joyeuse, se faufilait derrière le store et inondait toute la chambre. J'ai chaussé mes bottes et je suis sortie. Il faisait doux. La neige fondrait sûrement. En attendant, c'était tellement beau. J'avais envie de voir le lac.

Les grands sapins m'ont frappée tout de suite. La neige molle écrasait leurs branches. Le poids semblait énorme. Pourtant, ils se tenaient bien droits. Bravement.

J'ai décidé de parler à Antoine aujourd'hui.

Avant d'éclater.

Tant pis s'il ne m'aimait plus. S'il me trouvait ridicule et stupide. Je l'aimais encore, moi. Et je me sentais tellement seule. Il fallait que je lui dise...

Léandre m'a déposée à l'école avant d'aller travailler. J'avais inventé une histoire de projet à terminer à la bibliothèque. Je voulais arriver plus tôt. Avant Antoine.

La bande à Dubé était déjà dans la cour, derrière la polyvalente. Les gars jouaient au soccer dans la neige. Au printemps, ils jouent au hockey. Et ils mangeraient avec leurs oreilles pour se rendre intéressants.

J'ai filé vers le tilleul. Et j'ai attendu.

Vingt fois au moins, j'ai failli me sauver. Il le savait bien, Antoine, que j'étais malheureuse. Et il ne disait rien. Depuis des jours.

Dans le ciel, les nuages formaient des moutons et des géants, des oiseaux aussi. J'avais froid.

Soudain, je l'ai vu arriver. Il m'a aperçue de loin. Il s'est arrêté. Et il s'est dirigé vers moi. Plus il approchait, plus mon coeur battait fort. J'avais peur. J'avais hâte.

Il était maintenant tout près. Je ne voyais plus que ses yeux. Ils prenaient toute la place. J'avais déjà remarqué qu'ils changeaient souvent de couleur. Ce matin, ils étaient pleins de miettes d'or. Ils brillaient de loin. J'ai couru jusqu'à lui.

On s'est embrassés longtemps. Et on est restés enlacés plus longtemps encore. Sans dire un mot.

Plus tard, la cloche a sonné.

Betterave était absente aujourd'hui. Mario Levert en a profité. On peut toujours compter sur lui quand on a des remplaçants. Ce matin, c'était un nouveau sorti on ne sait d'où. Il n'avait pas l'air d'un pauvre diable échoué sur une île infestée de fauves. Il avait l'air baveux, tout simplement.

— Voici. Je suis monsieur Beaulieu et je ne suis pas ici pour perdre mon temps.

— Juste le nôtre, je suppose.

Claude Dubé était fier de son coup. Beaulieu est devenu rouge. Puis mauve. Enragé. Il serrait ses mâchoires tellement fort que sa tête tremblait, et les veines de son cou se gonflaient dangereusement.

— Allez vous expliquer chez le directeur, monsieur l'insolent.

Tout le monde n'adore pas Dubé, mais Beaulieu réagissait trop vite et trop sévèrement pour un remplaçant. La guerre était déclarée. C'était au tour de Mario de jouer.

Mario a le don d'exaspérer les profs. Sournoisement. Il n'est pas très subtil: il rote, il pète, il tousse et il éternue. Ce matin, en prime, il a simulé une crise d'appendicite aiguë. On était crampés.

J'ai vu Antoine à la cafétéria ce midi. De dos seulement. Il avait le nez plongé dans un grand évier. J'aurais aimé qu'il se retourne un peu. Il aurait pu sourire ou me faire un signe. J'ai fait exprès pour parler un peu plus fort. Peine perdue.

Mme Lirette m'a tendu une assiette de rat en souriant drôlement. J'ai compris pourquoi une fois assise devant mon plat. Un bout de papier, collé avec du ruban adhésif, dépassait sous l'assiette.

JE T'AIME ENCORE PLUS QU'AVANT.

Ce n'était pas signé, mais ce n'était pas nécessaire.

Sylvie aussi l'a lu. Elle me l'a presque arraché. Elle était très excitée.

— Wôw! Ça, c'est beau. Vas-tu l'encadrer?

J'ai failli me fâcher. Parfois, j'aimerais que Sylvie se mêle de ses affaires. Je l'aurais gardé pour moi, ce billet-là. Comme un secret, entre Antoine et moi.

Demain, c'est ma fête. Quinze ans. Enfin!

Ce soir, maman était presque gaie. Il était temps! Quand j'ai la grippe, elle dit toujours qu'il ne faut pas trop s'écouter, qu'il faut se secouer, mais elle, elle se vautre dans sa ménopause. Léandre a dû acheter un nouveau miroir pour la salle de bains.

— As-tu des plans pour demain soir, chérie?

Je n'y avais pas pensé. Cette semaine, je n'avais qu'Antoine en tête. J'avais presque oublié ma fête.

— Non... Je ne crois pas...

— Je travaille demain soir. Je suis désolée. J'aurais aimé t'amener au restaurant, mais le vendredi soir, on est tellement occupés au salon... Je ne pouvais pas demander congé.

Ma mère n'est pas vraiment l'être humain avec qui je souhaitais célébrer ma fête, mais ça m'a fait un peu de peine. Un anniversaire, c'est un anniversaire. Et une mère, une mère. Quand même!

— Si tu veux, on peut sortir ensemble, Marie-Lune...

Quoi! Seule avec mon père? Pour parler des nouvelles batteries d'autos vendues chez *Canadian Tire?* Pas question!

— Merci, papa... mais Sylvie serait fâchée si je n'étais pas avec elle le soir de ma fête. On écoutera de la musique...

— Ça tombe bien. La mère de Sylvie t'invite à manger demain soir. Elle est passée au salon aujourd'hui.

Quelle fête à l'horizon! Pas très olé olé.

Je donnerais la lune pour être avec Antoine demain soir.

Chapitre 6

L'oiseau de bois

Je n'avais pas sitôt enlevé mes bottes que Sylvie me faisait grimper quatre à quatre les marches de l'escalier.

— Viiiite! Accélère! Je veux te donner ton cadeau.

C'est quand même bon d'avoir une amie. Je pensais que ma fête s'était terminée ce matin, avant l'école, quand Fernande et Léandre m'avaient offert mon jean et mon chemisier.

Je les portais aujourd'hui. Antoine a dit que j'étais sexy. Ça m'a un peu gênée. C'était la première fois qu'un gars utilisait cet adjectif en parlant de moi. Je nous ai revus chez lui.

— Je t'aime.

J'ai réussi à le regarder droit dans les yeux en disant ça.

Antoine est imprévisible. Il a baissé les yeux. Il a pris ma main. Et il y a déposé un baiser. Au bout des doigts. Léger, léger.

La chambre de Sylvie ressemble à une vaste poubelle. Il y traîne souvent une pointe de pizza séchée, quelques vieux coeurs de pommes et des tas de boulettes de papier.

Au bout de quinze minutes, elle a fini par déterrer mon cadeau dans tout ce désordre. Une boîte minuscule, emballée dans un papier bleu et doré. J'ai mis un temps fou à l'ouvrir. C'était bardé de ruban adhésif. La boîte était légère. Il n'y avait qu'un bout de papier à l'intérieur:

DESCENDS AU SOUS-SOL.

Bon! Ça y est: Sylvie est retombée en enfance. Une course aux trésors à notre âge! Sylvie semblait s'amuser follement. Tant mieux pour elle!

La maison était sombre et tout à fait silencieuse. En ouvrant la porte de la cave, j'ai entendu un bruit. Comme un cri de moineau, suivi d'un éclat de rire. Les lumières se sont allumées d'un coup et une vingtaine de fous m'ont assaillie en hurlant des BONNE FÊTE! à tue-tête. Il y avait Josée, Valérie, Gaétan, Mario, Isabelle, Johanne, Mathieu et beaucoup d'autres.

Et un peu à l'écart, il y avait Antoine.

J'ai sauté dans les bras de Sylvie. Et je me suis mise à pleurer. Les chutes Niagara, c'est de la petite pluie à côté de mes larmes. Quand Marie-Lune Dumoulin-Marchand fabrique des larmes, attention, ce n'est pas au compte-gouttes!

Je pleurais parce que j'étais trop contente. Parce qu'il était là. Parce que tout le monde était là. Parce que c'était la première fête surprise de ma vie. Et un peu aussi parce que je m'en voulais d'avoir négligé ma meilleure amie depuis qu'Antoine était entré dans ma vie.

— Merci, la vieille!

— Vieille toi-même! Tu remercieras ta mère aussi quand tu la croiseras. L'idée vient d'elle. Mais attention! Je n'ai pas été inutile: si ton grand truc blond est ici ce soir, ce n'est sûrement pas grâce à elle...

— Tu es pleine de défauts, Sylvie. Et tu n'as vraiment pas d'allure... Mais je t'adore!

Les parents de Sylvie ne nous ont pas trop dérangés. Gaston est descendu une fois, au début, pour saluer tout le monde et expliquer les règlements.

— Amusez-vous, lâchez votre fou! Ceux qui veulent fumer, allez geler dehors: ma femme et moi, on est allergiques à la cigarette. Pas de drogue non plus dans ma maison: ça me donne des boutons. Embrassez-vous, si vous voulez, ce n'est pas péché. Mais ne vous arrangez pas pour que les pouponnières soient débordées dans neuf mois. Les becs, ça suffit. Compris?

C'était clair. Et sympathique.

Tous les gars m'ont invitée à danser. On aurait dit qu'ils faisaient exprès pour agacer Antoine. Mon grand blond se faisait discret. Il attendait son tour.

Finalement, on s'est retrouvés. Et comme par hasard, c'était sur une chanson des T.B., notre chanson, celle du party d'Halloween. Sans trop le savoir, j'attendais ce moment depuis des semaines. C'est ce que je voulais le plus au monde. Danser avec Antoine. Comme la première fois. J'étais un coureur de fond enfin arrivé à destination. Je ne voulais plus bouger. Pendant au moins deux ou trois milliers d'années.

Ma tête s'est creusé un nid contre l'épaule d'Antoine. Ses bras m'ont enveloppée tendrement. Le paradis doit ressembler à ça.

J'ai pensé à ma mère. Encore. Elle écoute souvent une chanson d'amour de Barbara. C'est une chanteuse française qui a un nez énorme. La musique est affreuse, et la voix de la fille encore pire, mais les paroles sont plutôt belles. Cette chanson m'est revenue:

Elle fut longue la route mais je l'ai faite la route
Celle-là qui menait jusqu'à vous
J'avais fini mon voyage
Je déposais mes bagages
Vous étiez venu au rendez-vous...

J'enlèverais les *vous*. On n'est pas au Moyen Âge! Mais le reste est parfait. Ça disait exactement ce que je ressentais. Ça prouve peut-être qu'à quinze ans, l'amour, ce n'est pas vraiment différent. C'est aussi grand, aussi fort, aussi important.

On dansait en respirant tout juste. On ne bougeait presque pas. Sa grande main a pressé mon dos. Nos corps se sont rapprochés. Je me sentais brûlante. De la tête aux pieds. On s'est embrassés.

Monique est descendue avec une assiette grande comme un navire prêt à sombrer sous le poids des sandwiches. J'ai reconnu les petits sandwiches ronds que Fernande prépare pour les grandes occasions.

Antoine m'a regardée. J'ai compris tout de suite.

Dehors, il neigeait. Une neige folle et fine. De minuscules papillons tombaient mollement en nous chatouillant le nez de temps en temps. On a fait à peine quelques pas avant de se coller contre le mur de pierres froides.

— Bonne fête, beauté!

Il disait ça avec des yeux espiègles.

— Si je l'avais su avant, je t'aurais acheté un beau gros cadeau.

J'ai ri. Même s'il l'avait su dix ans avant, Antoine n'aurait pas eu d'argent.

— Tiens! J'ai trouvé ça dans une poubelle, ce matin.

Les poubelles, je n'ai jamais trouvé ça romantique. Même quand le plus beau gars du monde fouille dedans. Antoine me tendait un petit sac de papier brun fermé comme une pochette avec un bout de ruban.

— Ne t'inquiète pas, ça ne sent pas trop la poubelle.

Il m'avait fait marcher. J'ai défait le ruban. Le vent l'a tout de suite emporté. Tant pis. Sinon, je l'aurais gardé. À l'intérieur du sac, il y avait un tout petit oiseau sculpté dans du bois. Je n'aurais pas pu deviner l'espèce. Mais c'était un oiseau bien vivant. Prêt à s'envoler. Pas un héron. Ni un pélican. Peut-être un peu les deux à la fois.

Antoine est dans ma classe de bio. Avant-hier, on a parlé d'oiseaux. Lenoir nous a demandé de nommer les espèces qu'on saurait identifier. J'ai parlé du pélican. Il était un peu surpris. Il m'a demandé si j'en avais déjà vu un. J'ai bafouillé un peu. C'était gênant. Surtout parce que Antoine était là. Antoine à qui je n'avais pas parlé depuis presque une semaine.

Finalement, je me suis lancée. J'ai tout raconté. J'ai même récité les plus beaux vers du poème d'Alfred de Musset. Personne n'a ri.

Lenoir a dit que c'est parfois dans les oeuvres de fiction qu'on trouve les meilleures descriptions de certains animaux. Il a ajouté que les artistes — les peintres, les poètes, les écrivains — pouvaient nous aider à découvrir la nature.

Je regardais le petit oiseau au creux de ma main. J'étais émue. C'est ce qui me fascine chez Antoine. Il parle si peu. Mais il écoute beaucoup. Chacun de ses gestes devient extrêmement important. Ça vient toujours de loin.

— Je t'aime.

Je me suis blottie contre son corps. Il m'a serrée très fort. J'avais un peu froid. On était sortis vite. Mon manteau était grand ouvert. Il m'a frictionné le dos, puis il s'est mis à attacher mes boutons un à un en commençant par ceux du bas. J'ai ri.

À mi-chemin, il s'est arrêté. Ses mains ont glissé autour de ma taille. Lentement, elles m'ont caressé le ventre avant de se poser sur mes seins. Elles tremblaient un peu. J'ai senti mon corps se tendre comme un arc. Mais je n'avais pas envie de lancer des flèches. Je n'avais pas peur. Je n'avais pas le goût de faire l'amour non plus. J'avais seulement envie de lui dire: «Je t'aime.» Des millions de fois.

Une portière a claqué. J'avais cru entendre une voiture arriver. Le moteur a démarré en trombe. Les pneus ont crissé.

Ma mère était au volant.

Fernande était venue embrasser sa fille et jaser avec Monique. Mais elle ne s'était même pas rendue jusqu'à la maison de Sylvie.

Cette fois, ma fête était vraiment finie. Je voulais rentrer maintenant. Je devinais ce qui m'attendait. Merde!

Chapitre 7

Crises, enfer et catastrophe

— C'est comme ça que tu nous remercies, ton père et moi? On a tout fait pour t'élever comme du monde. On ne mérite pas ça. Tu n'as pas le droit de te jeter dans les bras du premier venu. As-tu compris, Marie-Lune Dumoulin-Marchand?

Ma mère était déchaînée. C'était pire que tout ce que j'aurais pu imaginer. Et elle pleurait. Un véritable torrent! Je me disais que l'actrice en mettait trop. Mais elle était convaincante. De grosses larmes grises roulaient sur ses joues. Elle s'était maquillée un peu. C'est rare. Et le trait de crayon sous ses yeux salissait ses larmes. Ma mère faisait presque pitié.

— Tu sauras, ma petite fille, que la première fois que j'ai embrassé un garçon,
c'était ton père. Et ce n'était pas comme
ça. Je vous ai vus! Il te touchait...

— C'est vrai! Et j'aimais ça.

Sa colère est tombée d'un coup. Elle
était saisie. Elle m'a regardée avec ses
grands yeux verts, et j'ai eu un choc, moi
aussi. Ses yeux sont verts comme les grands
sapins, verts comme les yeux d'Antoine. Je
ne l'avais jamais remarqué avant.

— Je l'aime, maman. Pour vrai. Il ne
veut pas abuser de moi. Il ne veut pas me
manger tout rond. Quand on s'aime, on
veut se toucher. C'est normal. Tu m'avais
dit quelque chose comme ça, le jour où tu
m'avais expliqué ce que c'était faire
l'amour. Je le savais déjà depuis longtemps, mais je les trouvais beaux, tes mots.

— Tu mêles tout! Tu as quinze ans. Tu
ne vas quand même pas prendre la pilule à
quinze ans! Tous les psychologues disent
qu'il ne faut pas brûler les étapes. Si ça
continue, tu seras déjà vieille à dix-huit ans.

— Tu es bouchée! Si le père d'Antoine
ne faisait pas si dur, je me demande si tu
ferais un tel drame. Tu es snob! C'est tout.

— Non! Je ne suis pas snob. Mais j'ai

une fille ingrate. Et insolente. Ton Antoine, je le connais depuis qu'il est bébé. Sa mère était à l'asile, la moitié du temps. Et son père a toujours empesté le gros gin. Pour faire pousser des bons légumes, il faut du bon engrais. Antoine n'est pas un mauvais diable, il fait même pitié, mais ce n'est pas un gars pour toi.

— Mange de la *marde!*

Cette fois, c'est moi qui pleurais. Je la détestais. J'avais envie de lui sauter au visage. Elle n'avait pas le droit de salir Antoine comme ça. C'était fou. Méchant. Et tellement stupide, son histoire de légumes. Ma mère est snob. C'est tout.

J'ai couru jusqu'à ma chambre. J'ai claqué la porte et je me suis jetée sur mon lit. J'étais crevée. Je suis tombée endormie en pleurant dans mon oreiller.

Samedi soir, Sylvie est allée à la discothèque, à l'école. Antoine était là. Il m'attendait. D'habitude, je vais à toutes les danses comme à toutes les activités organisées par l'école. Pour Fernande et Léandre, l'école est une police d'assurance. Tout ce qui se passe entre les murs de cet édifice est béni d'avance. S'ils savaient...

— Il faisait pitié, ton Roméo.

— Pitié, mon oeil! Allez-vous arrêter de dire qu'il fait pitié! C'est peut-être moi qui fais pitié. Je ne suis pas allée à la discothèque, moi. Je n'avais personne avec qui danser.

J'étais furieuse, au téléphone.

— Calme-toi! Je devine ce qui t'énerve. Antoine n'a pas dansé non plus. Tu es contente? Il n'arrête pas de parler de toi. Même que, franchement, ça commence à me fatiguer. Je t'aime bien, mais comme sujet de conversation, je pourrais imaginer autre chose!

— Excuse-moi, Sylvie. C'est l'enfer ici! Viens-tu faire un tour?

— Je voudrais bien, mais on passe la journée chez mon parrain. C'est la fête d'Émilie, sa petite peste de deux ans. Ça promet...

J'ai enfilé mes bottes et mon manteau et je suis allée marcher. Je pensais faire le tour du lac à pied. Deux heures de randonnée, ça devrait me calmer. En passant devant l'église du lac, j'ai entendu chanter. L'abbé Grégoire chante comme un crapaud enrhumé, et sa chorale ne vaut guère mieux, mais la chaleur de leurs voix me faisait du bien.

L'église du lac est jolie. Derrière l'autel, on voit l'eau, les falaises, les montagnes. Il y a quelques années, j'allais souvent à l'église, maintenant je me contente des messes de minuit.

La porte a grincé quand je suis entrée. Le prêtre buvait du vin. Je ne me souvenais plus si c'était avant ou après la communion, ce bout-là. Je me suis assise. J'étais bien. Il fait toujours chaud dans l'église. C'est silencieux, mais c'est vivant en même temps. Peut-être parce qu'il y a des gens.

J'étais assise complètement à l'arrière. J'aurais pu m'étendre sur le banc, lire un livre, faire n'importe quoi. Personne ne m'observait. Je me suis agenouillée. Pour une fois, j'en avais vraiment envie. J'avais le goût de me ramasser en boule pour penser. Mais sans m'en apercevoir, j'ai prié.

C'était quand même drôle parce que je ne crois plus en Dieu depuis quelques années. Je pense qu'on meurt comme les chats. On raidit, on refroidit et puis on engraisse la terre. Ça fait presque mon affaire. C'est moins angoissant que l'idée de vivre éternellement. Surtout qu'au paradis, si j'ai bien compris, il n'y a pas grand-chose à faire.

Prier, c'est un bien grand mot. Disons que j'ai parlé dans ma tête. À quelqu'un qui n'existe probablement pas. Mais tant pis.

Je lui ai dit que j'avais mon voyage. Que ma mère n'était plus comme avant. Et que moi aussi, j'avais changé.

Je lui ai confié qu'en ce moment, je me sentais comme les feuilles tombées que le vent pousse de tous côtés. Elles n'ont rien pour s'agripper.

Je lui ai raconté que j'aimais quelqu'un. Beaucoup. Mais que l'amour laissait de grands trous dans ma vie.

À l'école, le lendemain, Antoine m'a demandé si mes parents me laisseraient sortir samedi prochain. Ça m'a fâchée. On était bien, en paix sous notre arbre. Pourquoi commencer à planifier? À s'inquiéter?

Au cours de maths, mercredi, Betterave m'a attrapée à copier. Je n'avais pas étudié. La veille, Fernande avait lancé un verre contre le mur de la cuisine. De toutes ses forces. Pour rien. C'est sa façon à elle de hurler, je crois. On ne sait même pas pourquoi. Elle a maigri. Elle a vieilli. Elle se promène avec un air de cimetière et de temps en temps, elle fait éclater du verre.

Ce n'est pas très gai au 281, chemin Tour du lac.

J'avais décidé que j'avais assez de problèmes dans ma vie sans m'en inventer avec des chiffres. C'est pour ça que je n'avais pas préparé l'examen de Miss Mathématiques.

— Puisque vous aimez copier, mademoiselle Marchand, nous allons vous gâter. Avant le prochain cours, copiez-moi cent fois: «À l'avenir, je ne copierai pas.»

L'imbécile. Elle se trouvait drôle.

Le cours de maths était le dernier de la journée. J'attendais l'autobus en compagnie d'Antoine quand un homme s'est dirigé vers nous. Il marchait lentement, et ses jambes semblaient si molles que chaque pas devenait un exploit. Ses yeux étaient trop rouges et sa barbe trop longue.

— Salut, mon petit gars! Ton père est venu te chercher. Tu diras pas que je m'occupe pas de toi. Si t'es fin, je vais t'acheter un bon cornet au dépanneur.

Le père d'Antoine était très soûl. Il devait s'imaginer que son fils avait cinq ans, et qu'on était en plein été. Ça fait deux mois que le dépanneur ne vend plus de crème glacée.

Antoine était très gêné. J'avais mal avec lui.

— Je pense que je vais y aller.

C'est tout ce qu'il a dit avant de partir. Son père l'a suivi en criant de l'attendre.

Fernande n'était pas à la maison quand je suis rentrée. C'était pourtant son jour de congé. Flavi m'attendait dans la cuisine. Elle portait un long tablier et roulait des cigares au chou.

— Ta mère est à l'hôpital...

La voix de Flavi était bizarre. Mal ajustée.

— On lui fait un traitement...

Sa voix était meilleure. Elle a souri.

— Ne t'inquiète pas, Marie. Ta mère avait mal au ventre depuis un bout de temps... Ils vont essayer de régler ça. Avec un peu de chance, ça devrait bien aller.

Un peu de chance! Ça veut dire quoi? Et s'ils ne réussissent pas?

— As-tu faim? Je vous prépare un bon repas...

J'ai embrassé Flavi et j'ai filé dans ma chambre faire mes devoirs.

Flavi est restée jusqu'à vendredi. Ce soir-là, j'ai encore demandé à Léandre de m'emmener avec lui à l'hôpital. Depuis mercredi, il refusait que je l'accompagne.

— Attends encore un peu, Marie-Lune. Ta mère prend des calmants. Elle dort presque tout le temps. Demain, peut-être qu'elle se sentira mieux.

Il m'a répété ce qu'il m'avait dit la veille et l'avant-veille. Il m'a aussi prévenue qu'il rentrerait très tard. Un dernier article à écrire pour l'édition de samedi.

Antoine est venu. Il a fait de l'auto-stop jusqu'au chemin Tour du lac et il a marché jusque chez nous. Je me suis rappelé combien je l'aime quand je l'ai vu, le manteau couvert de neige, les joues glacées et les yeux pleins de lumière.

Pauvre Antoine! Au lieu de l'inviter à entrer, j'ai sauté dans mes bottes et je l'ai entraîné jusqu'au lac. Au bord de l'eau, il y a un grand banc de bois. J'ai balayé la neige avec mes mitaines.

— Je voulais voir le lac avec toi. On ne restera pas longtemps. Juste quelques minutes...

Antoine a ri. On s'est enlacés. Autant parce qu'on s'aime que pour se réchauffer.

Il faisait déjà noir. Des tas de petits bruits trouaient la nuit. Ils venaient du vent, de l'eau, des oiseaux et des bêtes cachées que la lune réveillait. J'aime cette musique, lourde de silences.

— Viens...

Antoine s'est levé en m'attirant vers lui. Ses bras m'ont emprisonnée, et il m'a embrassée.

Je n'arrivais plus à entendre les sons de la nuit. Mon coeur s'est mis à battre plus fort. Mais je ne ressentais ni plaisir ni désir. Seule l'angoisse montait en moi. C'était la voix de Fernande que j'entendais. Des miettes de phrases, de tristes petits bouquets de mots. Et des cris étouffés. Comme des appels au secours.

Antoine a senti que je n'étais pas avec lui. Mais il n'a pas compris.

— Ça t'a refroidie de voir mon père cette semaine, hein? Dis-le. Je comprends ça...

Quelque chose en moi s'est rompu. Antoine aussi était loin de moi maintenant. J'étais vraiment seule sur mon île. Comme Jeff, dans *Le héron bleu.*

J'avais envie de hurler, de pleurer, de courir jusqu'au bout du monde. Mais sur une île, le bout du monde n'est jamais bien loin.

— Je m'en sacre de ton père! Et du

mien. Et de ma mère. Et de TOI! Je veux juste la paix!

Antoine est reparti. Aussi gelé que lorsqu'il était arrivé.

Pendant la nuit, j'ai fait un cauchemar. Je marchais tranquillement sur la route autour du lac. Antoine était avec moi. Il me tenait la main. Le temps était magnifique. Le soleil s'accrochait aux mottes de neige sur les branches des sapins.

Soudain, un camion a foncé sur nous. J'ai crié. Antoine m'a poussée vers la forêt. Le camion a frappé Antoine. Son grand corps a volé avant de rebondir sur le pavé.

J'ai eu le temps de voir le chauffard. C'était Fernande.

Je me suis réveillée en hurlant.

Léandre est venu. Il était gêné. Il n'a pas l'habitude de me consoler. Je tremblais comme un bouleau battu par le vent. J'étais incapable d'arrêter.

Je ne lui ai rien raconté. Mais il m'a pris dans ses bras. C'était doux et chaud. Mon père doit être à peu près grand comme Antoine. C'est un peu pareil dans ses bras. Ça m'a calmée.

Chapitre 8

Fernande est partie

J'ai dormi très tard. Et je me suis réveillée avec la drôle d'impression d'être en retard. Pour rien, puisqu'on était samedi matin. Sans réfléchir, j'ai enfilé rapidement un vieux costume de jogging. De gros bas de coton. Mes espadrilles. J'ai donné trois coups de peigne dans mes cheveux. Je me suis brossé les dents.

J'étais prête. J'ai su pourquoi en vissant le petit capuchon blanc sur le tube de pâte dentifrice.

Il fallait vite réveiller Léandre. Depuis quand dormait-il aussi tard? Je voulais voir Fernande. Et pas cet après-midi. Ce matin.

Tout de suite.

La chambre de Léandre était vide. Les couvertures du lit déjà tirées.

Sur le comptoir de la cuisine, il m'avait laissé un message.

PARTI À L'HÔPITAL.

J'ai attrapé mon manteau. Tant pis. Je marcherais jusqu'au dépanneur et de là, je trouverais quelqu'un qui descendrait au village.

Dehors, j'ai remarqué que j'avais oublié de mettre mes bottes. Tant pis. J'ai fait quelques pas dans la neige dure. L'auto de Léandre est arrivée.

Je me suis arrêtée.

Il est sorti.

— Elle est morte.

C'est tout ce qu'il a dit.

Chapitre 9

Le désert de pierres

Antoine est venu au salon. Sylvie aussi. Toute la classe est venue. Même des profs que je ne connais pas.

Ce n'est pas épeurant, un mort. Ce n'est pas épeurant, parce que ça n'a pas l'air vrai. Ça ressemble aux statues du musée de cire. Le bout des doigts est mince, aplati. Et la peau trop dure, trop sèche. On voit le maquillage épais. On dirait un déguisement.

On reconnaît la personne, mais en même temps, on a envie de dire:

— Ce n'est pas elle. Vous vous êtes trompés.

Je n'ai pas pleuré une seule fois. Mario a même réussi à me faire rire. Sans se forcer.

Je le regardais et j'avais le fou rire. C'est idiot, mais ça l'a gêné. Il n'est pas resté longtemps.

Antoine non plus. Il est venu le premier soir. Il avait l'air d'un homme dans son costume du dimanche. Je me demande où il l'a pris. Il a donné une poignée de main à Léandre et lui a offert ses condoléances.

Mon père m'a surprise. Il a pressé Antoine contre lui, comme s'ils étaient de vieux amis. Antoine avait les yeux mouillés quand il m'a enfin regardée. Il m'a enveloppée dans ses bras. Et il m'a murmuré à l'oreille:

— Je t'aime. Je suis là. Appelle-moi quand tu voudras.

Puis il est parti.

Je ne l'ai pas rappelé. Je n'ai peut-être pas eu le temps. J'étais comme une toupie au salon. Tout le monde m'étreignait en disant des sottises.

— Pauvre petite chatte.

— Elle a bien du courage.

— Mon Dieu, qu'elle ressemble à sa mère!

C'est pareil dans les zoos. On parle des animaux devant eux. Comme s'ils n'étaient pas là. Comme s'ils n'entendaient pas.

Ça pue, les salons. Pourtant, j'aime les fleurs. Mais ici, les fleurs sont comme les morts. Elles n'ont plus l'air vraies.

Lundi, c'était pire. On était tous tassés autour d'un trou. J'ai pensé à Camille, ma grosse chatte grise. Un matin, elle est rentrée en boitant. Une bête sauvage l'avait mordue. Elle pleurait comme pleurent les chats. De grands sifflements désespérés. Léandre l'avait enveloppée dans une serviette de bain et on avait filé jusqu'à Saint-Jovite chez le vétérinaire. C'était trop tard.

C'est toujours trop tard. L'an dernier, Léandre m'avait menti. C'était une tumeur maligne que les médecins avaient découverte dans le corps de Fernande. Ils l'ont enlevée, mais une autre est apparue. Fernande n'avait pas de problèmes de ménopause. C'est le cancer qui la grignotait.

Tout le monde le savait.

Sauf moi.

Léandre m'avait aidée à la mort de ma chatte Camille. On avait monté la côte à Dubé ensemble. Camille avait l'air de dormir, bien emmaillotée dans la grande serviette. Le Dr Lavoie lui avait fait une injection. Pour qu'elle puisse mourir plus vite. Pour qu'elle ne souffre pas.

Ma mère a-t-elle connu le même sort? Je me demande souvent si elle a beaucoup souffert.

Tout en haut de la côte à Dubé, il y a une cascade. L'eau gicle sur les grosses pierres lisses. C'est plein de vie, un torrent. On avait enterré Camille près de là. C'était triste. Mais pas trop. Léandre avait creusé un petit trou. J'y avais déposé ma chatte. Léandre m'avait aidée à la recouvrir de terre.

Les cimetières n'ont rien à voir avec les torrents. J'avais envie de hurler.

— NON! ARRÊTEZ! Vous vous êtes trompés. Fernande ne veut pas ça. Elle aime la vie. Le lac, la montagne, les sapins fouettés par le vent. Les chutes, les sources, les rivières, les torrents. Vous n'allez pas l'emprisonner ici!

Ils descendaient la grande boîte de bois au fond du trou. Je les trouvais tellement idiots. Camille était bien sur son matelas de terre. C'est tellement plus doux que du bois.

Un oiseau a crié. Il devait être loin, car il n'y a pas d'arbres au cimetière. C'est comme un désert. J'ai senti quelque chose débouler en moi. Une chute terrible. Un choc atroce.

J'ai crié. Plus fort que les oiseaux sauvages.

Léandre n'a pas bougé. Il criait peut-être, lui aussi, mais en silence.

Paul, le frère de ma mère, a voulu m'étreindre pour me consoler.

— Lâche-moi! Va-t'en! Ne me touche pas!

Je criais, je hurlais. Je le frappais le plus fort que je pouvais.

Il le méritait. On n'essaie pas de consoler une bête prise au piège. On la libère. Ou on se tait.

J'avais envie de tout détruire. De faire voler en éclats ce grand désert de fausses pierres. Et tous ces imbéciles, plantés autour d'un trou.

On ne sait jamais combien de temps durent les ouragans. Tout redevient calme d'un coup.

Léandre était maintenant près de moi. On est rentrés à la maison. J'étais épuisée. Mais je ne pleurais pas. Je n'avais pas versé une larme depuis que Fernande était morte.

J'ai souvent pensé à Antoine. Au salon. Au cimetière. Et souvent depuis. Il n'a pas fait l'imbécile, lui. Il n'est pas allé à la mascarade.

— Je t'aime. Je suis là. Appelle-moi quand tu voudras.

C'est tout ce qu'il a dit. C'est tout ce qu'il y avait à dire.

Chapitre 10

L'amour qui tue

J'ai passé la journée sans rien faire. Un long samedi vide. Aussi morne que chacun des jours de la dernière semaine.

Hier, Léandre est retourné au journal. Pour la première fois depuis. J'irai à l'école lundi. Pour la première fois depuis.

Mon jean neuf est déjà trop grand. Je mange juste un peu. Pour faire plaisir à Flavi. Je ne fais pas exprès. On dirait que j'ai un estomac de souris. Trois bouchées et j'ai fini.

Sylvie n'est pas venue aujourd'hui. Elle allait voir Les Détraqués, à Montréal.

— Viens donc! Ils sont tordants.

J'ai refusé. Je me sens assez détraquée

comme ça.

Léandre a travaillé au journal toute la journée. À dix-sept heures, il a téléphoné pour annoncer qu'il rentrerait très tard.

Flavi est retournée à Montréal avec Sylvie et Monique, en fin d'après-midi. J'ai dû lui promettre de mieux manger.

La maison était vide. Pendant les deux premières minutes, je me suis sentie heureuse d'être seule. J'ai ouvert la radio. On jouait une nouvelle chanson des T.B. Je ne comprends pas toujours l'anglais. Surtout sur de la musique. Mais certains mots revenaient souvent: *Killing love*. L'amour qui tue. C'était probablement le titre.

Ils avaient lancé leur nouvel album cette semaine. J'entendais cette chanson pour la première fois. La musique était belle. Puissante. Poignante. Un peu affolante aussi.

Le soleil fondait tranquillement derrière les montagnes. J'avais un peu faim. J'étais presque bien. J'ai étalé un linge sur la table à café du salon et j'ai allumé des bougies. J'avais envie de me gâter. Je me suis préparé un sous-marin et j'ai trouvé une bouteille de vin dans le fond du frigo. Je m'en suis servi un grand verre et j'ai pique-niqué seule en regardant le soleil disparaître.

Je ne me souvenais plus si la bouteille de vin était pleine quand je l'avais prise. À la dernière bouchée de mon sous-marin, elle était vide.

Je ne me sentais ni gaie ni fatiguée. Je me sentais seule. Affreusement seule. J'aurais enlacé un grand sapin glacé juste pour sentir quelque chose d'un peu vivant contre moi.

J'ai composé le numéro. Le téléphone a sonné trois fois. Pendant une seconde, j'ai eu peur que son père réponde. Non. C'était bien Antoine. Je reconnaissais sa voix.

— Marie-Lune? Qu'est-ce que tu fais? Où es-tu? Ça va?

— Tu m'avais dit que je pouvais t'appeler. Tu n'es plus fâché, hein?

— Je t'aime. Tu le sais.

— Je peux aller chez toi?

Il y a eu un silence. Il allait dire non.

— Non. Attends-moi, je monte au lac. Tu ne peux pas venir comme ça... À moins que ton père te conduise.

— Léandre travaille. Mais je ne veux pas que tu viennes. Je veux sortir. Je veux être chez toi. Comme la dernière fois.

J'ai raccroché. Je me suis habillée chaudement. Veste, tuque, mitaines, double paire de bas. Tout le tralala.

J'ai marché jusqu'au dépanneur. J'étais assez habillée pour visiter le Pôle Nord et pourtant, j'avais froid. Ça faisait exprès. Pas d'auto. Personne. J'ai continué à marcher. Tant pis. J'étais prête à faire vingt kilomètres à pied.

Des phares se sont approchés. Un gros camion. J'ai levé mon pouce. Je n'avais jamais fait ça. J'ai pensé à Fernande. Si elle me voyait, son coeur flancherait.

S'il battait encore.

Le camion a ralenti. J'ai sauté sur la petite marche, sous la portière. Le conducteur était plutôt vieux. Sûrement pas dangereux. Il faisait chaud à l'intérieur.

— T'as quel âge, toi?

Tu parles d'une façon d'aborder les gens. Je suis peut-être jeune pour faire de l'auto-stop mais lui, il est plutôt vieux pour conduire un douze roues. On est quittes.

— Dix-sept ans.

Je lui ai servi mon sourire le plus angélique.

— Je n'ai pas l'habitude de faire du pouce, mais mon père est malade. Et les taxis coûtent cher.

Il m'a regardée avec l'air de dire: «Ne

me prends pas pour un idiot», mais il s'est tu. Il m'a laissée à l'entrée du village.

Il faisait encore plus froid. J'ai couru. En tournant au coin de la rue, je me suis trouvée nez à nez avec Antoine.

— Tu es folle, Marie-Lune! J'étais tellement inquiet.

Je ne l'ai pas laissé parler. Je l'ai embrassé. J'avais envie de me noyer dans ses bras.

Tout était propre et rangé chez lui. J'ai enlevé mon manteau, mes bottes et plusieurs pelures. Je portais la chemise bleue du père de Sylvie.

— As-tu faim? As-tu froid?

J'ai dit non. Je l'ai embrassé encore.

— Ça va, Marie-Lune?

C'est fou. Je l'embrasse et il s'inquiète.

On était debout.

J'ai déboutonné mon chemisier. Antoine me regardait. Il ne disait rien.

Le chemisier est tombé sans faire de bruit en formant une petite flaque bleue à mes pieds.

Antoine m'a enlacée. Enfin. Il sentait encore la forêt d'automne, les feuilles mouillées et la terre. Tant pis pour l'hiver. Antoine sent l'automne, lui. Il est plus fort que les saisons.

Sa chemise était rude sur ma peau. Je l'ai déboutonnée. On s'est retrouvés nus devant la fenêtre du salon sans rideaux. Antoine m'a guidée jusqu'à sa chambre. Le matelas s'est creusé sous mon poids. J'étais bien. Comme dans un nid.

Je n'ai pas eu mal quand il a plongé en moi. C'était bon. Nos corps voguaient, secoués par de hautes vagues; la mer dansait autour de nous.

Mais le temps a brusquement changé. Ça tanguait trop. J'avais peur. Je voulais rentrer. M'étendre doucement sur la plage. Sans bouger.

La tempête s'est abattue sur nous. La mer était déchaînée. Les vagues allaient nous avaler.

J'ai crié. Trop tard. On a chaviré.

La mer allait m'engloutir. Tout était noir. J'étouffais.

J'ai crié encore. J'ai aperçu la forêt. Deux grandes taches vertes. Je me suis accrochée au regard d'Antoine, sinon j'allais me noyer. C'était ma seule bouée.

Il m'a caressé le front, les joues, le cou. Longtemps. Jusqu'à ce que les vents s'apaisent. Puis il m'a aidée à me rhabiller. Sans dire un mot.

J'ai vu qu'il pleurait.

Il a téléphoné à la maison. Puis au *Clairon*. Léandre ne répondait pas. Monique est venue me chercher. Elle n'a rien dit.

Au lac, Léandre ronflait sur le sofa du salon. Il n'avait pas enlevé son manteau, et la neige de ses bottes fondait sur l'imprimé fleuri. Il avait bu, lui aussi.

Monique m'a ramenée chez elle. J'ai dormi dans le lit de Sylvie.

Chapitre 11

Deux Miss Marathon

— Allez! Secoue ta carcasse, Marie-Lune la lune. Viens voir comme c'est beau. Il a neigé toute la nuit. Veux-tu faire du ski?

Je venais tout juste d'ouvrir un oeil. De comprendre où j'étais et pourquoi j'étais là. De me souvenir d'hier...

— Tu ne me demandes pas ce qui est arrivé hier soir?

— Euh!... Si tu veux... Mais je sais où tu étais...

— Tu sais aussi que j'ai fait une crise. Monique t'a dit autre chose?

— Non... Pas vraiment...

Sylvie aime les défis. Les compétitions,

les marathons et les longues randonnées de ski de fond. L'an dernier, elle m'a presque tuée. On a parcouru tous les sentiers du parc du Mont-Tremblant. Rien ne l'arrête. Elle s'est gelé les oreilles, seule sur les pistes un après-midi où il faisait 20 au-dessous de zéro.

Son lobe gauche est devenu tout blanc. Puis il a enflé, il a viré au noir et il est tombé. Pas tout d'un bloc. Un petit bout. Depuis, Sylvie a l'oreille gauche plus fluette que la droite. Pour la faire enrager, Claude Dubé l'appelle Zoreille. Ça marche à tous coups.

— C'est vrai qu'il fait beau. Penses-tu que les sentiers du parc sont déjà ouverts?

Monique a téléphoné. Toutes les pistes étaient skiables. C'est plutôt rare au début de décembre. On avait eu seulement trois tempêtes. Mais la neige n'avait pas fondu.

— O.K. Je te suis. Mais pas de singeries.

— Ne t'inquiète pas. Le pire qui puisse t'arriver, c'est que tu te gèles le nez. On t'appellera Narine. Penses-tu qu'Antoine t'aimerait quand même?

Antoine? Antoine qui? J'ai senti une onde de chaleur me courir le long des jambes et me monter à la tête. La nouvelle chanson des T.B. m'est revenue. Elle jouait à la radio, hier soir, pendant qu'on faisait l'amour. *Killing love*. L'amour qui tue. Des mots horribles. C'est là que j'avais paniqué. Les paroles de la chanson avaient déclenché la tempête.

Si Antoine n'était pas entré dans ma vie, Fernande serait-elle morte?

Le cancer, ça se dompte, je pense. On peut ralentir le cours des maladies. Mais quand l'inquiétude nous grignote les tripes, on devient vulnérable. C'est comme les animaux blessés: les loups sautent dessus.

Robert, notre patrouilleur-secouriste préféré, nous a accuillies au Centre communautaire du lac Monroe. C'est là que les skieurs doivent s'enregistrer avant de s'élancer sur les pistes. Robert est un peu mère poule. Il voulait s'assurer qu'on choisirait les bons farts.

— C'est du bleu aujourd'hui, les filles. Mais emportez du vert aussi. Ils annoncent du mauvais temps en fin d'après-midi. Ne traînez pas sur les pistes.

Miss Marathon a décidé que nous prenions La Mallard. Vingt kilomètres. La plus longue piste. Seule La Poisson est plus difficile. Un peu moins longue, mais plus traître. Le sentier de La Poisson monte à pic pendant plus d'une heure. La descente est terriblement casse-cou.

Les patrouilleurs ont l'habitude de grimper en motoneige jusqu'au sommet en tirant leur traîneau-civière pour ramener les blessés. Les accidents sont fréquents. Une bonne dizaine par année. C'est pour ça qu'entre nous, cette piste-là, on l'appelle La Diable, pas La Poisson.

La neige était bien froide. Nos skis glissaient comme des patins entre les conifères. D'habitude, Sylvie doit souvent m'attendre. Mais là, je filais à toute allure. Sylvie était contente. Nous avions atteint le premier refuge en moins de quarante minutes. Elle a proposé qu'on entre pique-niquer.

Miss Marathon a englouti deux sandwiches au beurre d'arachide, miel et confiture en croquant des cornichons. Ça me donne des frissons. Elle insistait pour que je goûte à tout: sandwich, fromage, noix, chocolat, biscuits. J'obéissais sans broncher. J'étais même prête à manger des cornichons pour avoir la paix et retourner au plus vite sur les pistes. Tant que j'avançais, je ne pensais à rien. J'étais bien.

J'ai pris les devants. Je roulais vite. Le

vent me soûlait. C'est encore mieux que le vin. En me gelant les joues, il m'anesthésiait aussi le cerveau.

Je pensais: Antoine. Rien. Le vide. Des nuages. Mon coeur ne battait ni plus vite ni moins vite.

Je pensais: Fernande. C'était pareil. De l'air. J'avais la cervelle creuse. Et je voulais qu'elle reste comme ça.

Arrivées à La Cache, le deuxième refuge, Sylvie a proposé une pause chocolat chaud. Elle était essoufflée. Moi aussi. Mais je n'avais pas envie d'arrêter.

La Cache est perchée sur un sommet. De là, on descend longtemps. J'ai décidé de foncer. Les arbres défilaient à toute vitesse. Le vent me fouettait le visage, et la neige blanche m'aveuglait. Mes skis ont dérapé sur une plaque de glace. Et j'ai fait une culbute avant de me réveiller sur le dos, les quatre fers en l'air.

— Qu'est-ce qui est arrivé? Tu saignes!

Sylvie avait vraiment l'air inquiète. Je me suis frotté la joue. Puis la tête. Je me suis levée et j'ai secoué mon pantalon. Ma jambe saignait. Ma mitaine blanche était tachée de sang. En tombant, je m'étais enfoncé la pointe d'un bâton dans la jambe droite. Je n'avais rien senti.

— Ce n'est rien. Viens!

— En arrivant au Centre communautaire, il faudra nettoyer ça. Après, on verra. Tu auras peut-être besoin d'une injection contre le tétanos. Tu roules trop vite, Marie-Lune. Je suis plus en forme que toi et je suis crevée. Ce n'est pas bon, au début de la saison. C'est comme ça qu'on se blesse. Tu le sais pourtant.

En apercevant le toit du grand chalet du lac Monroe, j'ai paniqué. Je ne voulais pas rentrer. Je ne voulais pas me remettre à penser. Tant que je skiais je me sentais bien.

Le stationnement était presque vide. Le soleil descendait doucement. Trois patrouilleurs fartaient leurs skis, prêts à fermer les sentiers.

— Salut, les filles! Rien à signaler avant qu'on fasse le ménage?

Sylvie a rougi. Les patrouilleurs, c'est son genre. Musclés, bronzés et pétants de santé. Ils allaient inspecter les refuges et s'assurer que plus personne ne traînait sur les sentiers.

Le ski de fond en montagne, ça peut être dangereux. Il suffit d'une spatule brisée, et on ne peut plus avancer. Sans skis, nos pieds enfoncent dans la neige. En quelques heures, la nuit tombe, et on gèle. Parfois, les skieurs paniquent et se perdent. Certains meurent d'hypothermie.

Moi, ce n'est pas le froid, mais les bêtes qui me font peur. Il y a des renards et des lynx dans la forêt. Des loups aussi. Le froid dévore lentement; il me semble qu'on doit avoir le temps de se sauver. Sinon, on s'endort lentement et on meurt sans s'en apercevoir. Les animaux sont plus sauvages. Ils bondissent sur leur proie.

— J'espère que maintenant j'ai droit à mon chocolat chaud? a demandé Sylvie.

— On peut le prendre au Centre communautaire. Il y a des sachets. Ce sera meilleur et plus chaud que le vieux fond qui reste dans ton thermos.

— Bonne idée! Mais avant, va nettoyer ta blessure. Le sang me coupe l'appétit.

— À vos ordres, madame!

J'avais du mal à paraître joyeuse. Les conversations amicales sont épuisantes quand le tonnerre gronde dans notre ventre. Quand tout dérape. Quand il grêle dans notre tête.

J'ai skié lentement jusqu'aux toilettes. Devant la porte, je me suis penchée pour libérer mes pieds des fixations.

Le vent hurlait. J'aimais sa musique. Elle enterrait tout. Lorsqu'on fonce dans un vent fou, plus rien n'existe. Il n'y a que notre corps qui avance et le vent qui souffle. C'est comme quand on danse sur une musique très électrique. La terre arrête de tourner. Il ne reste que des gestes et des sons.

Je me suis relevée. Les bottines de Monique étaient encore bien ancrées dans leurs fixations. J'ai décidé d'avancer. La Diable était devant.

Chapitre 12

Tempête sur La Diable

Du lac Monroe, le sentier des Falaises grimpe sur un dos d'âne, une bonne butte aux versants à pic. C'est très beau. On a l'impression de franchir une passerelle. Au loin, les falaises sont noires et mystérieuses. L'an dernier, Robert nous a raconté que des hérons bleus nichent au faîte de la montagne l'été. Ils s'installent presque toujours sur de vieux pins mourants.

Tout en haut, après des kilomètres de pentes abruptes, la vue est magnifique. En route, on peut reprendre son souffle à La Perdriole.

Pour oublier la fatigue, il faut se laisser envoûter par les falaises. La glace épaisse accrochée aux flancs brille sous le soleil. C'est fascinant. Les reflets bleus et verts se teintent de violet parfois.

J'avançais rapidement. C'est toujours facile de glisser dans des traces fraîches. Robert était devant. Je l'avais vu filer vers La Diable.

De nouveau, j'étais bien. Pas besoin de parler. Pas besoin de penser.

Mais il faisait froid. Pendant les quelques minutes d'arrêt au lac Monroe, devant le Centre communautaire, mon corps s'était refroidi, et mes vêtements humides de transpiration étaient rapidement devenus glacés. Il fallait que j'avance vite pour me réchauffer. Que j'avance vite aussi parce qu'il était tard. En partant derrière un patrouilleur, j'avais enfreint le règlement.

AUCUN DÉPART APRÈS 14 H 00

C'est bien écrit au Centre communautaire. Vers quatorze heures trente, les patrouilleurs plongent dans la forêt pour fermer les pistes. Ils ramassent les skieurs en panne ou trop fatigués. Au début de l'hiver, la nuit tombe vite. Elle avale tout, d'un coup, en quelques minutes. À seize heures trente, il fait déjà noir. Ceux qui partent trop tard risquent de se faire prendre par la nuit.

Je savais que Sylvie serait inquiète. Au début, elle croirait que j'avais eu du mal à nettoyer ma blessure. Ensuite, elle me chercherait un peu partout. Elle mettrait un bon moment avant de comprendre que j'étais repartie. Comment savoir sur quel sentier? En skiant vite, j'avais peut-être le temps de rentrer avant qu'elle s'affole complètement. J'arriverais à boucler la piste en moins de deux heures. Avant la noirceur.

C'était bête de faire ça à une amie. Je le savais. J'aurais pu simplement revenir sur mes pas. Rentrer sagement. Mais à l'idée de cesser d'avancer, de recommencer à vivre avec les rafales dans ma tête et les volcans dans mon ventre, j'avais envie de hurler.

Les conifères agitaient furieusement leurs branches. De vrais cinglés. Le vent soufflait la neige un peu partout. Une pluie de confettis glacés me fouettait le visage.

Autant, cet après-midi, la forêt était pleine de vie, autant les bois étaient maintenant de plus en plus gris. On n'entendait plus criailler les geais et les sittelles. Les mésanges placoteuses s'étaient tues. Les piverts devaient ronfler déjà.

J'avais l'impression de grimper depuis des heures. J'avançais maintenant comme un robot. L'effet euphorique du vent faiblissait. Je me sentais de plus en plus fatiguée. J'avançais mécaniquement. De plus en plus péniblement. À ce train-là, je ne serais jamais au Centre communautaire avant dix-sept heures.

Lentement d'abord, puis de plus en plus fort, la tempête s'est levée en moi. J'étais prise dans un ouragan, ballottée aux quatre vents. Des mots refaisaient surface.

Lorsque le pélican, lassé d'un long voyage
Dans les brouillards du soir retourne
à ses roseaux
Ses petits affamés courent sur le rivage

C'était moi, ce grand oiseau. J'étais tellement fatiguée. Mais je n'avais pas fini mon voyage.

Qu'est-ce que c'est, des roseaux? Je ne suis pas sûre. Est-ce comme les quenouilles?

Il n'y a pas de quenouilles l'hiver. Il n'y a rien l'hiver. Seulement de la neige.

Et puis je n'ai pas d'enfants, moi, comme la mère pélican. Je n'ai même plus de mère.

Alors il se soulève, ouvre son aile au vent
Et, se frappant le coeur avec un cri sauvage,
Il pousse dans la nuit un si funèbre adieu,
Que les oiseaux des mers désertent le rivage

Il hurle, le pélican. Il souffre, le pélican. Il n'en peut plus. Mais personne ne l'entend.

Ce n'est pas moi, le pélican. Je suis seulement son enfant. La fille d'un oiseau mort. D'une pauvre bête que je n'ai pas vue partir. D'un grand oiseau que je n'ai pas pu embrasser. D'un grand oiseau qui est mort fâché.

Je l'entends maintenant, le cri du pélican. Un grand cri de mort crevant le ciel, déchirant les montagnes. Un long gémissement. À fendre l'âme. Il n'est pas funèbre, le cri du pélican. Juste désespéré.

J'ai soif. Pouah! La neige est dure et glacée. Elle m'égratigne la gorge.

Je ne m'arrêterai pas vraiment. Une mini-pause. Le temps de me coller contre un sapin géant.

Son écorce est rude. J'y presse mon oreille. Comme si je pouvais entendre son coeur battre.

C'est Antoine. Sa chemise est rude, mais son corps est doux et chaud. J'ai envie d'enlever mes vêtements pour mieux le sentir contre moi.

Est-ce qu'on a vraiment fait l'amour? Faire l'amour, ce n'est pas la même chose que faire naufrage. On allait faire l'amour pour la première fois. Et puis, on s'est trompés. On a fait naufrage. C'est tout. On n'est sûrement pas les premiers. Il n'y a pas de quoi fouetter un chat.

Il fait noir et il fait froid. Il faut avancer. Fernande voudrait que j'avance. Antoine aussi, je pense.

Mais je vois mal. On ne sait jamais si le sentier va tourner ou pas. Je devrais déjà être au sommet. Où sont les falaises glacées?

J'ai mal partout. J'ai tellement froid. Le vent me mange tout rond. Bientôt, il ne restera plus rien. J'aurai disparu complètement.

La neige semble plus chaude. Plus enveloppante. Une grosse douillette. Épaisse.
Moelleuse. On se glisse dessous. Puis on
dort. Le lendemain, tout va mieux.

Je n'ai pas d'oreiller, mais tant pis. En
camping, il ne faut pas se plaindre.

Je pense que je vais mourir.

Mourir, ce n'est pas grave. Qui sait?
Peut-être que ce n'est même pas doulou-
reux. Fernande est peut-être très heureuse.
Elle se dit peut-être: «Wôw! J'aurais dû
mourir avant.»

Peut-être qu'elle crie:

— Viiiiiiens, Marie-Lune! Viiiiiite!
Dépêche-toi. Mourir, ça ne fait presque pas
mal. Ça ne dure pas longtemps. Ensuite, on
est bien.

J'ai mal à la jambe. Mais ça ne saigne
plus.

J'aimerais qu'Antoine soit ici. Il me ré-
chaufferait. Mais Fernande se fâcherait, je
crois.

Elle ne voulait pas mourir. Elle m'en
veut. Elle en veut à Antoine aussi. On l'a
poussée vers le précipice. On l'a fait mourir plus vite. Mais on ne le savait pas.

— Comprends-tu ça? ON NE LE SAVAIT
PAS.

Ça fait du bien de crier.

— COMPRENDS-TU ÇA? ON NE LE SAVAIT PAAAAAAS!

Et puis non. C'est trop fatigant. Le mieux, c'est de fermer les yeux.

Il y a eu juste un voile bleu. Léger, léger.

J'aime le bleu.

Le vert aussi. Le vert doré des yeux d'Antoine. Et de Fernande.

J'aime le violet. Sur les falaises glacées.

Et l'ombre noire des montagnes.

J'aime le gris doux des ailes d'oiseau.

Et le blanc lumineux de la première neige.

J'aime les champs blonds, juste avant.

Et l'or blanc des étoiles sur un ciel d'encre.

Mais ça ne compte pas. Tant pis.

Je n'aime plus la vie.

Chapitre 13

Trois lettres

C'est drôle! Le ciel est blanc et les étoiles noires. Elles ne clignotent même pas.

Non. Ce ne sont pas des étoiles, mais des trous. Des milliers de petits trous.

Je comprends! Ce n'est pas le ciel, mais un plafond au-dessus de ma tête.

Si je suis dans un cercueil, je suis dans la Cadillac des boîtes de bois. Très confortable. Juste assez mou. J'ai deux draps blancs et une grosse couverture jaune. Je ne savais pas qu'ils nous enveloppaient comme ça.

Mais non! C'est ridicule. Ce n'est pas un cercueil, le plafond est cent fois trop haut. À moins que j'aie ratatiné en mourant.

Je pense que je ne suis pas morte.

Ce n'est pas grave. C'est peut-être mieux ainsi.

— Bonjour, beauté!

Je me relève tranquillement. Ouille! J'ai mal à la tête.

Un homme me soulève un peu, cale un oreiller dans mon dos.

C'est Robert! Et je suis à l'hôpital. La preuve? J'ai un bracelet de plastique autour du poignet. Rien de très élégant.

— Salut, Marie-Lune! T'as failli voyager dans le firmament. Je vais dire aux infirmières que t'es réveillée...

— Non. Attends! S'il te plaît...

— *Ben* sûr...

— Qu'est-ce qui est arrivé?

— Ça serait plutôt à toi de raconter... Je venais d'atteindre La Perdriole... Je roulais vite parce qu'il faisait un froid de canard. C'est là que j'ai entendu quelqu'un crier. Je me suis dit que c'était impossible. Que j'avais dû rêver. Il fallait être fou pour traîner derrière moi par un temps pareil. J'ai continué d'avancer, mais ça me tracassait. Je suis redescendu un peu pour voir.

C'était chouette d'entendre Robert. Il racontait une histoire. J'écoutais comme si je ne connaissais pas la suite.

— J'ai failli te manquer. T'étais sortie du sentier. Heureusement que tes skis sont orange. J'ai aperçu une spatule entre les branches. C'est comme ça que je t'ai trouvée. Un petit paquet gelé.

Il s'est éclairci la voix en grognant un peu.

— T'aurais pu mourir... Tu le sais?

Je l'ai regardé droit dans les yeux.

— Oui. Je le sais.

Il a continué.

— Là, j'ai décollé. Dieu merci, je suis assez en forme. J'ai descendu au lac Monroe d'une traite. Sans piquer de plonge. Une chance! Les patrouilleurs avaient déjà accroché des traîneaux aux motoneiges. Mais ils partaient à l'aveuglette. J'ai demandé à André de m'aider, et on est venus te chercher.

Il parlait vite. Lui aussi avait eu peur.

— Il y avait un peu de sang sur ton pantalon. Et sur tes mitaines. Rien de grave. Mais tes lèvres étaient bleues et tes doigts blancs. Ton nez aussi.

J'ai ri. Robert avait l'air de penser que j'étais complètement marteau.

— Ils vont m'appeler Narine!

J'ai expliqué à Robert l'histoire de Zoreille et de Narine. Il semblait soulagé.

— Ne t'inquiète pas, va! Ton nez est beau. Mais tu vas peut-être perdre un ou deux orteils... Si ton chum ne t'aime plus, il ne te méritait pas. Moi, si j'avais quinze ans, je te trouverais belle même sans orteil.

J'ai dû faire une grimace. J'avais vraiment mal à la tête.

Il m'a embrassée gentiment sur le front. Je me suis soudain sentie terriblement triste. J'ai attrapé son bras.

— Merci...

Il m'a lancé un clin d'oeil et il est parti.

Ils m'ont vite assaillie. Léandre, Sylvie, Monique. Je leur bâillais au nez; je voulais seulement dormir. Alors, ils m'ont embrassée, minouchée, dorlotée et ils ont disparu.

Léandre n'a pas parlé de sa brosse. Ni de la mienne. Ni de La Diable. Ni de Fernande.

— Ça va aller, ma chouette! C'est une grosse côte à remonter. Mais on est deux.

C'est à peu près tout ce qu'il a dit. J'ai failli répondre que les côtes, j'en avais assez.

Flavi aussi est venue. Seule. Ce matin. Elle se tenait bien droite. Elle ne semblait pas gênée comme tous les autres. Elle en a vu d'autres, Flavi. La mort, la folie, la furie, ça ne l'impressionne plus.

— Ça va, Marie?

Elle était la première à me le demander. Les autres répondaient d'avance pour moi. Ils juraient tous que j'allais bien. Qu'est-ce qu'ils en savaient?

Flavi m'a laissé une grande enveloppe contenant trois lettres.

De Fernande.

— Je triche, Marie. J'avais promis de te les remettre beaucoup plus tard. Ta mère voulait attendre que tu aies vingt ans. Mais je pense que tu es prête. Prends ton temps pour les lire. C'est à toi.

Je n'ai pas ouvert l'enveloppe. J'attends. Je reprends des forces. Ce midi, j'ai même mangé les pois. Quand j'étais enfant, je refusais d'avaler ces petites billes dégueulasses. Je disais que c'étaient des crottes de poules malades.

En pensant aux poules, j'ai ri. L'infirmière m'a regardée bizarrement. Je me demande ce que les infirmières racontent à mon sujet lorsqu'elles bavardent ensemble au bout du corridor.

Demain... Peut-être... J'ouvrirai l'enveloppe. Ensuite, j'attendrai. Quelques heures ou quelques jours. Pour m'habituer à ces petits morceaux d'elle. Les lettres portent peut-être son parfum. Je sens qu'il faudra les apprivoiser.

J'ai décidé de marcher un peu avant de dormir. Dans le corridor, une infirmière m'a fusillée du regard.

— Prend ça cool! Je n'ai pas mes skis...

C'est ce que j'avais envie de lui dire. Mais je suis polie.

J'avais déjà arpenté deux étages quand je l'ai aperçu... Antoine! Que faisait-il ici? Ma chambre n'était pas dans cette aile, ni à cet étage. Pourtant, il avançait sans hésiter, comme s'il savait où il allait.

Il s'est arrêté devant une porte. Il a frappé doucement et il est entré.

Je m'attendais à ce qu'il ressorte tout de suite. Il verrait bien que Marie-Lune n'y était pas.

Mais il est resté. Longtemps.

Je me suis approchée. Antoine me tournait le dos. Il tenait la main d'un homme.

Son père!

Mon Dieu, que je suis bête! Sylvie ne m'avait pas donné de nouvelles d'Antoine. Léandre et Monique non plus. Et je n'en avais pas demandé. Il aurait pu lui arriver des millions de choses pendant tout ce temps. Il aurait pu déménager à Tombouctou, gagner la Super Loto. Ou mourir. Son père aussi.

— Antoine!

Il s'est retourné. Il a rougi.

— Marie-Lune!

C'est moi maintenant qui étais gênée.

— Je t'ai vu. Je marchais. Je pensais que tu venais me voir... Excuse-moi...

— Non. Attends! Ne te sauve pas. Mon père a eu une crise de foie. Je voulais te voir... Mais je ne savais pas si je devais. Je t'ai fait assez de mal comme ça...

— Quoi? Pourquoi?

Son père dormait. Mais les trois autres malades dans la chambre nous écoutaient. Tant pis.

— Je n'aurais pas dû, Marie-Lune. Je m'excuse. Je savais que tu étais en miettes. Mais quand je t'ai vue à moitié nue... J'ai oublié... Ça faisait longtemps que je t'imaginais comme ça. Tu es encore plus belle que je pensais.

Il a pris mes mains et les a délicatement emprisonnées dans les siennes. Comme la première fois.

J'ai fermé les yeux. Je voulais partir. Tout de suite. Pour passer la nuit avec ce doux souvenir.

Je craignais que l'ouragan ne s'éveille en moi. Qu'il gonfle et se déchaîne. J'avais peur d'éclater. Mais avant de quitter Antoine, j'ai réussi à réunir suffisamment de courage pour sourire. Bravement. Afin qu'Antoine ne se sente pas trop seul. Afin qu'il sache que j'avais compris. Que ça allait. Que j'étais peut-être en miettes, mais bien vivante.

Avant de m'endormir, j'ai ouvert la grande enveloppe brune. Je ne pouvais plus attendre. Les trois enveloppes à l'intérieur étaient blanches et plus petites. Fernande avait écrit sur chacune d'entre elles «À Marie-Lune», suivi d'une date:

23 novembre 1976
28 octobre 1991
30 novembre 1991

Elles avaient l'air bien mystérieuses, ces lettres.

J'ai fermé les yeux. Demain... Peut-être....

Chapitre 14

Tu es née ce matin, ma belle

— Allô!

Je me suis réveillée avec un Martien à côté de moi.

— La madame a dit que je pouvais te visiter... T'es pas dangereuse. Ni contagieuse. T'as juste essayé de mourir.

Un drôle de petit bonhomme était installé sur la chaise à côté de mon lit. Son crâne presque chauve était hérissé de quelques poils d'un blond roux. Il portait un pyjama rayé avec des tas de dinosaures rouges, bleus et verts. Et ses grands yeux caramel me dévoraient comme si c'était moi, l'extra-terrestre.

— C'est vrai que tu voulais mourir? Les

infirmières disent que c'est pas si sûr...

— Un instant, monsieur! Ça ne serait pas plutôt à moi de poser les questions? C'est ma chambre ici. Non? Comment t'appelles-tu?

— Bruno.

— Bon! Bonjour, monsieur Bruno. Oui, oui, vous pouvez entrer. C'est gentil d'avoir frappé avant...

Il a éclaté de rire. Un beau rire pétillant. Clair et léger. Plein de bulles.

— Que faites-vous à l'hôpital, monsieur Bruno? Amygdalite? Appendicite?

Il riait encore.

— *Ben* non! J'ai le cancer, voyons.

Un grand frisson m'a parcourue. Du bout des orteils jusqu'à la pointe des cheveux.

— T'es drôle, toi! D'habitude, le monde devine. J'ai perdu mes cheveux. C'est la chimo qui fait ça.

— La chiMIO. Pas la chimo.

— Tu vois. Tu connais ça. C'est à mon tour, là?

— Ton tour de quoi?

— De poser les questions, voyons. C'est vrai que t'es partie dans la forêt quand c'était presque la nuit? Le savais-tu que c'était dangereux? Voulais-tu mourir?

— Trois questions d'un coup, c'est beaucoup! La prochaine fois, une seule suffira. Disons que c'est une exception.

Il me regardait comme si j'étais le père Noël. Ou Superman. Quelqu'un de grand et d'important, en tout cas.

— Je suis partie en skis trop tard. Je le savais. Mais je ne voulais pas mourir. Voyons donc!

— T'es sûre?

Il était petit mais pas nono.

— Au début, oui. Je voulais simplement continuer à skier. Parce que ça m'empêchait de penser. Après... peut-être que j'ai voulu mourir.

Ça faisait drôle de m'entendre dire ça. Mais c'était vrai. C'est plus facile de parler aux extra-terrestres.

— Tu voulais mourir? Pourquoi?

Il est devenu tout rouge. J'ai pensé que ça le gênait de parler de ça.

— Euh!... *escuse!* Je pense que j'ai posé deux questions, là... Hein?

J'ai éclaté de rire et j'ai ébouriffé les quelques poils roux sur son crâne.

— Je voulais mourir parce que ma mère est morte. Elle est morte très vite. Je ne savais pas qu'elle avait... une maladie grave.

J'aurais dû m'en douter. Peut-être que je ne voulais pas le savoir. Elle est morte quelques minutes avant que je puisse aller la voir à l'hôpital. Et quelques jours après une grosse chicane...

— *Ouin...* T'es pas chanceuse, chanceuse. Qui va te consoler?

Je n'étais pas sûre de la réponse.

— J'ai mon père, des amis. Un amoureux....

— Un AMOUREUX? Moi aussi, j'ai une amoureuse! Anne-Marie. Mais elle est plus grande que moi. Mon ami Guillaume dit qu'on ne pourra jamais se marier à cause de ça. Toi..., qu'est-ce que tu penses? De toute façon, Anne-Marie ne sait pas que je l'aime...

Il s'est arrêté pour reprendre son souffle.

— Je peux monter dans ton lit?

— Si Anne-Marie te voyait, elle ne serait pas fâchée?

Il n'a pas répondu. Il s'est glissé sous les couvertures. Son petit corps était chaud. Cinq minutes plus tard, il était endormi.

J'ai pris la première lettre. La plus vieille.

23 novembre 1976

À Marie-Lune,

Tu es née ce matin, ma belle.

Je voudrais te dire tant de choses. Mais je suis fatiguée et je ne suis pas très douée pour l'écriture.

J'aimerais que tu lises cette lettre dans vingt ans. Ou quand tu auras des enfants. On verra.

Je ne sais pas du tout ce qui va nous arriver. Qui je vais devenir ni qui tu seras. Mais c'est le plus beau jour de ma vie.

Ça fait mal accoucher. Je ne pensais pas que ça faisait aussi mal. Dans les cours prénatals, on nous enseigne qu'en respirant bien, c'est possible de contrôler la douleur.

C'était atroce. Pourtant, je respirais exactement comme on me l'avait enseigné. Il y a eu des secondes, des minutes peut-être, où j'ai presque regretté de t'avoir fabriquée.

Je me demandais dans quelle galère je m'étais embarquée. J'avais l'impression que mon ventre allait éclater.

Pauvre Léandre — c'est ton père ça —, chaque fois que je criais, il pâlissait. Si tu

n'étais pas sortie, je pense qu'il serait de-
venu transparent.

J'ai repris courage quand ils m'ont an-
noncé qu'ils voyaient tes cheveux. Tu t'en
venais! Je ne savais pas si tu étais une fille
ou un garçon. Ça ne me dérangeait pas. Du
moment que tu étais là.

Je savais que tu n'aurais probablement
pas de frère ni de soeur. C'était déjà un
petit miracle que tu sois là. Je te raconte-
rai ça une autre fois...

Mais ma petite bonjour, tu me faisais mal
en creusant ton chemin. À un moment don-
né, le Dr Lazure a lancé: «Arrêtez de pous-
ser, Fernande.» Je l'aurais étripé! Ça paraît
qu'il n'a jamais accouché, lui. C'est facile
à dire, ça: «Arrêtez de pousser.» Mais ce
n'était pas moi, c'était toi qui poussais. Tu
étais déjà toute là. Avec ton petit carac-
tère, tes désirs et tes idées.

Je me suis dit: «Au diable le beau doc-
teur. Elle veut sortir, elle va sortir.» Je t'ai
aidée. J'ai pris une grande respiration et
j'ai poussé comme si j'avais une montagne
à déplacer.

Soudain, je t'ai entendue. Tu n'étais pas
grosse, mais tu en faisais, du vacarme! Tu
ne pleurais pas, tu beuglais. Ça me faisait

peur. J'ai pensé que quelque chose n'allait pas.

Tu avais peut-être un cordon enroulé trois fois autour du cou. Je n'avais pas le courage de regarder.

L'infirmière a crié: «C'est une belle fille!»

Au ton de sa voix, je savais que tout était parfait.

Mais les bébés, moi, je ne connaissais pas ça. Tu étais toute rouge et tu hurlais. J'ai cru que je ne saurais jamais comment faire. Trouver les bons gestes, les bons mots. Qu'est-ce qu'on fait avec un petit paquet de chair qui hurle à ébranler les maisons?

Ils t'ont déposée sur mon ventre mou. J'ai failli crier: Non! Attendez! Montrez-moi comment faire avant.

Tu étais encore gluante. Mais tu avais un nez mignon, une belle petite bouche et deux grands yeux qui me regardaient comme s'ils me connaissaient. Tu étais toute chaude. Moi aussi. On avait fait tout un marathon ensemble.

C'est là que je me suis aperçue que tu ne pleurais plus. Depuis que nos corps s'étaient touchés. Un vrai miracle.

Tu ressemblais à un petit oiseau affamé avec ton bec qui cherchait mes seins. Je t'ai aidée. Tu faisais presque pitié, tellement tu avais faim. Déjà. Ou peur. Je ne sais pas.

Pendant que tu tétais, je ronronnais.

C'est à ce moment-là que j'ai compris qu'on était unies pour la vie. Ce qu'il y avait entre nous, c'était déjà plus fort que tout.

Je ne sais pas ce qu'on va devenir, Marie-Lune. J'espère que je serai une bonne mère.

Quand je ne saurai plus, tu m'aideras. Mais je serai toujours là. C'est sûr.

Je t'aime, Marie-Lune.

Bonne vie!

Ta mère

Bruno dormait toujours à côté de moi. Sa présence m'aidait. Une infirmière est venue avec un plateau d'oeufs brouillés et de jambon. Ça sentait bon.

— Chut!

Je lui ai fait signe de se taire, en désignant Bruno. Elle a souri et elle est repartie avec son plateau. Tant pis, je mangerais plus tard. Je ne voulais pas le réveiller.

Sitôt fermée, la porte s'est rouverte en coup de vent.

— Salut, ma cocotte! Je passe vite. Je ne peux pas rester. Monique avait une course à faire à côté...

Sylvie s'est arrêtée d'un coup. Elle venait de voir une autre tête sur mon oreiller.

— Qu'est-ce que c'est ça?

— Un chimpanzé!

— Ne fais pas la drôle...

— Excuse-moi. J'étais gênée de te le dire: «C'est un orignal!»

Bruno était réveillé. Et mort de rire.

— Allez, Bruno, brame. Si j'ai bien appris mes leçons de français, c'est ça, le bruit d'un orignal. Si tu ne *bramasses* pas, mon amie va penser qu'on se paie sa tête. Vite, brame!

Il riait tellement qu'il s'étouffait. Sylvie aussi. Ensuite, j'ai fait les présentations.

— Je pense que je vais le dire à son amoureux. Il ne sera pas content de savoir qu'elle le trompe.

— Je le sais qu'elle a un amoureux. Il s'appelle comment?

— Antoine...

C'est moi qui ai prononcé son nom. Ça me faisait du bien de le dire.

L'infirmière est entrée. Marielle Lajoie.
La même que tout à l'heure. Avec le même
plateau. Et elle avait l'air de dire: «Cette
fois, tu manges, ma fille.»

— Je pense que tu nous quittes demain,
Marie-Lune...

Elle voulait seulement faire la conversation. Mais Bruno a frémi sous les couvertures.

— Non, j'ai changé d'idée.

Sylvie a failli s'étouffer avec sa gomme.
Garde Marielle m'a regardée, l'air de dire
cette fois-ci: «Tout le monde a raison: elle
est folle!»

— Je ne peux quand même pas laisser
mon mari seul. Il va trop s'ennuyer. Alors,
je reste.

En parlant, j'avais entouré Bruno de mes
bras. Et il s'était collé contre moi. La bouche fendue jusqu'aux oreilles.

Marielle a tout saisi.

— Je comprends très bien, madame.
Mais, vous savez, votre mari aura droit à
des visites. Tous les jours, si vous voulez.
Normalement, on visite les gens en s'as-
soyant *à côté* du lit. Pas dedans. Mais si
vous trichez un peu, on n'en fera pas tout
un plat. Venez visiter votre mari en pyja-

ma, si vous y tenez. Ou en costume de bain, tiens. Pourquoi pas?

Bruno riait. J'étais contente.

— Votre mari a-t-il faim, madame? Je pourrais peut-être apporter son plateau ici?

Chapitre 15

Les sapins dansent
dans la tourmente

Je voulais lire une autre lettre aujour-
d'hui. J'ai attendu d'être seule. L'après-
midi, dans les hôpitaux, c'est comme dans
les garderies. Tout le monde fait la sieste.

28 octobre 1991

Marie-Lune,

*Je pense qu'ils ont tous tort. Tu devrais
le savoir. Mais je n'ose pas.*
*Si je me trompais... Si c'était pire de sa-
voir...*
*Je vais mourir. C'est sûr, maintenant.
L'an dernier, j'ai trouvé la petite bosse sur*

mon sein, trop tard. Depuis, le cancer s'est répandu.

J'ai peur.

Le pire, ce n'est pas de mourir. C'est de mourir au mauvais moment. J'aurais aimé que tu sois plus vieille. Mariée peut-être. Avec des enfants, si possible. Je sais que ça fait ancien, mais je partirais moins inquiète. Depuis hier, j'ai encore plus peur. Tu es revenue de ta danse d'Halloween, le coeur en feu. Le corps aussi.

Ce n'est pas le temps de tomber amoureuse. Mais tu ne le sais pas. Ce n'est pas de ta faute.

Si j'avais toute la vie devant moi, je m'inquiéterais moins. Je pourrais te suivre pas à pas. Même quand tu ne veux pas.

Mais je suis à court de temps, et toi, tu cours trop vite.

C'est vrai qu'il est beau, ton Antoine. Je ne suis pas aveugle. Et il n'a pas l'air méchant pour deux sous. Il a de grands yeux doux...

Mais je connais sa vie. Sa mère, son père. Je ne veux pas prendre de risque. Je voudrais que tu attendes. Que tu en choisisses un autre. Plus tard.

Hier soir, malgré ma peur, je trouvais ça

beau de t'entendre. Tu étais tellement heureuse. Tu flottais. Ça se voyait.

Ça m'a ramené une grosse pelletée de souvenirs.

La nuit dernière, j'ai rêvé à ton père. À nous, il y a presque vingt ans. Le jour où on s'est rencontrés. Je ne te l'ai jamais raconté...

Au dépanneur, chez Flavi, il y avait deux ou trois tables et des chaises. On servait du Coke et du café. Un matin, Léandre est entré. Je l'avais déjà vu. De loin, seulement. Ton père n'est pas né ici, tu le sais. Il vivait dans le Nord depuis seulement quelques mois.

Il s'est assis, il a commandé un Coke. Je me rappelle chaque mot, chaque geste.

— As-tu du Coke, ma belle noire?

J'ai rougi jusqu'aux orteils.

Je pense que je l'ai aimé tout de suite, passionnément. Sans le connaître vraiment. Je savais que c'était lui, l'homme de ma vie.

Ce soir-là, à l'heure où on range tout avant de fermer le dépanneur, je l'ai vu arriver. Il m'attendait. Il m'a invitée à aller marcher avec lui. Il faisait un froid de canard, mais j'ai accepté.

Je ne l'ai jamais dit à personne. Même

pas à lui. Mais j'ai su ce soir-là qu'on se marierait.

Ne ris pas. Je te jure que c'est vrai. Je l'aimais déjà. Et lui aussi m'aimait. Je le savais.

Dans sa façon d'être beau, on voyait qu'il était bon aussi. Je ne peux pas te donner plus d'explications.

Un an après, on était mariés. Onze mois plus tard, tu es née.

Mais tu aurais pu naître avant...

Flavi n'est pas au courant. Je ne sais pas si les mères racontent ces choses-là à leurs filles quand elles sont plus vieilles... Mais je n'aurai pas la chance de me reprendre. Et je veux te le dire.

C'est arrivé un soir de tempête. Flavi était partie passer deux jours à Montréal. Son père avait eu un accident. Il fallait que je reste dans le Nord. À cause du dépanneur.

Léandre est venu ce soir-là. Tard. Après son ouvrage. Il travaillait déjà au journal. Je fermais le dépanneur. Il ne savait pas que Flavi était partie.

Quand on s'est retrouvés seuls, chez nous, j'ai su tout de suite qu'on allait faire l'amour. Il y avait de l'électricité dans l'air.

Je ne l'ai jamais dit à ton père, mais je pense qu'il a deviné: je n'ai pas tellement aimé ça, la première fois.

Faire l'amour, pour moi, c'était un peu la fin du monde.

Aujourd'hui, je sais que ça peut être grand, et beau, et magique. Mais pas chaque fois... Et pas toujours la première fois.

Après ça, j'ai eu peur. On allait se marier dans quelques mois, et je me demandais presque si je l'aimais. Je me disais que si on s'aimait vraiment, ç'aurait dû être merveilleux tout de suite. Dès la première fois. Je serais partie en Boeing pour le septième ciel.

C'est Léandre qui m'a aidée à me retrouver. À le retrouver. Il a senti que quelque chose n'allait pas. Mais il ne me poussait pas, il ne me pressait pas. Il m'aimait. Tout simplement. Je le sentais tout le temps.

Petit à petit, j'ai compris que c'est l'amour qui compte. Le reste, ça s'apprend. Ça s'apprivoise. La nuit où on t'a fabriquée, quelques mois plus tard, on était déjà des vrais pros...

Je te souhaite d'aimer quelqu'un, Marie-Lune. Très, très fort. Et qu'il t'aime, lui aussi. Aussi fort. C'est tout ce qui compte dans le fond.

Je ne sais pas qui ce sera, ma chouette. Le pire, c'est que je ne le saurai jamais. Ça me fait tellement mal quand j'y pense.

La lettre n'était pas signée. Les derniers mots étaient mal tracés. L'encre avait coulé... Fernande avait pleuré.

Mon coeur battait trop fort. Il se fracassait contre le mur de mon corps.

J'ai ouvert la dernière enveloppe sans même m'en apercevoir.

30 novembre 1991

À ma Marie-Lune,

Hier soir, je leur ai dit que je voulais être un peu plus lucide pendant quelques heures ce matin.

Je ne souffre pas beaucoup. Il faut que tu le saches. On me donne des injections qui me font flotter. Mais ce matin, j'ai refusé l'injection.

Je pensais t'écrire mes adieux en pleurant toutes les larmes de mon corps.

Mais ce n'est pas ça... Je suis bien, Marie-Lune.

C'est triste de partir. C'est sûr. J'aimerais mieux rester...

Mais je me sens comme les voiliers qui glissent sur le lac, l'été, par temps clair. Ils dérivent doucement. Poussés par le vent.

Je pensais que je te ferais des adieux, mais je n'avais rien compris. Je ne pars pas vraiment, Marie-Lune. Je le sais maintenant. J'en suis certaine. Hier après-midi, Flavi m'a apporté une lettre que je t'avais écrite le jour de ta naissance. Je ne l'avais jamais relue.

En relisant la lettre, j'ai compris.

On est un peu la même personne. Moi, je t'ai fabriquée. Toi, tu m'as transformée. En quinze ans, on a fait tellement de choses ensemble. De toutes petites et de très grandes.

J'ai dû attacher au moins un million de fois les boutons de tes chemisiers, de tes manteaux, de tes robes et de tes pantalons. C'est impressionnant, quand on y pense...

Et entre les boutonnages, il s'en passait des choses. Toutes les fois que je t'ai consolée. Tous les sourires que tu m'as donnés.

Tes caresses, tes sourires, tes mots gentils transformaient ma vie. Ils me donnaient confiance en moi. Tu me souriais, et je me sentais unique au monde.

Quand je serai partie, Marie-Lune, je veux que tu fouilles un peu en toi. Tu verras: je serai là. Toujours. À chaque instant.

Au creux de toi.

À bientôt, Marie-Lune,

Je t'aime,

Fernande

Le barrage a sauté. D'un coup. Le mur a volé en éclats. L'eau a tout défoncé. Elle n'en pouvait plus d'être emprisonnée.

Elle coulait librement. Enfin.

Je n'aurais jamais cru que c'était si bon de pleurer.

C'était la première fois. Depuis.

L'orage a duré longtemps. Très, très longtemps. Jusqu'à ce que je sois bien à sec.

J'étais épuisée maintenant. J'allais m'endormir quand j'ai vu Antoine. Il était là. À trois pas. Il hésitait. Il avait l'air gêné, à moitié caché derrière la porte.

— Viens.

Il s'est approché lentement et il a caressé tendrement mes cheveux emmêlés sur l'oreiller.

J'ai fermé les yeux.

Je revoyais Antoine dansant avec Nathalie Gadouas, le soir de l'Halloween. Soudain, sa grande forêt verte réapparaissait devant mes yeux. Nous dansions sous le tilleul. Il m'embrassait pour la première fois. Nous courions dans la tempête, puis nous faisions l'amour comme on fait naufrage. Nous étions maintenant étendus sur la plage. Fatigués, perdus, blessés...

— Je t'aime, Antoine.

Je ne l'avais pas dit très fort. Alors, j'ai répété:

— Je t'aime, Antoine.

Il n'a pas répondu.

— Je ne sais pas si on sera capables... Si c'est possible. Je suis vivante. Plus forte aussi. Mais les tempêtes vont revenir.

La preuve, c'est que j'avais envie d'éclater.

— J'ai peur, Antoine. Tellement, tellement peur.

Sa forêt. Mon Dieu que j'aime ses yeux!

Ses yeux me répondaient. Qu'il serait patient. Qu'il avait peur, lui aussi. Qu'il était prêt à partir sur tous les ruisseaux, les lacs, les rivières et les mers. Avec moi. Sans savoir où ça mènerait. Tant pis, si ça ne menait nulle part.

On ne pouvait s'empêcher d'essayer.

Les grands arbres n'ont pas peur des tempêtes. De la neige, de la pluie, de la grêle. Ils se tiennent droits dans le vent. Hauts et puissants. Leurs longs bras ploient sans craquer. Ils dansent, eux, dans la tourmente. Leurs gestes sont souples. On sent qu'ils sont résistants.

Les grands sapins ne tombent pas. Ils attendent d'être très vieux. Secs et usés. Des centaines d'années. Et jusqu'à la fin, ils restent droits.

Table des matières

Achevé d'imprimer
sur les presses de Litho Acme Inc.